SECRET SOCIETIES

SECRET SOCIETIES

*From the Ancient and Arcane to the
Modern and Clandestine*

DAVID V. BARRETT

BLANDFORD

A BLANDFORD BOOK

First published in the UK 1997 by Blandford
A Cassell Imprint
Cassell Plc, Wellington House,
125 Strand, London WC2R 0BB

Distributed in the United States by Sterling Publishing Co., Inc.,
387 Park Avenue South, New York, NY 10016–8810

British Library Cataloguing-in-Publication Data
A catalogue entry for this title is available from the British Library

ISBN 0–7137–2647–4

Typeset by Falcon Oast Graphic Art
Printed and bound in Great Britain by Hartnolls Ltd, Bodmin, Cornwall.

'I know that's a secret, for it's whispered everywhere.'
William Congreve (1670–1729)

CONTENTS

ACKNOWLEDGEMENTS

I am indebted to all the authors whose works I have plundered, whether I have quoted them directly or not; their insights (even when I have completely disagreed with them) have been invaluable. Of the many I shall single out Richard Cavendish and the late Dame Frances Yates, whose sheer common sense and sound scholarship have helped keep me to a fairly steady path in a field renowned for its oddball ideas; also A.E. Waite, whose deep knowledge of this subject matter caused him not to suffer fools gladly.

Belated thanks to my college lecturer Gordon Aldrick who, though he probably didn't realize it at the time (I certainly didn't), was largely responsible for stimulating a scholarly interest in esoteric religion in what must have seemed a most unlikely student some 25 years ago. It doesn't seem like a quarter of a century since I first learnt to say 'phenomenological' without tripping over my tongue.

Particular thanks to R.A. Gilbert for his invaluable corrections to one section, and to Diana Rosalyn Atkins, Chris Bell, Mary Gentle and John Hamill for reading and commenting on different parts of the manuscript. All opinions, and any errors of fact or logic which remain, are my responsibility. Thanks also to Matthew Scanlon, The Board of General Purposes, United Grand Lodge of England, the Rosicrucian Fellowship and Builders of the Adytum for providing and granting permission to use photographs.

INTRODUCTION

SECRET SOCIETIES are rooted in our everyday experience. Everyone loves to hear secrets, to know things which most other people don't know. If it's something important, something significant, there can be a feeling of power in being one of the few people who know it; even if not, there's a satisfaction in knowing that you are one of the select few.

As small children, many individuals – especially those raised on Enid Blyton's Famous Five and Secret Seven, or Malcolm Saville's Lone Pine Club – formed a secret society of their own, a private club. Usually these had very few members; in some cases, only two, including the long-suffering dog.

At school, it's important to join in. If you're not in the First XI or the First XV, or the football, hockey or netball team, you have to join the philatelic club, the astronomy society, or some other group. If you don't, you're really a loner. Sometimes two or three loners group together; there's security in numbers, as well as companionship. And there's always some kid who is even more of a loner than the rest of you; you don't really want him, but you sometimes let him tag along with you, on the understanding that he's on the outside, not really 'one of you'; you let him know that there are secrets you're not going to share with him – even if there aren't.

When we leave school there is still that need to belong. For some this is satisfied by membership of a church; for others, by sports; for others by being one of a group of regulars at a pub. For some, folk clubs; for others, science fiction fandom. If you play football, your team is better than anyone else's; if an SF fan, you might speak dismissively of 'mundanes', those not part of your group.

Some groups have more kudos than others. If a leading member of your university debating society, you are on a powerful launch-pad; you might end up in the select company of lawyers, or in the British House of Commons.

If you're a businessman, or a small-town solicitor, or a schoolteacher, or a policeman, you might find yourself joining a Rotary Club or the

Freemasons. For most, the same need is being satisfied: the need to belong, the need to be one of the gang.

And for some, that need is to know things that other people don't: to have secrets; to be one of the select few. Knowledge is power, and the fewer people who share that knowledge, the more powerful they are. If invited to join such a society, you feel good about it. It might be the Freemasons; it might be a local amateur dramatic society. In this one respect at least, there is little difference. You are on the inside at last and, among other things, are now in a position to keep other people out.

Nobody likes to feel left out. 'The psychology of perceived exclusion' – feeling left out – can cause jealousy and envy. Whether they admit it or not, many of those who attack the Freemasons, for example, may be harbouring bitterness that they have never been asked to join. But the same thing applies in all aspects of life: in the professions, church, clubs, and other social groups. A common complaint is that the people who share out all the best jobs among themselves all know each other. One doesn't have to look at secret societies to find self-perpetuating inner circles. Why are some people more powerful and successful than others with equal ability? 'It's not what you know, it's whom you know' is a common grumble, especially when you're trying to break into a new field and find that all the plum assignments go to people who have connections in that field.

It's easy to ignore the counter-argument, that it's perfectly natural to give a job to someone who you know (from his or her track record) can do it, and who you know (from personal contact) you can trust. Self-perpetuating inner circles sometimes have a perfectly rational reason for existing.

But when someone who is known to shake hands in a particular way lands a decent job, whether a local building contract or the chairmanship of a major company, human nature would have us point a finger of suspicion at the Freemasons. And when sensationalist newspapers and books fearlessly expose corruption supposedly riddling Freemasonry, it's hardly surprising that some people believe it.

This is *not* yet another book of that type.

Having said that, I'm quite sure that there are corrupt Freemasons. It would be astonishing if there were not. I'm equally sure that there are corrupt members of the Institute of Directors, the Trades Unions and, for all I know, the Mothers' Union.

Whether it's a child in his own special club of two or three members, or whether it's a businessman in the Freemasons, there's nothing unusual about wanting to belong to a secret society. It can be fun; there is the delight in knowing secrets that few others know; the satisfaction of being included in the in-group; a feeling of importance, and sometimes of power; and sometimes there *is* genuine power through being one of the decision-makers, one of the élite.

But are you one of the real élite? Outsiders sometimes suspect there is a hidden group of people making the major decisions which affect all our lives. People sometimes joke about 'The Secret Masters of the Universe'. But once finally a member of the Freemasons, or the Yachting Club, are you any nearer to being one of these 'Masters'? Or do you suspect that an inner group of members are actually pulling the strings? You climb higher and higher up the ladder, and the thousands at your level become hundreds, and then tens. Compared to those further down the ladder, and even more to those who are right outside, the Great Unwashed, the mundanes, the profanes, you're one of the élite – but are you really one of the powerful decision-makers? Even the Grand Master of your Order (or the president of your golf club) seems to be constrained by the decisions of others. Perhaps he's just a puppet himself, a figurehead for public consumption; perhaps, behind him, there's a shadowy group who *really* run things. Perhaps *they* are 'The Secret Masters of the Universe'.

Conspiracy theorists have a field day with this sort of thing. Always, beyond the top, there's another level; always, behind the leaders, there are the secret leaders; and behind the secret societies that we know about, there are even more secret societies that no one has ever heard of.

I'll be touching on such theories throughout this book.

For the record, I'm not a Secret Master of the Universe myself. I'm not at the time of writing (nor, in the words of the McCarthyites, have I ever been) even an ordinary, common-or-garden Freemason or Rosicrucian. You won't find the names of any Secret Masters in this book, except by accident. I don't know who they are. Neither does any other author on the subject.

By definition such Secret Masters (if they have any existence beyond the paranoid minds of conspiracy theorists) are unknown and unknowable to all except themselves. You can't apply to become a Secret Master of the Universe, as you can to become a Rosicrucian; membership is by invitation only. I imagine such membership would be extended to very, very few.

DEFINITIONS AND CAVEATS

From the moment one first looks at secret societies, it becomes apparent that most of them have some sort of religious basis. It may be useful to examine the origins of a few terms, many of them religious, often associated with secret societies.

Alchemy was never really to do with the transmutation of base metals into gold; this was symbolic of the transmutation of the base nature of man to the godly nature of the transformed man.

'As above, so below' refers to the mirroring of the macrocosm (the world, the universe, the cosmos, the God without) and the microcosm (the individual man, the soul, the God within).

Arcane comes from the Latin for 'something that is shut up', or locked in a chest.

Christ spark is a term sometimes used to refer to the spark of the divine flame, or the tiny fragment of God, within each human being.

Esoteric comes from the Greek for 'inner' or 'within', and applies to something taught to or understood by the initiated only.

Exoteric, from the Greek for 'outside' or 'the outward form', applies to knowledge available to the uninitiated.

Heresy and heretical beliefs are always defined as such by the establishment Church (of whatever religion), usually as a means of enforcing their control over spiritual dissidents. The word actually comes from the Greek for 'choice', which religious hierarchies have always denied to individuals.

Hermetic, often as in Hermetic Philosophy, comes from the name Hermes Trismegistus, Hermes the thrice-greatest, the mythical author of the occult Egyptian texts which lay behind fifteenth- to seventeenth-century alchemy; he was named for the Greek messenger of the Gods, equivalent to the Roman Mercury.

Immanent, immanence (from the Latin *manere*, 'remain') refer to the indwelling nature of God; see also *Transcendent/ence*.

Initiate, as a noun or a verb, comes from the Latin for 'beginning', and generally refers to the admission of someone into secret knowledge.

Magic, mage, magus, magician come from the Greek for 'art' as in 'skill' – artful rather than artistic.

Myth, in its technical sense rather than its everyday sense, means a story whose importance rests on the message it carries, rather than on whether or not it is historically factual. Use of the word does *not* imply that a story never actually happened; in its correct usage, the Masonic tale of Hiram the Architect, the stories about King Arthur, and incidents in the life of Jesus are all myths. The phrase 'the Jesus myth' includes not just the New Testament account, but also the centuries of popular accretions, such as the three wise men, not numbered in the Bible.

Occult comes from the Latin for 'hidden'; it is used in that sense in both astrology and astronomy today, without any devilish connotations.

Rite, ritual, from the Latin, mean a solemn or religious ceremony or observance.

Transcendent, transcendence (from the Latin *trans*, 'beyond', and *scandere*, 'climb') refer to God being 'out there somewhere', beyond human apprehension; see also *Immanent/ence*.

Western mystery tradition: Depending on the particular emphasis of a school, this can include the study of the Arthurian cycle, or Greek, Roman and Egyptian mythology. It usually includes study of the Cabala and Tarot, and the spiritual alchemical teachings of the Hermetic Philosophers.

Note that the word 'orthodox', except in one or two places where with a capital letter it clearly refers to the Eastern Orthodox Churches, is used throughout in the sense of mainstream, establishment, 'normal' beliefs, in contradistinction to unorthodox, heterodox, unusual and probably heretical beliefs. Exoteric Christian beliefs and practices are orthodox; esoteric ones are not.

The capitalized word 'Church' refers to the authority of the Christian establishment, of whatever denomination. In many places, historically, this means the Roman Catholic Church; in other places, depending on the context, it can mean the Protestant authorities. The word 'church' with a lower-case 'c' means a church building.

The word 'God' is capitalized throughout, both for convenience and to avoid the implied value judgement of showing discrimination between 'the one true Christian God' and 'false pagan gods'.

The word 'Mason' means Freemason; without the capital letter it refers to stonemasons.

Throughout this book I mention several varieties (as opposed to denominations) of Christianity. These should be defined in the sense in which I am using them, as follows.

Such terms as *mainstream, traditional, orthodox, establishment*, and *standard* are used to refer to the majority of Christians in the major denominations, who generally follow the teachings of their Church. Historically, in the Roman Catholic and Anglican Churches, they regard their priest as the intermediary between themselves and God, though this has changed quite a lot in the last few decades. Many are devout believers, well versed in their faith. Others, while holding a sincere belief in the main tenets of orthodox Christianity, would be hard put to argue theological points. Some, whom I refer to as 'pew-sitters', have only a vague, generalized understanding of Christian doctrine; the Church is a familiar, comfortable part of the establishment in their life, and little more than that. Having said that, most of Christian history – Roman Catholic, Eastern Orthodox and Protestant – is mainstream; most normal Christian doctrine is mainstream; most Christian scholarship is mainstream. Mainstream Christian doctrine ranges from Evangelical to liberal.

Evangelical Christians have asked Jesus Christ to be their personal Saviour, and believe that they have assurance of salvation. They know the Bible well, and they can argue their theology. They believe that the Bible is the inspired word of God, though there is some range of belief on this. For example, there are Evangelical Biblical scholars (e.g. Professor F.F. Bruce) who accept many of the findings of Biblical criticism of the last hundred years or so, but whose faith in Jesus as Lord is not affected by this. In recent decades Evangelicalism has grown in importance within the Church of England, and there are now numerous Evangelical bishops.

Only a minority of Evangelicals are Fundamentalists, but they are an outspoken minority. A Fundamentalist Evangelical Christian believes absolutely in the literal truth of the Bible: God created the world in six days, Adam and Eve were real people, Moses parted the Red Sea, and so on. If anyone suggests any doubt about the factuality of such events, they are to be condemned; true Fundamentalists even regard most Evangelicals as having a fairly wishy-washy, watered-down belief, while most other people who call themselves Christians simply aren't: Roman Catholics, for example, are the Whore of Babylon. Fundamentalists reject Biblical criticism out of hand; the suggestions that people may have edited books of the Bible to support their beliefs, or that the choice of which gospels and epistles ended up in the New Testament was a human decision, or that parts of the Bible should be interpreted allegorically, are regarded as outright blasphemy.

Liberal theology, to Fundamentalists, is simply not Christian. Liberal beliefs again have a very wide range, from almost-mainstream right up to God-is-dead. Generally, liberal Christians are likely to doubt the Virgin Birth, the physical resurrection, and many miracles in the Bible. They accept Biblical criticism into their views, and regard parts of the Bible as allegorical rather than factual. Some would speak of Jesus the man, and Christ the Saviour; they would distinguish between the mainstream belief in the deity (Godhood) of Jesus Christ, and the more liberal belief in the divinity, or divine indwelling, of the man Jesus.

Some readers may be offended by some of the ideas discussed in this book: the suggestions that there might be some truth in all religions, that the Bible was compiled by human hands, and that the majority of Christian doctrine wasn't formulated until several hundred years after the birth and death of Jesus. But such concepts are hardly new.

The vast majority of ordinary Christians are kept ignorant of the scholarly findings and debates of the last century or so pertaining to their religion.

Anglican and Roman Catholic priests all study the development of biblical criticism during their training for the priesthood, but they rarely pass any of this knowledge on to their congregations. In the early 1990s the Bishop of Durham, the Right Rev. David Jenkins, caused controversy by saying that it is permissible to have doubts about such matters as the Virgin Birth and the resurrection, and still remain a Christian. Fundamentalists condemned him, as might be expected; but the media behaved as if no-one had ever voiced such thoughts before, and that the Bishop had no right to do so. Many said he shouldn't be a Bishop; some said he wasn't a Christian.

A century of biblical criticism and religious scholarship might as well never have existed. Any writer discussing varieties of belief constantly meets such popular ignorance and condemnation. For an excellent discussion of this problem, see the first chapter of *The Messianic Legacy* by Michael Baigent, Richard Leigh and Henry Lincoln.

In places this book is critical of previous books in one or another specific area of this overall subject; this is most apparent in the chapter on Freemasonry. This is not a case of authorial infighting; more importantly, it does not mean that I am acting as an advocate for Freemasonry or for any other movement. Such books are criticised in order to point out sloppy scholarship, poor argument, factual errors, or what might be seen as outright deceit.

This book is a phenomenological exploration of the beliefs of certain organisations, movements and individuals, rather than a statement of my own beliefs. I am not personally either approving or antagonistic towards any secret society, or any branch of Christianity or any other religion. Where there is criticism it is of bigotry, small-mindedness and tunnel vision, and such faults are by no means restricted to Christian, or indeed any other religious movements.

In many ways this book can be seen as a companion volume to my *Sects, 'Cults' and Alternative Religions* (Blandford 1996). Inevitably there is some overlap between the two, though I have tried to keep repetition to a minimum.

One further point must be made right at the start. Most of the present-day organizations mentioned in this book say firmly that they are *not* secret societies. The Freemasons are often quoted as saying that they are 'a society with secrets, rather than a secret society'. The various Rosicrucian groups generally call themselves schools of religious philosophy, or something similar. One organization, the Lemurian Fellowship, wrote: 'though we understand the basis for your proposing to include the Fellowship in a book about these [secret societies], it simply would not be accurate'. They go on to say that 'the Lemurian lesson material is available only to qualified students. Not because it is "secret" but because each lesson's information provides a basis for the next; along with this the Fellowship teachers' guidance to each student according to his individual needs makes the deeper benefits possible and adds to the uniqueness of Lemurian Training.'[1]

There is no simple definition of a secret society, but this comes as close as anything to describing four of the major characteristics of secret societies:

- carefully graded and progressive teachings
- available only to selected individuals
- leading to hidden (and 'unique') truths
- and to personal benefits beyond the reach and even the understanding of the uninitiated.

A further characteristic common to most of them is the practice of rituals which non-members are not permitted to observe, or even to know the details of.

Whether or not they call themselves secret societies, the movements – whether historical or present-day – mentioned in this book exhibit some or all of these characteristics.

Secrecy is endemic in our society. It always has been. Later in the book I shall look at secrecy in crime and government; before that I examine the Freemasons to see where they came from, and the Rosicrucians and where they came from; and the whole confusion of secretive philosophical and religious organizations throughout the centuries. Everywhere there will be found connections: the Freemasons, the Rosicrucians, the Knights Templar, the Cathars. There are links of ideas and ideals between all of them, and they all share common roots: with these roots my discussion begins.

Movements and individuals are covered more or less in chronological order throughout the book, except where discussion of one leads naturally into discussion of another. Certain subjects, such as Architecture, Tarot, Magic and others, which span centuries, are explored where it has been most convenient to place them.

CHAPTER ONE

THE ROOTS

T HE HISTORY of secret societies is the history of esoteric religion, and is the history of magic. Whatever their current practices and teachings, appearances and priorities, the majority of secret societies have religious roots. Religion is as old as man, and the priest vies with the prostitute and the spy among the world's oldest professions. This chapter examines briefly some of the many religious influences on present-day secret societies, from the earliest times up to the late Middle Ages.

It should be noted that the dates given for some of the early teachers and writers vary from source to source. Also, the mythologies, philosophies and religious movements in this chapter do not necessarily follow each other sequentially; many of them overlap each other.

PRIMITIVE SOCIETY

The origins of religion are both external and internal. Primitive man was far more at the mercy of the elements than we are today: thunder, lightning, wind, rain, floods, scorching sun and drought, all affected his daily life. Above him was the sky, with the mysteries of the sun by day, and the moon and stars by night. What were these lights? Why did they move across the heavens at different times of day and month and year, and why did they change in brilliance and shape and size? The heat and light of the sun gave life. When it was at its weakest in midwinter, how could they be sure that it would return to life-giving strength again? You put a seed into the ground, and it becomes food. The corn dies, and then comes back to life again.

It's easy to see how Gods developed, from the great powers of nature, powers beyond man's control. Could the powers be entreated? If sacrifices were made to them, would they respond favourably? What was the most efficacious way to approach the powers? Was it dangerous to do so? Could anyone do this, or was it a specialist task, a skill, an art, a power in itself?

And so priests developed.

There were other questions to which man wanted answers. What happens when someone dies? Will I die? What will happen to *me* when I die? If there is another life after death, of what form is it? Where is it? Is it good or bad? How can I ensure it will be good? If there is life after death, was there life before birth? If crops live and die and come to life again, does the same hold true for people? And then a further set of questions. Where do I go to in my dreams? Why can't I bring things back from them? Do dreams foretell the future? Who can tell me what they mean?

Further, in a time where injury or illness could easily lead to death, the person with knowledge of the right treatments, the right herbs, became honoured, one of the most important members of the tribe.

The priest, or shaman, or medicine man knew the right rituals to ensure the return of the sun each year. He knew how best to bring rain, or to bring good crops, or a good hunt, or a victory over a neighbouring tribe. He knew the meanings of signs and omens, and the hidden meanings of dreams, and he could travel at will in his own dreams to the lands of the spirits. He knew how to heal, and how to curse. He was a man of wisdom, whom even the tribal chieftain would consult for advice.

No one lives forever, so one of the priest's most important jobs, for the well-being of the tribe, was to train his own successor in the complicated lore of his work. As the role became more powerful, so the knowledge became more closely guarded; the link between power and secrecy was formed. As societies developed and became more complex, so did religion in its outer, more public, forms: exoteric religion – and so did the secret knowledge, and the secrecy of the knowledge, at the heart of religion: esoteric religion. The two became more and more separate, until the inner secrets of religion became hidden not just from the public, but also from many of the priesthood.

BETWEEN THE TIGRIS AND THE EUPHRATES

In the light of late twentieth-century political and religious repression, it is perhaps strange to remember that the cradle of civilization lay in present-day Iraq, in the fertile land which included the rivers Tigris and Euphrates, and the cities of Baghdad to the north and Basra to the south, at the top of the Persian Gulf. The Sumerians lived around the southern Euphrates over 6,000 years ago; the Akkadians, the name given to a Semitic race who settled in Sumer and Akkad – specifically Babylon – 5,000 years ago.

These peoples had agriculture, cities, and a sophisticated society, with an organized religion and priesthood, and stepped temples, the ziggurats. Sumerian, Babylonian and Assyrian mythology lies behind the mythology of the tribe of Abraham, Isaac and Jacob from which sprang the Jewish religion and, later, Christianity. It has been shown that many of the Hebrew myths can be traced back to the much earlier Babylonian or Sumerian versions.

Islam, which also honours the Jewish patriarchs and prophets, began on what is now the southwest coast of Saudi Arabia in the early seventh century AD, and spread rapidly, moving into present-day Iraq and Iran within a few years of Muhammad's death, with the effect that there was a strong Persian influence on the religion in its very early days.

It is worth noting that when the people now known as Akkadians moved into Sumer, gradually assimilating rather than displacing the Sumerians, they brought their own language, though they adopted the cuneiform writing of the Sumerians. But they continued to use the Sumerian language, rather than their own, for religious ritual, which meant that eventually, priestly secrets were spoken in 'the language of the Gods', and were hidden from the ordinary people.

There is not space to outline all the Mesopotamian myths – Sumerian, Babylonian/Akkadian and Assyrian – but many are still known today: the Creation myth and the Flood myth, with their Biblical counterparts, the descent of Inanna or Ishtar into the Underworld, the Gilgamesh myth, and others.

One reason for Evangelical Christians' distrust of Freemasonry, Rosicrucianism and other esoteric forms of religious belief is the Evangelicals' insistence on both the literal truth and the uniqueness of the Bible stories, and the more liberal esoteric movements' acceptance of them, and of their non-Biblical equivalent myths, as allegorical and as equal in value.

All pantheons (to use the Greek term) have family relationships between Gods, sometimes with rival families, and usually with rivalry within families. Gods argue, trick, fight and kill each other, resembling humans in this respect. The myths of disputes between Gods, such as Dumuzi and Enkimdu in Sumerian mythology, or between men, such as Cain and Abel in Hebrew mythology, often reflect major societal changes in the peoples, such as (in both these cases) the shift from a nomadic, pastoral lifestyle to a settled, agri- cultural life. Other conflicts between the Gods might be folk-memories of battles for supremacy between different cities, different cultures, different peoples. It has long been observed that in Celtic countries, when a new race of people move in and take control from the original peoples – who are often more primitive and closer to the land, and have a relationship with the spirits of the land which the newcomers fear and envy – the original peoples eventually become 'the little people' in the folk memory of the invaders.

ZOROASTRIANISM

Zoroastrianism, named after the Persian priest Zoroaster or Zarathustra, can lay claim to be the first significant monotheistic religion, with tremendous influence on the 'Religions of the Book' (Judaism, Christianity and Islam) which followed it. (These religions' beliefs in one God, heaven and hell, the resurrection of the dead, the final judgement and the eventual victory of good over evil all stem from Zoroastrianism.) It eventually became the state religion of the Persian Empire, and remained strong until the Muslim invasions of the seventh century AD.

Zarathustra, who lived either around 660–583 BC or possibly as early as 1000 or even 1400 BC, reformed the complex ritual- and sacrifice-ridden polytheism of Persia (modern-day Iran) by declaring that there was only one God, Ahura Mazda, the Wise Lord; all the other Gods worshipped by the Persians were but assistants and servants of the supreme being. The purity of Ahura Mazda was represented by the purity of the flame, and Zoroastrians still worship over a living fire today. It is significant both that the Jewish God I AM spoke to Moses from a burning bush (Exodus 3:2, 14), and that many present-day esoteric religious movements, including the Rosicrucians and the I AM-inspired Church Universal and Triumphant, represent God, and the God-presence within man, as a flame.

Although monotheistic, Zoroastrianism also taught the principle of a good power and an evil power. The latter, Angra Mainyu, with his demons is in control of the world though man, with his knowledge of God's law, is able to turn away from the dark to the light. This is probably the origin of the dualistic beliefs of the Gnostics.

The Wise Men of Matthew's Gospel and of every nativity play were Zoroastrians; there was much trade between the Persians, the Jews, the Greeks and the Egyptians, and the Syrian capital of Antioch, where Matthew probably wrote his Gospel, was a busy trading port.

Some Zoroastrians today are known as Parsis or Parsees (Persians), especially in India, or as Mazda-yasnians (worshippers of Ahura Mazda).

MITHRAISM

Mithra, or Mithras, was one of the Persian Gods subsumed into Zoroastrianism; he was lord of contracts and agreements, and was linked with the Sun. Mithraism was the popular religion in the Roman Empire from the second century to the fifth century AD, particularly with soldiers and officials of the Empire. While Zoroastrianism gave fairly equal treatment to men and women, Mithraism was a religion for men only.

Roman archaeological remains in Britain show that Mithraism was a far more widespread and important religion among the Romans than was Christianity. The latter religion as it developed borrowed much from the former. Mithras was both a sun-God (the Persian *Mihr* means 'sun') and a saviour God; Plutarch referred to him as the Mediator between man and the supreme God. It is probable that the Mithraic day of worship was Sunday; one of the main festivals was held on the winter solstice, which was celebrated on 25 December. There is also evidence that followers of Mithras celebrated some form of ritual meal, though with bread and a cup of water rather than wine.

Rituals were held in caves, cellars or temples decorated to look like caves to represent the 'cosmic cave' or universe. There were seven levels of initiation: *Corvus* (Raven), *Nymphus* (Bride), *Miles* (Soldier), *Leo* (Lion), *Perses* (Persian), *Heliodromus* (Runner of the Sun), and *Pater* (Father). It was not uncommon, for example, for a medium-ranking soldier to have progressed to a higher level of initiation than that of his military superior. Little is known of the rituals, except that they were held in secret, with only the initiated allowed to be present. It is thought that new initiates had to find their way through dark passages until they found the light: a clear symbolism. The ritual also apparently included a symbolic representation of death and resurrection. By no means all soldiers were members; but those who were had a special feeling of comradeship with each other in the outer world, and probably recognized each other with secret signs.

Although historically there can be little or no direct link between them, there are clear parallels with the structure, secrecy, rituals and men-only comradeship and mutual support of Freemasonry and other later initiatory societies.

Mithraism was only one of several mystery religions in the centuries immediately before and after Christ. A mystery religion was a religio-magical cult, or society, which revealed its secrets, teachings and rituals only to the initiated; the word 'mystery' comes from Greek roots meaning 'secret thing or ceremony' and 'initiated one'. Initiation often involved a symbolic death and rebirth, and symbolism featured strongly in the other rituals. Furthermore, the secrets of the religion were revealed progressively, through a series of initiations, to fewer and fewer people as the initiates climbed the 'spiritual career path' (see also p. 11).

Other mystery religions were based on, among other Gods, Dionysus, Isis and Osiris, Cybele and Attis, Demeter and Persephone (the Eleusinian mysteries), and Orpheus; this last, the Orphic movement, taught that there is a spark of the divine imprisoned deep inside the material nature of each person: a concept to be encountered throughout this book.

PYTHAGORAS

Although Pythagoras (581–497 BC) is chiefly known today for his mathematical work, he was one of the foremost religious philosophers of the centuries before Christ, and his influence on esoteric religion, and on secret societies, cannot be over-estimated.

The *Encyclopaedia of Dates and Events* says of him tersely, 'great philosopher and mathematician, but scientific approach was prejudiced by mysticism.'[1] This is rather like saying that William Blake was a great poet and artist whose work was spoilt by his mysticism.

Pythagoras is said to have wandered for many years in Egypt and Mesopotamia, and perhaps as far east as India, studying religion, philosophy and science in an attempt to find a 'unified field theory' covering all knowledge. (Several founders of recent esoteric movements, including H.P. Blavatsky and Georgei Ivanovitch Gurdjieff, followed his example – whether in reality or in self-created myth.) In about 530 BC Pythagoras settled in the Greek community of Croton in southern Italy, and set up an academy with very strict membership criteria.

Mathematics, music and astronomy all formed part of the teaching, not as discrete subjects in their own right, but as part of Pythagoras's system of belief, to which E.M. Forster's famous dictum 'Only connect!' would have applied admirably. Mathematics and geometry, the occult properties of numbers and the relationship between them, lay behind the whole world, and the heavens above. Pythagoras is believed to have formulated the idea of the musical octave, and explained the mathematical basis for musical intervals and harmonics. The entire universe is in vibration, singing, producing the 'music of the spheres'. He is reputed to have worked out the Golden Section, the mathematical ratio which lies behind much of the esoteric meaning of architecture (and hence ties in with the symbolism of Freemasonry).

He taught reincarnation, a staple belief of the Western Mystery Tradition. He taught the relationship between man and the cosmos, microcosm and macrocosm; this naturally links with astrology, which at that time and for many more centuries was the same thing as astronomy. His teaching on the esoteric meaning of numbers still lies behind modern numerology.

Like many other founders of occult societies, Pythagoras took on semi-divine characteristics to his followers; he was referred to as 'the harmonic deity', halfway between the Gods and men. He insisted on a strictly ascetic way of life, with many prohibitions on his followers; they had to follow a vegetarian diet, for example, but must not eat beans. Purity of body and behaviour, and complete dedication of mind, were essential.

It took three years to pass through the first stage of initiation, and five years to pass through the second; being a Pythagorean follower took great commitment.

The ideas of Pythagoras greatly influenced Plato (429–347 BC), one of the most influential Greek philosophers. It could fairly be said that without Pythagoras there would have been no Plato, and without Plato, no Neo-Platonism (which included Neo-Pythagoreanism), which was supremely influential in esoteric thought at the start of the Christian era, and during the Renaissance.

It has been suggested by some authorities either that Pythagoras was at some stage taught by the Druids of northwest Europe, or that he or his followers taught them.

NEO-PLATONISM

Neo-Platonism, which developed through the first five or six centuries AD, was the last flowering of the Greek philosophers; it absorbed teachings from various sources, and it strongly influenced both exoteric and esoteric Christianity. Many of the Church Fathers knew of Neo-Platonist thought – it was impossible for educated men, including Saint Paul, not to know of Greek philosophy in those early centuries – and some of the theological battles which ultimately resulted in the fixing of Christian dogma had their basis in the disagreements between proponents and opponents of Neo-Platonist ideas.

More important for present consideration, however, is the influence that Neo-Platonism had on the esoteric side of Christianity and other major religions, and thus, ultimately, on secret societies.

The Neo-Platonist movement, or School, changed and developed over the centuries, as different leaders built on the teachings of their predecessors. Thus, Plotinus (204–262) – who was opposed to magic – advocated virtue, chastity and the mystical contemplation of God. His pupil and successor, Porphyry (232–304), however, stressed religious rituals and magical rites; this emphasis was to cause conflict between Neo-Platonism and the nascent Christianity, and would also give the Roman Emperors an excuse to clamp down on non-Christian religious practices from time to time.

So far as this book is concerned, perhaps the most important long-term effect of Neo-Platonism was that, in a nutshell, it found a solution to the dichotomy between polytheism and monotheism. There was one infinite, universal, incomprehensible God, above everything; philosophy (Greek: the love of wisdom) was the true means of approaching this God, while religions were lesser attempts to approach lesser Gods, who were effectively servants, or *dæmons*, of the One God (see also Zoroastrianism p. 20).

The word 'demon' is an incorrect rendering of *dæmon*, which included both good and evil beings, and both lesser Gods and spirits of the dead. Its pejorative use specifically to mean evil spirits is a later Christian alteration of its meaning. Within Christian theology the term might be better replaced by 'principalities and powers' (Colossians 1:16), which are created by the one God, and which can be good or evil. Angels fall into much the same category.

The distinction between demons and *dæmons* is important. The Neo-Platonists taught *theurgy*, which might be called the raising of spirits, but is more correctly the calling down or invocation of good *dæmons*. In the later ritual magic of the Hermetic Philosophers and alchemists, and the late nineteenth- and early twentieth-century Hermetic Order of the Golden Dawn (trivialized and misrepresented as 'black magic' by, for example, Dennis Wheatley novels), the idea was not usually to call on the devil and the infernal host – in fact, this was very rare and acknowledged to be extremely dangerous – but on the *dæmons*, the lesser Gods, the angels, the principalities and powers, and the powerful spirits of those who had been spiritually powerful in their lives.

The concept of the One God, above and beyond all Gods, is central to the spiritual beliefs of secret societies. It explains why, although both Freemasonry and Rosicrucianism are essentially Christian in origin and expression, they are also open to those of other faiths, particularly the other Religions of the Book. The Great Architect of the Universe is not limited to Christianity.

Evangelical Christian opponents of Freemasonry, and anti-Masonic authors such as Stephen Knight and Martin Short, in attempting to tackle this point, really miss it entirely. The God of Freemasonry is not, as Knight and others claim, 'a compound deity composed of three separate personalities fused in one',[2] an amalgam of Yahweh, Baal and Osiris in the sacred name Jahbulon (see pp. 117–120). God might indeed be approached through this compound name, or through any of its constituent parts (assuming that this is the correct derivation) – or through any of the many other names of God over the millennia. Man is, after all, only human; it helps to have a name, a label, a set of attributes, to help one approach the ineffable. But God is not limited to these human-applied labels.

The Christian Church turned dæmons into demons
(Francis Barrett, *The Magus*, 1801)

This belief in the One Supreme God also explains how mystical Jews, Christians and Muslims have been able to share their understanding throughout the centuries, as will be seen in discussions following.

The Eastern Church was always more able to cope with the mystical aspects of Christianity, even before its formal split with Rome. Byzantium, or Constantinople, was a more flexible melting pot of different cultures and ideas than Rome could ever be. Byzantium-born St Maximus (580–662), for example, taught what in the West would have been seen as rampant heresy, 'that the ultimate aim of the worshipper is to *become* God. This position unites both the Neo-Platonist desire for ecstatic communion with pure being, and the early-Christian belief that full initiation made the devotee a christ.'[3]

Such beliefs lie at the heart of esoteric Christianity; it is hardly surprising that the Church, with its monopoly on salvation, has always tried to stamp out such an affront to its authority.

EGYPT

It is significant that the word 'alchemy', which will recur throughout this book, derives from the Arabic *al kimiya*, which almost certainly comes, via the Greek *chemeia*, from the old name for the Nile Delta in Egypt, *khem*, which means 'black earth': the deeply fertile, life-giving soil, dark silt from the Nile, amidst the arid desert. The allegorical connotations are unlikely to be accidental.

Although the true alchemy is the transformation of the soul, it should not be forgotten that the first (and the later) alchemists were also chemists. (Similarly, the distinction between astrologers and astronomers is relatively recent.) Those who knew the often spectacular effects of adding different amounts of different powders to each other, and heating them to specific temperatures, could combine being a scientist and a showman; and for outside observers, for ordinary people, both are forms of magic.

As far back as 2900 BC, the Egyptians had discovered the secret of refining gold which, as a precious metal difficult to obtain, was reserved for royalty. The priests who guarded this secret were not just metal-workers but, in effect, early chemists. Religion, magic, secrecy, scientific knowledge, and the physical production of gold have thus been linked together for millennia.

Egyptian mythology is complex. As with all mythologies, it evolved over the centuries. But in contrast with Judaism, which developed into universal monotheism, it appears that the familiar pantheon of Osiris, Isis, Anubis and the rest was a later development, and that the earliest Egyptian belief was in one God, the Sun God Re or Ra.

In one of the earliest versions of the Egyptian creation myth, the Creator God Atum-Re, who has risen out of the primeval chaos alone, masturbates to create life. In early religion, sex was seen as a potent force. With humans, as with all animals, sex gives birth to new life; with the Gods it must surely be the same. Sexual energy, and the sexual fluids, are life-giving, powerful, sacred.

Just as Pythagoras travelled around the Middle East and possibly the Far East in his search for knowledge, and eventually settled his school in a Greek community in Italy, other philosophers spent years in countries not their own, learning and studying, comparing and assimilating knowledge.

The study of comparative religion of the nineteenth and twentieth centuries is nothing new; 2,000 years ago or more, scholars around the Mediterranean – i.e. the whole civilized, cultured world – looked at their Gods and the Gods of their neighbours and drew comparisons. The Roman and Greek Gods were easy enough to match up, the Egyptian Gods a little less so, though when the Greeks ruled Egypt they were happy to identify Atum-Re, the Creator God, with their own Zeus.

Christianity spread into Egypt from its very beginning. Unlike the Greeks and Romans, the early Christians could not allow any other Gods under any other names; they could not accept that God the Father of Jesus could be identified with Zeus or Jove or Amun-Re as the One Creator God. In addition, the early Christians looked at the openly sexual nature of Egyptian mythology and were horrified. Origen, an Egyptian Christian, castrated himself in order to purify himself. The sinfulness, guilt and shame which Christianity has attached to sex from the time of the Church Fathers onwards quite possibly originated in an over-reaction against the religion of Egypt, and a determination to show itself to be different.

HERMES TRISMEGISTUS

There is considerable doubt as to when the works of Hermes Trismegistus were written, but it is certain that no one person by that name ever existed. The name means Hermes the thrice-greatest, Hermes being the Greek God of the spoken word – the *logos* – identified with Mercury, the winged messenger God of the Romans, and with Thoth, the Egyptian God of writing, itself a magical activity not understood by the common man. (Note that Mercury – both the astrological planet and the liquid metal – was of

'As Above, So Below', the famous dictum of Hermes Trismegistus
(Robert Macoy, *General History, Cyclopedia and*
Dictionary of Freemasonry, 1850)

supreme importance in alchemy.) Thoth was the historian, and the creator of
the all-important calendar by which not only history, but the movements of
the Sun, Moon and stars could be measured. As the scribe of the Gods Thoth
was the custodian of all knowledge. Knowledge is power; knowledge known
only to the few is even more so. Under the intermingling of philosophers and
religious scholars of different cultures, Thoth/Hermes became the God of
esoteric knowledge and power. A priest, philosopher or magician whose
works were ascribed to Hermes Trismegistus, was the human amanuensis of
the Gods.

Whoever or how many people 'he' was, Hermes Trismegistus was the
author of what became known as the Hermetic texts, or the *Corpus
Hermeticum*, a vast amount of writing on esoteric religion. (The complete
Corpus Hermeticum in English translation fills three large volumes.)

It was thought at one time that Hermes Trismegistus lived at around the
time of Pythagoras, or perhaps of Moses; references in the Hermetic texts to
the teachings of Jesus were believed to be prophetic foreshadowings of these
great truths. Later scholarship, however, has shown that the *Corpus
Hermeticum* was written sometime in the first five centuries AD, largely in
Egypt, as a fusion of Greek and Egyptian esoteric teachings.

The Hermetic texts were known to Islamic scholars in medieval times, but did not come to the attention of the West until they were translated into Latin in 1471 by the Italian Marsilio Ficini. The texts included works on religion, philosophy, magic, medicine, alchemy and astrology, all of which were closely linked. They include among many others the *Emerald Tablet*, or *Tabula Smaragdina*, which begins with the saying usually shortened to 'As above, so below', and which discusses the Philosopher's Stone; *Poimandres, The Good Shepherd*, a Gnostic text about the infinite light of God, and man's journey to enlightenment; and the *Perfect Sermon* of Asclepius, which speaks of the divine creative Unity above a hierarchy of spiritual beings, and of man, who possesses both body and spirit, having a divine nature.

The *Emerald Tablet* begins:

It is true, without falsehood, and most real: that which is above is like that which is below, to perpetrate the miracles of one thing. And as all things have been derived from one, by the thought of one, so all things are born from this thing . . .

It continues:

Here is the father of every perfection in the world. His strength and power are absolute when changed into earth; thou wilt separate the earth from fire, the subtle from the gross, gently and with care . . . By this means thou wilt have the glory of the world. And because of this, all obscurity will flee from thee. Within this is the power, most powerful of all powers. For it will overcome all subtle things, and penetrate every solid thing. Thus the world was created.

Within one short passage we have the ideas of the link between the macrocosm and the microcosm, of the One Creator God, and of the power of God being available to man. The words 'thou wilt separate the earth from fire, the subtle from the gross' refer to two of the traditional elements but, more importantly, speak – in what became known as alchemical terms – of spiritual transformation: the separation of the pure gold from the dross of base metals, the purification of the spirit from within the material body.

The translation of the Hermetic texts spurred the sixteenth-century alchemists and the seventeenth-century Hermetic Philosophers who, as will be seen, were of great significance not only in the continuation of esoteric teachings, but also in the development of modern-day science. The usage 'hermetic seal' reflects the strength of the secrecy: permanent and air-tight. This was not knowledge for the common man.

GNOSTICISM

As with Pythagoras, the influence of Gnosticism on secret societies through the ages cannot be overstated.

The term Gnosticism comes from the Greek word *gnosis* meaning 'knowledge'. One writer[4] calls it 'religious existentialism', in that it deals with direct experience of the divine. The Gnostic looks within himself for the divine spark and, finding the God within, can apprehend the God without.

(Although the word 'apprehension' today usually means fear, uncertainty or disquiet, the *SOED* gives as a more primary meaning of 'apprehend', 'to lay hold of with the intellect; to see; to catch the meaning of'. The Gnostic would, in this sense of the word, apprehend, or take hold of, divine knowledge. Similarly the word 'comprehend' includes the meanings of 'to lay hold of; to overtake, or attain to; to accomplish; to grasp with the mind, take in; to apprehend with the senses.' The well-known verse of John 1:5, 'And the light shineth in darkness; and the darkness comprehended it not' is a clear Gnostic reference.)

Knowledge, here, equates with secret knowledge, hidden knowledge. The Bible has an exoteric meaning, open to all; but the Gnostic studies its esoteric meaning, open only to the few: the secrets of God, and of his creation.

It should be stressed, though, that the *gnosis* is not simply an intellectual knowledge, a learning of certain secret doctrines; late twentieth-century Gnostics, of whatever religion or movement, stress that it is the *realization* of God within. Like love, it is a knowledge of the heart as well as of the mind: a state of inner *being*.

Gnosticism is almost certainly pre-Christian, taking in elements of Zoroastrianism, Greek/Egyptian philosophy, and esoteric Judaism. There is a strong argument that the Essenes (whether based at Qumran or not[5]) were Gnostic, and some believe that Jesus was an Essene; if this was the case, though proof is lacking, it is only a short step to suggest that standard exoteric Christianity could actually be a debased descendant of Gnosticism, rather than vice versa. Certainly Gnosticism, though always attacked as a heresy, has had a major influence on Christian thinking, exoteric as well as esoteric.

Gnosticism has never been one religion in its own right, but more an approach to religion – or rather, to spirituality. Thus, although most Gnostics in the first few centuries were linked with Christianity, there have also been those within Judaism and Islam who have been Gnostic – and who have also usually been regarded as heretics by the orthodox establishment of their own religion.

It is easy to see why.

One of the primary problems confronting all religious thinkers is the presence of evil. How could the good Creator God allow suffering on his Earth? If God is all-powerful, why is there pain, sorrow, death? All religions struggle with this question. Few answers are as logically compelling as that of Gnosticism.

We have seen how Zoroastrianism, although monotheistic, has both a spirit of light and a spirit of darkness. Some Gnostics took this idea further: there is not just a spirit but a God of good, and a God of evil: dualism rather than monotheism. Above all is the great God, the One, but below him is another God, who is actually the Creator God. This is the ultimate logical extension of the more common dualistic belief in body and soul, that the pure, eternal spirit is imprisoned in the dross of the material human body. That which is spiritual is of the good God; that which is material is of the evil God, and this includes the physical world, thus accounting for evil, pain, disease, earthquakes and the tsetse fly. The God who created the world, the demiurge, by whatever name he is known (including Yahweh), is the sub-ordinate God (or one of them) and therefore, in some forms of Gnosticism, the evil God. Ordinary people, through their ordinary religions, are thus worshipping the Evil One.

This is a simplification of the complexities of one variant of Gnosticism, but it shows how far the beliefs could be from traditional Judæo-Christian theology.

Dualism lies at the heart of Gnosticism. Good and evil, light and dark, spirit and matter, life and death, truth and error, knowledge (*gnosis*) and ignorance, and similar paired opposites occur in all Gnostic teachings.

Gnostic beliefs were strong in the early centuries of Christianity, when the complexities of Christian dogma were being codified.[6] Many of the more vitriolic pronouncements of the Church Fathers were attempts to counter the often appealing arguments and teachings of the Gnostics.

There was also the not unimportant matter that the teachings of orthodox Christianity came via the bishops and priests of the Church, where-as Gnostics claimed special knowledge of and an individual revelatory rela-tionship with God, and so were out of the control of the Church. A related, but more theological, issue was that the Church taught that God and man were separated by sin, and could only be brought together through the medi-ation of the priesthood, representing Christ. Gnostics, in contrast, believed that the spark of God was in each one of them; the *gnosis* was the revelation or knowledge that they had divinity within them – that they were themselves, in effect, God, or at least, that God could be found within them.

Without its monopoly on salvation, both bestowing it and removing it through excommunication, the Church would have no power.

One of the earliest Christian writings, *Against Heresy* by Irenæus, Bishop of Lyons – written in AD 180 – was a polemic against Gnosticism. The battle for supremacy against Gnosticism was no doubt also reflected in editorial changes to the nascent New Testament, which did not take its final authorized form until as late as AD 367.[7] Many gospels and epistles completely unfamiliar to later Christians were in circulation in the early centuries. The Church Fathers eventually defined orthodoxy (though many of them had heterodox beliefs themselves; Saint Augustine was a follower of the major Gnostic religion Manichæism for twelve years), and effectively selected for the New Testament those writings which best reflected the Church's official teachings. A lot of writings were condemned as heretical, and suppressed; many of these were completely lost until a collection of early documents was found at Nag Hammadi in Egypt in 1945. *The Gospel of Thomas* and *The Acts of Thomas* are strongly Gnostic, while the beautiful poem *The Thunder, Perfect Mind* is a hymn not so much to the Goddess as to Sophia, the female wisdom aspect of God, who is found in early heterodox beliefs.

The Gospel of Thomas is very likely the lost source document known by scholars as *Q*, or the Sayings of Jesus, which lies behind *Matthew*, *Mark* and *Luke*, the Synoptic Gospels; at the very least, it is closely related to that source. It contains a number of sayings which have been excised from orthodox scripture, including several with a distinctively Gnostic flavour. It begins, 'These are the secret sayings which the living Jesus spoke and which Didymos Judas Thomas wrote down'; Didymos means 'twin', and in early Syrian Christian tradition the apostle Thomas was Jesus' twin brother. (The doctrine of the 'perpetual virginity' of Mary, stressing Jesus' physical uniqueness as the child of Mary, is among other things a clear attempt to dispose of such troublesome characters as Didymos.)

> Jesus said to them, 'When you make the two one, and when you make the inside like the outside and the outside like the inside, and the above like the below, and when you make the male and the female one and the same . . . then you will enter the kingdom' (*The Gospel of Thomas*: 22).[8]

Note the echo of 'that which is above is like that which is below' from Hermes Trismegistus's *Emerald Tablet*.

In the *Acts of the Apostles* (8:9–24) there is an account of one Simon, who 'beforetime in the same city used sorcery'; he believes and is baptized, but when he sees 'the miracles and signs' of the apostles, he tries to buy the same power for himself, and is rebuked by Peter. (He bequeathed to us the word 'simony', meaning the purchase of offices in the Church.) There are non-biblical stories of Simon Magus, a powerful Gnostic magician, and his battle of magical powers with Simon Peter. They may have some basis in fact, but it is more likely that these tales developed later as an expansion of the brief biblical account, for Christian propaganda purposes (after a succession of tit-for-tat magic, Simon Peter takes away Simon Magus's power of flight, and the latter plunges to his death, thereby proving the supremacy of the Christian God) – but the very fact that the stories were told shows that the early Christians saw Gnosticism, including Simonian Gnosticism, as a force to be reckoned with. Irenæus claimed that 'all heresies take their origin' from Simon Magus. Note also that Gnostics were seen not just as people with a false religion, but as people with real magical powers.

St Paul, who was certainly familiar with Neo-Platonist thought, inveighed against heretical beliefs in his epistles. He writes of 'another Jesus, whom we have not preached' (II Corinthians 11:4), and rebukes those who preach 'a different gospel' (Galatians 1:6–9). Most Gnostics, and indeed many early Christians, believed in reincarnation; this may be why the writer of the *Epistle to the Hebrews* emphasized in contrast that 'it is appointed unto men once to die, but after this the judgement' (9:27).

Many Gnostics were extreme ascetics, denying themselves all pleasures of the (evil) flesh in order to purify or set free the spirit. Others, however, believed either that the evil God Yahweh, who was responsible for this world, thus bore the responsibility for all wickedness in it, which absolved them from responsibility for their actions; or that the spirituality of the *gnosis* put them above the petty restrictions of morality in the physical world; or, as the second-century Basilides seemed to teach, that in order to speed their soul's way through its reincarnations, they must perform as many acts of immorality as they could, as if to get them out of the way. Needless to say, whatever the rationale, the established Church did not look kindly on such behaviour.

But even with those whose lives were exemplary, the Church has always been suspicious of anyone claiming direct communication with God. Mystics are a classic example. Those who were clearly spiritual – living saints – and who kept to the rules in their outward behaviour, were tolerated – just. Those who seemed to put themselves above Church authority were not.

It would be wrong to suggest that all mystics were Gnostic in their beliefs, but the emphasis on an individual, personal relationship with God which is the heart of mysticism is a hallmark of Gnosticism. It has always been wiser by far for those with Gnostic leanings to stay within the main body of their religion; and if they have to speak publicly about their mystical experiences, to do so in acceptable terms; and to keep the more radical aspects of their beliefs to themselves. Those who were less careful, over the centuries, were likely to meet the stake. After the first three or four centuries of the Christian era, Gnosticism, where it existed, kept very quiet.

The stake, or the sword, was the establishment's answer when Gnosticism resurfaced (via Manichæist offshoots) in the Cathars or Albigensians of the eleventh to thirteenth centuries (see p. 46). Manichæism, founded by the Persian teacher Mani (AD 216–76), was in its early days a strong competitor to Christianity; it maintained a presence around the Mediterranean, and in parts of Asia and India until the thirteenth century, and traces of its beliefs were found in China as late as the seventeenth century.

Manichæism was not so much a Christian heresy as an alternative religion, drawing on Christianity, Gnosticism, Zoroastrianism, and very likely Buddhism. Two deities, of Light and Darkness, are in perpetual conflict; the God of Light is the creator of the soul, but we live in an evil world of matter created by the God of Darkness: the God of the Old Testament. The serpent in the garden was not evil, but good; it was attempting to bring Adam and Eve to true knowledge. Mankind contains sparks of the original divine light. As in Gnosticism, salvation comes from realizing the truth about God and man, or rather, God *in* man. Manichæans also believed in reincarnation. Most Manichæans, the 'hearers', would die and return, but the elect would be liberated from this cycle; the elect lived an ascetic life, eating no meat and abstaining from sex, on the grounds that procreation condemned more divine sparks to be trapped in human flesh. (It is worth noting that it was very likely Augustine's background in Manichæism which caused him to formulate the doctrine of Original Sin, and the sinfulness of sexual enjoyment.)

One feature to distinguish Manichæism from other Gnostic movements was that Mani set up an organization, a Church hierarchy with apostles and bishops, right from the start; this is probably why it survived longer than the others.

As well as in the Cathars, forms of Gnosticism – suitably veiled – also became apparent in the Sufis, possibly the Knights Templar, and certainly the Cabalists.

In different forms Gnosticism has resurfaced in more recent centuries, both in religious movements and in more secretive societies. The Hermetic Philosophers of the sixteenth and seventeenth centuries were influenced by Gnosticism, and they in their turn influenced many organizations including the Rosicrucians, the Freemasons and the Hermetic Order of the Golden Dawn.

There is still a small Gnostic religion in late twentieth-century Iran and Iraq, called the Mandæans, who claim spiritual descent from John the Baptist rather than from Jesus. They believe in the Gnostic (and Zoroastrian) dualism of light and dark, and the soul imprisoned in the material body, and they look forward to a coming saviour, Manda d'Hayye (Knowledge of Life), from whom they take their name.

CABALISM

In a phrase, Cabalism is esoteric Judaism practised also by esoteric Christians. The Cabala, or Kabbalah, or Qabala, is not just a set of texts, but a means of approaching these texts. The meaning of the Hebrew word *qbl* is variously given as 'received tradition' or 'mouth to ear'; in other words, its teachings were originally passed by word of mouth, only to those thought fit to receive them.

Although one recent scholar differentiates three different meanings for the three spellings[9] – he sees Kabbalah as the original Jewish system, Cabala as the Renaissance Christian version of it, and Qabala as the modern occultist use of it – this is something of an *ex post facto* discrimination. There have been many varieties and uses of Cabalism over the centuries, and different people of different countries at different times have spelled it in different ways. 'Cabala' is used in this book (except in quotations or book titles) for three reasons: it is the simplest spelling; it avoids whatever specific resonances might be seen in the other spellings; and it is more clearly seen as the root of the word 'cabal', which has entered the language to mean a secret intrigue or a small powerful group, without any religious connotations.

There is some truth behind the affectionate stereotype of the Jewish love for telling stories with a moral. Cabalist writings delight in stories-with-a-message, allegories, parables, myths. So, of course, does the Bible, including the teachings of Jesus – a point missed by those who insist on a wholly literal interpretation of the Bible.

The essence of Cabalism, as described in the *Zohar*, is that most people reading the Scriptures see only the outer story or, as it were, a suit of clothes; a few see the person within the clothes; a very few see the soul within the person. Cabalists look for the inner meaning, the secret meaning, the esoteric meaning; they seek to discern the secrets of God and of creation. One might recognize the beauty of a friend's clothes, and even admire them; but the true value of the friend is somewhat deeper.

Cabalism originated some 2,000 years ago. Educated Jews at the time of Christ were split into several factions, of which the rabbinical Pharisees – who followed oral tradition in their interpretation of the scriptures and the law – and the more conservative, aristocratic and literalist Sadducees – who did not believe in angels, demons or resurrection – are mentioned in the New Testament. There were also the nationalistic Zealots, who had political motivations, and the pious Essenes, who were probably Gnostic. Although they all shared the *Torah* – the Law, the Pentateuch, and by extension the whole Old Testament – they had very different ways of approaching it and interpreting it. So did the Jewish mystics, later known as Cabalists. Based in rabbinical Judaism, in their search for spiritual enlightenment they borrowed over the years both from Jewish Gnosticism and from Jewish Neo-Platonism and Neo-Aristotelianism.

As the Jews were scattered and persecuted throughout Europe over the next millennium and a half, it was important for them to maintain both their scholarship and their spirituality. While medieval Christian priests were often almost completely uneducated, and their bishops often morally and political-ly corrupt, medieval Jewish rabbis were renowned for their learning and their piety. 'Rabbi' is Hebrew for 'my master', and rabbis were teachers and judges of their people, and interpreters of the Law, rather than priests, though they did conduct ritual ceremonies.

Spirituality and scholarship is a powerful combination. In seeking a greater understanding of and closeness to God, many rabbis delved deeper into their studies of the *Torah* and the *Talmud*, the written body of rabbinical tradition and interpretation of the Law. The Babylonian *Talmud* dates in its written form to around AD 500, but the *Talmud* could in one sense be said to be ever-unfinished, as later rabbis have added their interpretations and com-mentaries on it right up to the present day.

With a religion so based on Law, the interpretation of Law is vitally important: hence the importance of, and the deep respect given to, rabbis. In any organization there is always a conflict between those who insist on obey-ing the letter of the law, and those who believe it more important to follow the spirit of the law; there are traditionalists and legalists (by no means always the same thing), and liberals, and supporters of a variety of different emphases. Legalists should not automatically be condemned – in the way that liberals are prone to condemning them – for small-mindedness; some follow the letter of the law *because of* the importance to them of the spirit of the law, i.e. the underlying reasons behind what might appear to others to be petty legalisms. This can apply to Cabalists, and certainly includes devoted mem-bers of some ritual-based societies today.

Cabalists always favoured a more allegorical rather than a literalist approach to the *Torah* and the *Talmud*. They also believed that truth could be found deep within the texts themselves, within the words and even the letters. One of the first Cabalistic works was the *Sefer Yesirah*, the Book of the Creation (second- to fifth-century); this first set down the concept of the 10 *sephiroth* (singular, *sephira*) and the 22 paths between them, showing already the importance that the 10 numbers and 22 letters of the Hebrew alphabet would have to Cabalism. As with Roman numerals, Hebrew letters also represented numbers, and numbers, as Pythagoras taught, are powerfully symbolic of God and man and the relationship between them.[10]

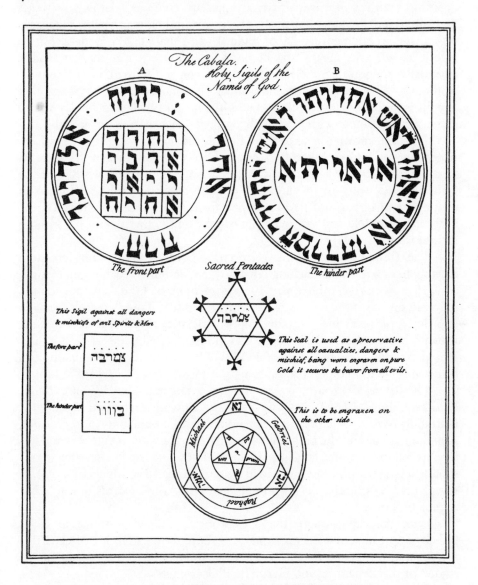

The Cabala: Holy Sigils of the Name of God
(Francis Barrett, *The Magus*, 1801)

Cabalism became more formalized in the tenth century, initially in Italy and then in Germany. The twelfth-century *Sefer ha-Bahir* (Book of Brilliance) emphasized the concept of the *Shekhinah* (Hebrew: 'dwelling'), or presence or immanence, as the female aspect of God. Cabalism came of age in the thirteenth century in Provence in Southern France, then shortly afterwards in Spain, where the *Zohar* was written (or perhaps compiled), largely by Moses de León, around 1285 – though the myth surrounding it attributes the teachings to the second-century Rabbi Simeon bar Yohai. The *Sefer ha-Zohar*, to give it its full title, means 'the Book of Splendour'; it teaches that God is essentially unknowable and indescribable, using the term *Ain-Sof* (Hebrew: 'without end'). Everything in the universe is connected to everything else, and all is an expression of God. The ultimate purpose of humankind is to attain mystical union with God, and Cabalism teaches ways towards this.

The best-known aspect of the Cabala is the diagram of the Tree of Life. According to Dolores Ashcroft-Nowicki, Director of Studies of the Servants of the Light school of occult science, it contains 'the entire wisdom of the Qabalah ... Owing to its simplicity ... the glyph is easily committed to memory; and because of its profundity, from this sparse simplicity can be derived a complete and satisfying philosophy and knowledge of life in both its inner and outer aspects.'[11]

The Tree of Life shows the relationship between God and his creation; it symbolizes both God reaching down to man, and man reaching up to God. The 10 *sephiroth* symbolize the 10 rays of light of God's creation of the universe, and thus the secrets of the universe. They show the levels of man's knowledge of the divine, but more importantly, they reveal attributes of God, which can be thought of as names of God. The sacred name of God, represented by the Hebrew letters for YHWH, or the tetragrammaton, was believed to be too holy to pronounce.

The 10 *sephiroth* are *Kether*, the Crown, *Chokmah*, Wisdom, *Binah*, Understanding, *Chesed*, Mercy, *Geburah*, Power, *Tiphareth*, Beauty or Harmony, *Netzach*, Victory, *Hod*, Splendour, *Yesod*, Foundation, and *Malkuth*, Kingdom. They and the paths between them correspond to numbers and letters, to colours, planets, angels, parts of the body, and much else; such correspondences are at the heart of ritual magic (see p. 165). Much later, correspondences were found between the 22 paths and the 22 cards of the Major Arcana of Tarot.

With the expulsion of the Jews from Spain and Portugal in 1492, Cabalism spread across Europe, and came more to the attention of Christian mystics and occultists. By the sixteenth century it was a major part of the studies of the alchemists and Hermetic Philosophers.

The complex symbolism of the Cabala, embodying both the theoretical and the practical, exemplifies the link between mysticism and magic, and also the importance of myth as a means of expressing truths. The deep spiritual teachings within it became central to all esoteric religion in the West, and remain so today in many secret societies.

SUFISM

Sufism is mystical Islam; but it is much more than that. In the same way that Cabalists made orthodox Jews uneasy, Sufis raised an uncomfortable mixture of respect and fear among orthodox Muslims. And in the same way that Cabalist teachings have extended way beyond Judaism, Sufi writings have been an inspiration to Jewish and Christian mystics and, today, to followers of other esoteric paths, including those with 'New Age' beliefs.

The early history of Islam is complex. Briefly, the split into the two main divisions of the religion, Sunni and Shi'ite, occurred within half a century of Muhammad's death, and the more radical Shi'ites then split into several more groups over the centuries. Although the origins of Sufism are veiled in that confused state between history and myth, it is known that mystical Islam began very early, probably in the seventh century AD. Sufis claim that Muhammad himself, and his son-in-law Ali, were Sufis.

The name Sufi derives from the Arabic word for 'wool-clad', and refers to the rough wool robe worn by many ascetic mystics, Christian as well as Muslim. There are also possible links to the Arabic *safa*, 'purity'; the Hebrew *Ain Sof*, 'without end', the Cabalist term for the unknowable God; and even *Sophia*, the Greek term for the (female) Wisdom persona of God.

As with the Gnostic and the Cabalist, the Sufi seeks to know the unknowable, to find unity with God. God is in all things, and all things are in God: a common mystical belief, but one which critics have always claimed smacks of pantheism. As with all mysticism, within paradox is found truth; it is both infinitely complex, and ultimately simple. The Sufi interpretation of the Koran is esoteric and allegorical. Sufis, by seeking an individual, personal union with God above all else, put themselves beyond the control of the hierarchy of formal Islam.

It is easy to see how Jewish Cabalists, Christian Gnostics and Muslim Sufis have more in common with each other than with their parent religions – and also to see why the orthodox 'establishments' of all three religions have persecuted those with such heterodox beliefs. Heresy, as always, is defined by orthodoxy.

After several centuries of persecution Sufism became accepted, even respected, in the twelfth and thirteenth centuries; as in Judaism, spirituality and scholarship were a strong combination, and many orthodox Muslim theologians of the time embraced and helped define Sufi teachings. The

Shi'ites, however, remained antagonistic towards Sufism and, even today in Pakistan, members of the Ahmadi sect of Sufism can be arrested, and have been killed, for doing or saying anything 'to injure the feelings of a Muslim'.

For outsiders, Sufism is known mainly for the famous 'whirling dervishes' who dance themselves into an ecstatic state, and for its beautiful poetry which often describes the loving union between man and God in erotic terms. (While no doubt horrifying to devout Muslims and Christians alike, this is not unique to Sufism; a modern comparison could be the work of the Canadian Jewish poet and singer Leonard Cohen, which focuses almost entirely on sex and God.)

In its early days, Sufism was influenced by Eastern Orthodox Christian mystics, by Neo-Platonism, and even by some aspects of Hinduism, particularly Advaita Vedantism. Sufis have always had a close relationship with mystics and philosophers of other religious traditions; the experience of a deep loving union with God transcends religious boundaries. It is known that in medieval times, even at the time of the Crusades, some Christians and some Muslims cooperated with each other, and learned about each other's mystical beliefs. Similarly, particularly in Spain, Cabalistic Jews and Muslim Moors shared their teachings.

Although most secret societies and the vast majority of Freemasons today probably know little about Sufism, it holds a vital place in the development of esoteric thought from two millennia or more ago, and into the late twentieth century.

The poet and historical novelist Robert Graves calls the Sufis 'an ancient spiritual freemasonry', and goes on to state as fact, 'Indeed, Freemasonry itself began as a Sufi society. It first reached England in the reign of King Aethelstan (924–939) and was introduced into Scotland disguised as a craft guild at the beginning of the fourteenth century, doubtless by the Knights Templar.[12]

THE ASSASSINS

Once again, the complexities of Islamic history will be dealt with very briefly. The Shi'ite branch of Islam had a number of schisms, the best-known being between the Seveners and the Twelvers, who believed that the seventh and twelfth imams respectively were the concealed and later-to-return Mahdi, or saviour-leader, who would restore Islamic purity. The Seveners, or Sabiyya, were Ismailis, named after the eighth-century Muhammad ibn Ismail, who died before becoming the seventh imam; a related Ismaili sect were the Nizari, named after the unsuccessful attempt to establish Nizar as the caliph or leader of the Ismailis on his father's death in AD 1094.

Hasan-i Sabbah was a Persian Twelver who converted to Ismailism and became an enthusiastic missionary for its cause, and a supporter of Nizar. In his youth he studied alongside the future tentmaker, astronomer and poet Omar Khayyám, and the future prime minister of Persia, Nizam ul-Mulk, whom he later had murdered. In 1090 he took control of Alamut (Eagle's Nest), a Sunni fortress high in the mountains of northern Persia, and established it as the centre of his operations.

Hasan's followers were named Assassins by the Christian Crusaders who encountered them. They were utterly dedicated to Hasan – sometimes known as the Old Man of the Mountains – and would kill or die on his order. There are stories, probably apocryphal, of Hasan demonstrating his power to honoured visitors by signalling to a follower standing guard on a high peak, who then cast himself to his death.

The mythic basis of this unquestioning loyalty is that Hasan had a beautiful garden in a hidden fertile valley in the mountains. The valley ran with streams of milk, honey, wine and pure water; its trees were heavy with fruit. Initiates were drugged, then taken to the valley, where for a few days they lived among its delights, which included palaces, musicians, singers, dancers and *houris*. Drugged again, they were returned to Hasan, and were told they had been given a glimpse of Paradise. If they swore an oath of absolute obedience to Hasan they would return there on their deaths.

There is some archæological evidence of water cisterns carved in the rock at Alamut – and it is said that a narrow cleft in the rocks leads to a small fertile valley. The drug with which Hasan introduced his initiates to blissful happiness was cannabis; it was the Arabic word *hashshashin* (users of hashish) which the Crusaders adapted to Assassins – the word still used for high political murders 900 years later. (Some authorities say that the name was simply applied to the Ismailis as an insult by their more orthodox Muslim enemies, to suggest that they were addicted to vices; others claim the name comes instead from the Arabic *Assasseen*, meaning 'guardians'.)

Hasan was a brilliant and ruthless ruler. He took advantage of the political chaos in Persia – he probably helped cause most of it – and he eliminated potential rivals. Within a very short time he had more real power than the supposed rulers, and was feared by Muslims and Christians alike.

Hasan died in 1124, aged 90, having ruled through the fanatical devotion of his followers for nearly 35 years. His successors continued the tradition, having major political and religious figures killed, the killers being assured that if they died they would go straight to that Paradise of which they had already tasted. One very successful technique they used was to plant 'sleepers' in the Courts of rulers. They would not reveal themselves for years, even decades, until they received a signal, at which point they would kill the completely unsuspecting ruler.

By the time of the fourth Grand Master, also called Hasan, his position as leader, or imam, was so strong that he could claim openly to be the Hidden Imam, the Mahdi, the direct mouthpiece of God. In the earlier years the Assassins had behaved outwardly as ordinary Muslims, but under Hasan II and his son Muhammad II they threw caution to the winds. The laws of Islam no longer applied; wine could be drunk, and pork eaten. This policy of open heresy was abandoned by their successors who, at least on the surface, adopted a form of Sunni Islam; the Alamut Assassins became relatively tame for a while.

Meanwhile the Syrian branch of the Assassins became effectively an independent body, continuing to kill at will – or on commission. They were in regular contact with the Crusaders in Syria, and not always as antagonists. If it suited their purpose to fight on the side of the Crusaders to maintain their own position against their common Muslim enemies, they would do so. These were the Assassins who had most involvement with the Knights Templar, for a while paying the Templars 2,000 gold pieces a year to avoid direct military conflict with them.

The Assassins were eventually defeated by the Mongols in the middle of the thirteenth century. They were not wholly wiped out, however; in their two centuries of influence they had spread over much of the civilized world, including parts of India and southern Russia. Although no longer known as the Assassins, the Nizari (also called Khojas) still exist today as a small Ismaili sect, whose spiritual (and to some extent temporal) leader is the Aga Khan.

The Assassins are important to the current narrative for several reasons. They were a powerful, self-sustaining Order with several levels of initiation, oaths of obedience, and secret signs. Their beliefs varied from those of standard Islam, having something in common with Gnostic ideas. Among their beliefs were the teachings that heaven and hell were the same, and that no acts were sinful in themselves because the only good and evil were in obeying or disobeying the imam.

The Assassins are believed by some to have influenced the Knights Templar in a number of ways. Their uniform was a white tunic with a red sash, hat or boots: the colours of innocence, or purity, and blood. The Templars wore a white tunic with a red cross. The Assassins were organized, under their chief *da'i* or Grand Master, into senior *da'is* and ordinary *da'is* (missionaries); *rafiqs* (companions); *fidais, fidavis* or *fedayeen* (literally 'faithful', or devotees) who were the actual assassins, in the modern sense of the word; and *lasiqs* (laymen). The Templars, under their Grand Master, had grand priors, priors, knights, esquires and lay brothers. It is widely believed that the originally orthodox beliefs of this Christian warrior Order were affected by the beliefs of this most decidedly unorthodox Muslim Order.

CHRISTIAN HERESIES

Before looking at the Cathars and the Knights Templar it will be useful to see how the religious climate of Europe was anything but settled at the time. Indeed, the Roman Catholic Church was having to deal with more heresies than at any time since the Church Fathers had defined Christianity.

In its first four centuries the Christian religion was beset with heresies,[13] several of which could very easily have become the dominant form of Christianity, and so might still have been with us today. (A heresy, after all, is only a belief that the current religious establishment wishes to crush.) One of these was Arianism which, if the Council of Nicaea had swung the other way in AD 325, would have saved generations of catechismal youngsters from wrestling with the complexities of Three-in-One and One-in-Three. As it is, Arianism has never entirely vanished, being with us today not only, in different ways, in the Unitarian movement and the Jehovah's Witnesses, but also, quietly, among the pews (and sometimes even in the pulpits) of many perfectly ordinary Anglican and Catholic parish churches. In its several varieties, Arianism basically said that if the Father was God, Jesus couldn't be. Or, to put it another way, there is only One Creator God.

Another heresy, Dynamic Monarchianism, held that Jesus was a normal man with divine power in him, a belief which, in one form or another, is quite widespread on the fringes of Christianity today.

One of the others, a very British heresy, was Pelagianism, founded by Pelagius, a fourth- to fifth-century Scots or Irish monk. Briefly, it taught that we can haul ourselves up by our own bootstraps; it is possible, albeit with a great deal of effort, to live a sinless life, and so to earn salvation. Even at the highest levels, the theological argument over salvation through faith versus works has never entirely gone away; while every day parish priests hear non-church-goers saying, 'But I try to lead a good life, Vicar; doesn't that count for anything with God?'

The next half millennium saw few new heresies, though it is worth noting that the ninth-century Irish scholar John Scotus Erigena taught that evil does not really exist (see p. 42, Assassins), that individual reason is more important than authority (see p. 31, Gnostics), and that creation came from rays emanating from God (see p. 38, Cabalists).

But by the twelfth century, central Europe was awash with heretical teachings. In the early part of the century in southern France, for example, Peter de Bruys taught that Christians should disparage the cross rather than revering it, as it had been the means of torturing and killing Christ; this might well have been the source of the later allegation that the Knights Templar spat on the cross.

The Waldenses, founded by Peter Waldo around 1176, were in effect the first Protestants; they rejected everything about the Catholic Church that the Reformation would later also reject. They were condemned as heretics and persecuted, and many were burned by the Inquisition; but they have survived to the present day.

Meanwhile the Manichæans (see p. 84) lingered on around the Mediterranean. Manichæism had an offshoot, the Paulicians, though some authorities see the latter as an independently-arising movement with similar beliefs because of their common Gnostic inspiration. The Paulicians may have been in existence as early as the fourth century, but they became prominent when they moved to Armenia in the mid-seventh century. Opposed to the theological complexity, the idolatry and the wealth of the Catholic Church, they reached their height in the ninth century, when they actually founded their own short-lived state in the Balkans.

They in turn seem to have inspired the Bogomils, or Friends of God, founded (at least in legend) by a tenth-century Eastern Orthodox priest, Bogomil. He taught the Gnostic dualist belief that the world was created by an evil being, not by God, and that Christ had come to free people from the Devil's hold. (Later they saw this being, Satanaei or Satan, as Christ's elder brother; Mormons today believe that Lucifer was Christ's brother.) Bogomil also preached a social gospel to the oppressed peasants of newly-feudal Bulgaria: the nobles and priests were the Devil's servants. Despite the Catholic Church's opposition and persecution (an eleventh- to twelfth-century Bogomil monk, Basil, was burned to death) the religion took hold, eventually becoming the state religion in Bosnia and Hungary, and also very strong in Serbia. The Bogomils lasted until the fourteenth century, when the Balkans were invaded by Muslims, and many Bogomils converted to Islam.

In their heyday, however, the influence of the Bogomils extended as far as Italy and France. Their priests and monks were called *perfecti*; stressing purity of spirit they ate no meat and abstained from sex, both being seen as part of the evil material world. Although most Bogomils lived ordinary lives, they often took the *consolamentum*, a ceremony which purified them, shortly before death.

The better-known Cathars, who will be discussed shortly, did not suddenly spring out of nowhere.

One of the commonest charges against heretics was sodomy.[14] The Cathars and the Knights Templar, among others, were accused of this; so were the Bogomils, who came from Bulgaria, and so were referred to by the French as *bougres* (Bulgars), giving us the English word 'bugger'. Sodomy, said the Catholic Church, was how Bogomils and Cathars had sex without bringing more babies into the world.

Although the Beguines and the Brethren of the Free Spirit came into existence after the Cathars began, discussion of them still helps to illustrate the variety and complexity of the religious situation in Europe in the late Middle Ages.

The Beguines, a largely female grassroots religious movement in western and central Europe from *c.* AD 1200, are thought by some to have taken their name from the Albigensians (Cathars), though there was no overlap in beliefs. Some lived in communities, while many others travelled from place to place. Although initially unsanctioned by the Church, they took a vow of chastity, seeing themselves as a religious Order. They worked in the community, caring for the sick and supporting themselves by their crafts and by begging. From the start their independence and their emphasis on the virtues of poverty irritated the Church.

In southern Europe, male followers were called Beguines; in northern Europe they were called Beghards.

As the movement developed, some Beguines moved towards mysticism, and some took on heretical beliefs, studying and preserving the works of the twelfth-century French philosopher Amalric of Bena, whose teachings were a development of those of John Scotus Erigena: the world emanated from God, and God is in everything. Other Beghards and Beguines became Brothers and Sisters of the Free Spirit; they believed that as the Holy Spirit indwelt them, they were completely pure, and to the pure, all things are pure (Titus 1:15). Although there is little evidence (beyond accusations by the Inquisition) that they behaved licentiously, they believed, at least in theory, that they were above the law, whether moral, religious or state. Those who were sanctified could no longer sin.

> Sin is the will to offend God, and he whose will has become God's will cannot offend God. His will is God's will, and God's will is his will. A man may become so completely Divine that his very body is sanctified, and then what it does is a Divine act. In this state the instincts and impulses of the body take on a holy significance.[15]

This extreme belief still exists; I once heard a Pentecostal preacher say, 'God came into my heart in 1956. Since that day I have not sinned.' No doubt that preacher would be horrified at the logical comparison with Aleister Crowley's famous dictum, 'Do what thou wilt shall be the whole of the Law' (see p. 168).

Beyond sin or not, the Brethren of the Free Spirit saw no need to obey the Church, or to receive the sacraments from priests. They also believed that there was no hell, and that all would be saved, the latter a doctrine to re-surface later in America with the late eighteenth-century Universalists, now merged with the Unitarian Church there.

The Brethren of the Free Spirit, inevitably bringing the Church's per-secution on themselves, brought it also on many other Beguines whose beliefs were more orthodox. By now the Church, through practice with the Cathars, met any suspicion of heresy with torture and death.

THE CATHARS

Like the Manichæans in the first few centuries of the Christian era, the Cathars were not so much a troublesome heresy within the Church as a fully-fledged alternative to mainstream Christianity. Like the Manichæans also, they quickly set up a Church hierarchy, complete with bishops; there were eleven by the end of the twelfth century. This made them even more dangerous in the eyes of the Catholic Church – which had problems enough of its own, with a series of schismatic 'antipopes' supported by the Holy Roman Emperor. The Church was a political power, reinforced by its power over men's souls. A competing religion, which condemned the riches of the Catholic Church, was a threat to its temporal power as well as to its spiritual power.

It is clear that the Cathars of what is now southern France were deeply influenced by the Bogomils; it is likely that they were a direct spiritual descendant. A Bogomil bishop, Nicetas, presided over a major Cathar coun-cil in 1167, and helped plan their organization. 'Cathari' comes from the Latin for 'pure ones', or *perfecti*; Emmanuel Le Roy Ladurie disputes this, saying that 'In fact "Cathar" comes from a German word the meaning of which has nothing to do with purity,'[16] though unfortunately he doesn't iden-tify the word. Their other common name, the Albigensians, is taken from the town of Albi, a major Cathar centre in the Languedoc region of southern France.

(The people of the Languedoc had their own language and very much their own culture; unlike the northern French, they were literate, educated, artistic and tolerant of different views. They are perhaps best known for the wandering poet-musicians, the *troubadours*. Their culture and group of language dialects are now generally known as Provençal. The two language groups – loosely the far Southern and the Northern French – were distinguished by the words used for 'yes': *langue d'oc* and *langue d'oïl*, the latter becoming *oui*.)

Like the Bogomils and the Manichæans, the Cathars believed in a Good Principle (Spirit) and an Evil Principle (Matter). Spirit was trapped in matter by the Evil One; Christ had come, as a spirit being and not as a man, to show how it might be freed. The crucifixion and resurrection were not physical events; the cross, therefore, had no relevance and inspired no reverence.

One could be saved from the round of reincarnation by living a perfect life. The *perfecti*, both male and female, were the spiritually pure; they ate no meat, eggs or milk (some hardly ate at all), and they abstained from sex, for the same reasons that the Bogomils had done so. Clearly this ascetic lifestyle would not appeal to ordinary people. The majority of members, known as *credentes* (believers), or in France as *bonshommes*, lived good but fairly normal lives, taking on the rigours of the *perfecti* only when they were close to death, through the ritual or sacrament of the *consolamentum*, the Baptism of the Holy Spirit. This was administered by a *perfectus* initiator placing his hand on a person's head, much as in the Catholic sacraments of confirmation and ordination. From the ordinary member's point of view, leaving this till his deathbed meant that he could enjoy an ordinary life, including meat and sex; from the *perfecti* point of view, there was less chance of a new *perfectus* backsliding into temptation. There are accounts, whether true or not, of people recovering from a seemingly mortal illness after having been given the *consolamentum*, and being denied food while still in a weakened state; it was better to die through this *endura* than to return to the world and yield to temptation.

The appeal of Catharism to ordinary people and nobility alike was its contrast with the wealth and hypocrisy of the Catholic Church and its clergy. The *perfecti* were genuinely pious, while the *bonshommes* were indeed good men – and women: Catharism both believed and practised equality of the sexes. For the nobility, the appeal was as much political as spiritual; the Counts of Toulouse and Foix, and the other leaders of what is now southern France, were effectively independent rulers, and resented being vassals of the Catholic king of France.

The Cathars first appeared not in France but in Germany; the first mention of them is in 1143, in Cologne. Within a few years they had spread to France, and by the 1160s they had found their home in southern France and northern Italy. Thirty German missionaries sent to England in the winter of 1166 were quickly dealt with by Henry II; they were branded, flogged and stripped, and sent out to die from exposure.

In 1184 Pope Lucius III, worried by the growing numbers and strength of the heretics, instituted the Inquisition; those suspected of heresy had to prove their innocence; the guilty were to be excommunicated from the Church, then handed over to the secular authorities for punishment. It didn't have a great deal of success until, in 1199, Pope Innocent III declared that heresy was high treason against God, and that convicted heretics' possessions should be split between the Inquisition and local civil authorities, thus ensuring their enthusiastic cooperation.

In 1208 Peter of Castelnau, a papal legate, was sent by Innocent III to convert the Cathars, and perhaps to negotiate with the recently-excommunicated Raymond VI, Count of Toulouse, ruler of much of the Cathar lands. He was murdered by one of Raymond's knights, and the pope took immediate revenge. Until now, crusades had been against Muslims, non-Christians who could be killed without harm to one's soul. Now, for the first time, the pope called a crusade against Christian heretics, declaring it God's will that orthodox Christians should kill heterodox Christians. Under the command of the brutal Simon de Montfort, father and namesake of the future anti-royalist leader of the barons in Britain, over 30,000[17] lords, knights and other Crusaders from the north of France (which was somewhat less civilized and sophisticated than the Mediterranean south) descended on the Languedoc, with the promise of two years' indulgence and as much booty as they wanted. Tens of thousands of Cathars died during the twenty years of the Albigensian Crusade.

One of the most disgraceful episodes occurred right at the beginning of the crusade in 1209, at the town of Béziers near the Mediterranean coast, where, as in many Cathar-dominated areas, Catholics and Cathars lived peaceably and agreeably side-by-side. As the troops prepared to storm the town a soldier asked the papal legate Arnaud, Abbot of Cîteaux, how they should distinguish between true believers and heretics, Catholics and Cathars. Arnaud's response was 'Kill them all; God will know his own'. Between 15,000 and 20,000 men, women and children were massacred at Béziers, some of them while claiming sanctuary in the church.

The sackings, sieges and massacres continued for years. The Cathars' walled city of Carcassonne fell; in Minerve 140 people died in the first mass burning in 1210, and in Lavaur, 400 people. A well-respected and pious Cathar noblewoman, Giraude de Lavaur, was stoned to death in 1211. In 1213 Raymond VI, who had swung from side to side over the years, accepting and then renouncing Catharism, depending on the political pressure put on him, was killed in battle. De Montfort died in 1218, but the campaign continued. In 1229 the northern French annexed the Languedoc by force. Raymond VII of Toulouse gave in, swearing allegiance to the new King Louis IX, and giving up most of his wealth to the Church and the king.

For some years, Cathars had to practise their faith in secret. Many withdrew, along with many Catholic nobles and knights from the Languedoc, to Montségur, a Pyrennean fortress which had withstood de Montfort in 1209. In 1243 a band of Crusaders, realizing they could not storm the fortress, laid siege to it. The siege lasted ten months, because local villagers smuggled food in to the fortress. In 1244 those in the fortress finally surrendered. The Catholics were allowed to live, but over 200 *perfecti* were burned to death; the stories say that they walked into the flames joyfully, singing hymns.

Legend also says that the night before the surrender, four Cathars were seen climbing down from the fortress on ropes; they escaped, taking with them 'the treasure of the Cathars'. Romantic legend says that this treasure was the Grail; it is perhaps more likely to have been their teachings.

The final stronghold of the Cathars, Queribus, fell in 1255. Officially this was the end of Catharism, but many Cathars had gone to northern Italy, where they managed to escape persecution for the remainder of the century; and some went into the Alps, where they survived even longer. It is possible that some went into the Balkans, to merge back into the Bogomils.

There was a minor Cathar revival around the village of Montaillou in the Comté de Foix between 1300 and 1318. The records of the Inquisition conducted by Jacques Fournier (later the Avignon Pope Benedict III) from 1318 to 1325 form the basis of Ladurie's famous historical portrait of the village.

The Albigensian Crusade was a shameful episode in French history. It is perhaps hardly surprising that many French historians skate over it as quickly as possible. An early nineteenth-century English school textbook, W.C. Taylor's *A History of France and Normandy*, has three brief but telling paragraphs; André Maurois' *A History of France* (1949) has six lines; and Achille Luchaire's *Social France at the Time of Philip Augustus* – exactly the right period – only has scattered references, in passing, when discussing something else entirely.

The culture of the Languedoc has already been mentioned. Provençal (sometimes called Occitan) culture was way ahead of that of northern France, which some authorities describe as 'barbaric', even in the twelfth century. It might not be too fanciful to suggest that the Languedoc was moving from the Middle Ages into the Renaissance a good two centuries before this occurred in Italy – and it was this flowering of culture which was wiped out by de Montfort's 'Crusaders'.

If the Cathars had not been exterminated, and the cultural as well as the spiritual influence of the Languedoc had spread, French history – indeed, European history – might have been entirely different.

But what has been left to us from this period is something which itself greatly affected French and English history and literature. The concepts of chivalry, of courtly love, of questing knights, of the Grail, of the entire Arthurian *œuvre*, are something we shall return to later. The significance of the Cathars will become more apparent as this book proceeds.

The hundred years of the Cathars in the late Middle Ages were the strongest and most visible resurgence of Gnostic beliefs until the present day. But from the viewpoint of later history, the Cathars are of most importance for one thing: they were responsible for the development of the Inquisition.

The Order of Dominicans came into being when a certain Dominic (1170–1221), a Catholic preacher of orthodox faith, travelled through the Languedoc with the Bishop of Osma, talking to Cathars, debating the two faiths with them, preaching 'the true faith' to them, and winning some conversions in 1206. Dominic took no part in the Albigensian Crusade which began in 1208, when Cathars were killed without any attempt at conversion; he just kept on debating and preaching. Pope Honorius III was so impressed with his work that in 1216–1217 he sanctioned a new Order, the Order of Friars Preachers, commonly known as the Dominicans, specifically to deal with the Cathars and other heretics; Dominic, through his work, had led to their foundation in 1215, in Toulouse, right in the midst of the Cathars.

Dominic was first and foremost a preacher and a teacher of preachers, a monk who did not believe that poverty had to include poverty of mind. But in 1233, twelve years after Dominic's death and a year before his canonization, Pope Gregory IX put the Dominicans in charge of the Inquisition. The rest is history. Dominic, who by all accounts was a gentle and good man, would have been horrified.

It is interesting to read a Roman Catholic comment on the 'poison' of the Cathars, and the work of

> the office of Inquisitors, to whom it belonged to sift all cases of suspected
> heresy, to save those whom ignorant zeal or jealous malice accused
> unjustly, to teach and reclaim those who had been led astray, and in case
> of obstinacy to declare the offender an enemy of the Christian name,
> one whom the Church, unable truthfully to claim, left to the vengeance
> of the Christian State against whose fundamental laws he rebelled.
>
> The long and arduous task was at length successful, and by the end
> of the fourteenth century Albigensianism, with all other forms of
> Catharism, was practically extinct.'[18]

THE KNIGHTS TEMPLAR

Much of what has been written about the Knights Templar is speculation, but there is a certain amount of factual information. It must be remembered, though, that even contemporary or near-contemporary accounts – here as in any area of history – are not necessarily any more reliable than those in newspapers of today. For example, William of Tyre was a twelfth-century Palestinian bishop who disliked the power and prestige of the Templars; his account of the Crusades may or may not be entirely accurate factually, but its interpretations of events are certainly coloured by their author's views. Walter Mapp, who borrowed heavily from William, was basically a twelfth-century gossip columnist and, like all such, was not averse to adding a little creative colour to his stories. The thirteenth-century St Albans writer Matthew Paris might have been a more conscientious chronicler, but even he could only rely on his sources, and some of those are known to have been anti-Templar. The blurring of fact and fiction about the Templars, then, began even in their own day.

The Templars were founded by Hugues de Payen, a noble knight from Champagne, with eight other knights, around 1119 – which was towards the end of the first Hasan's rule over the Assassins. Their aim was to protect pilgrims going to Jerusalem, which had been captured by the Crusaders and established as a Christian kingdom in 1099. Their cause was taken up by Bernard of Clairvaux, head of the Cistercian Order, who helped draw up their statutes; they were formally established at the Council of Troyes in 1129 as the Order of the Poor Knights of Christ and the Temple of Solomon.

Their connection with the Temple of Solomon, originally, was that they were given rooms in the royal palace of Baudouin I, the king of Jerusalem; the palace was, according to tradition, built over the ruins of Solomon's Temple. The name was to assume far greater significance in the future.

Templar knights made the usual monastic vows of poverty, chastity and obedience. The Order grew quickly; by 1130 there were some 300 Templar knights in Palestine. It is interesting to note that among the requirements for entry to the Knights Templar, in addition to being from a knightly family, born in wedlock, and unmarried, a candidate had to be an adult, free from all obligations, not a member of any other Order, and not in debt; these last four requirements are also demanded by some of today's esoteric societies.

They were tough and brilliant fighters, and were respected for this, but right from the beginning there was suspicion of the Knights Templar. Until then knights had done a necessary but bloody job, and monks had resolutely kept their hands clean of blood; the Templars were the first to combine the two in a military order, and many in the Church didn't like this.

Initially, at least, they were highly regarded at the very head of the Church; in 1139 Pope Innocent II granted them independence of any authority, religious or secular, save that of the Pope himself. In 1161 Pope Alexander III granted them exemption from all tithes, and allowed them to receive tithes themselves, and to have their own chaplains, and their own burial grounds. Although bestowed by popes, these privileges – and the Templars' open use and probable abuse of them – angered many bishops who saw their own power being eroded.

Kings and nobles, while not able or willing to join the Templars themselves, granted them land and the rents from land; lay members gave them money. (One King of Spain left them a third of his country in his will, though his bequest was never carried out.) Over time, the Templars came to own not only land and fortresses, but ports and fleets as well. So that pilgrims need not risk carrying large amounts of money with them, they gave their money and valuables to the Order, which issued them with promissory notes – effectively an early form of cheque – which could be exchanged for money when needed. In a fairly short time the Knights Templar were the bankers of Europe; like all bankers they became very wealthy, and were able to lend money to merchants, nobles and kings. Because of their expertise, they were put in charge of the state coffers of several countries, including those of France.

In 1187 Saladin, leader of the Muslim Saracens, captured Tiberias and Hattin, and the Christians began to lose power in the Holy Land. Over the next century more and more battles were lost, and more and more cities fell, culminating with Tripoli and Acre in 1291. Long before this, although the Templars maintained their bases in the Holy Land, it was clear that their real power was now in Europe. It was also clear that – especially now that they were no longer really doing the job for which they had been founded – they had become far more powerful than many people liked. In 1252, for example, the English king Henry III accused them of 'pride and haughtiness', and suggested that their liberties be constrained and their possessions reduced.

Nobody likes bankers, especially when they are as powerful as the Knights Templar. The crowned heads of Europe began to look for ways to reduce the Templars' power over them; some, heavily in debt, wanted to find a way to escape their debts. One of these was King Philippe le Bel of France. With the support of the Avignon Pope Clement V (who owed him a favour: Philippe had helped secure the papacy for him) he took action on 13 October 1307, arresting large numbers of Templars in co-ordinated raids. Unfortunately for Philippe's empty coffers, the Templars seem to have learned of the plan in advance; the treasury at their Paris preceptory, which Philippe seized, had already been cleared out – according to some stories, filling eighteen Templar ships.

Rather than facing civil or criminal charges, the arrested Templars were charged with heresy, and many were tortured. The last Grand Master of the Knights Templar, Jacques de Molay, was held in the royal château of Chinon, in the Loire Valley, before being taken to Paris and burned at the stake in 1314.

(According to one recent historian, the term Grand Master is erroneous; his actual title was the Master of the Order of the Temple of Solomon of Jerusalem.[19] Regional Templar leaders, however, such as the Commanders of Antioch and Tripoli, were known as Masters, and there were even Masters of England and France; the term Grand Master to distinguish the Master of Jerusalem, the head of the whole Order, is thus allowable.)

In France in particular, and also in much of mainland Europe, the Templars were destroyed; but in Spain and Portugal they were allowed to transfer to newly-created Orders, the Order of Montesa and the Order of Christ respectively. The latter became an important maritime body; Vasco da Gama and Christopher Columbus both sailed under its flag – which was the Templar red cross. It is widely claimed, with much evidence but little proof,[20] that many Templars fled to Scotland, where they were quietly influential for a few centuries, and eventually formed the Freemasons. This last claim will be examined later.

The well-known charges made against the Templars included their secret alliance with the Saracens, and their working to let the Holy Land go to the Muslims rather than to the Christians; indulging in debauchery and abominations, including homosexual acts; scorning the sacraments; trampling, spitting or urinating on the cross; blaspheming against Christ, and worshipping the head of Baphomet; making any crime or vice committed for the benefit of the Order not sinful. There is little doubt that on at least some of these charges the Templars were falsely accused, but the most effective slanders always contain an element of the truth.

The accusation about being on the side of the Saracens cleverly links two charges with an implied 'therefore'; the first was undoubtedly true on various occasions, but the second did not logically follow – though enemies were quick to point out that since the formation of the Templars, Christian possessions in the Holy Land had decreased. Some even argued that if the Holy Land were won for Christ, and the Muslims routed altogether, the Templars would have put themselves out of a job.

Debauchery and assorted abominations are standard charges against those whom one wishes to destroy; true or not, they work just as well today against politicians, for example. But in any case, the Church was hardly in a position to cast slurs; there were many priests, bishops and popes not living morally blameless lives.

Blasphemy was a far more serious charge. If true, it spelled death for the Templars. The Catholic Church was beginning at this time to flex its muscles against heretics; Pope Lucius III instituted the Inquisition in 1188, Pope Gregory IX put it under the control of the Dominicans in 1233, and Pope Innocent IV authorized torture to obtain confessions in 1257. In purely practical terms the Inquisition was brilliantly conceived: suspects were assumed guilty until proven innocent, ensuring plenty of convictions; and the Church and local civil authorities confiscated the belongings of those convicted, ensuring cooperation, enthusiasm and income. The Church had won a resounding victory against the heretical Cathars half a century earlier; although more powerful, the Templars were far fewer in number.

Were the Templars guilty as charged? Most authorities think not. Many of the charges made against the Templars by Guillaume de Nogaret, one of Philippe of France's chief ministers, had previously been levelled by Nogaret against others, including Pope Boniface VIII – sodomy and spitting on the cross among them. They were standard charges if you wanted to accuse someone of heresy and magic. The fact that many Templars confessed to them is irrelevant; study of Inquisition transcripts shows that most people tell their torturers what they wish to hear. Such behaviour as spitting on the cross would have been unlikely – but it made for a very serious accusation, and a very lurid confession. As Leonard George says, 'Torture is a poor way to get at the truth, but it can be an impressive method of verifying one's worst fears.'[21]

Thirty-six Templars died under torture: another incentive for others to confess.

The fact that the Templars' initiation rites were held in secret counted against them; they could not prove, through outside witnesses, that they were innocent of the charges of heretical behaviour brought against them.

Jacques de Molay, the final Grand Master, confessed to some charges under interrogation, though he strongly denied others, but he later retracted his confession, saying that the Templars were innocent and that his only infamy was that he had lied in confessing to the charges. His confession would have meant life imprisonment; his retraction meant death the following day.

As for Baphomet, scholarly opinions differ. Some believe that Baphomet was a demon or deity actually worshipped by the Templars; others that the word was a corruption of Mahomet, or Muhammad (in Spanish the name became Mafomat, and in Provençal, Bafomet); or alternatively of the Arabic *abufihamat*, meaning 'Father of Wisdom', the title of a Sufi Master, which would strengthen the esoteric Muslim connection; and one authority claims that Baphomet is an early Jewish code for the Greek Sophia, the female wisdom persona of the Godhead.

Admission of a novice to the vows of the Order of the Temple:
a nineteenth-century impression
(Robert Macoy, *General History, Cyclopedia and*
Dictionary of Freemasonry, 1850)

It is quite possible that the demon/deity Baphomet was entirely the creation of the Inquisitors, but a mythology grew around him through the centuries, culminating in the twentieth-century magician and charlatan Aleister Crowley using the name as one of his own titles. As Peter Partner says of the charges against the Templars, 'it can be said to be a case in which medieval witch-hunting was the direct ancestor of modern occultism.'[22]

Baphomet is usually described as a head, and could thus tie in with the (real or apocryphal) speaking brazen head of the thirteenth-century monk–scientists Albertus Magnus or Roger Bacon, depending on the version of the story; or with some early versions of the Grail myth, as will be discussed in due course. The Templars, like the Cathars, were sometimes thought of as the Guardians of the Grail.

The final charge, mentioned on p. 53, of all behaviour being lawful if it was to the benefit of the Order, is familiar policy from that of the Assassins at their height, and also from those at the libertarian rather than the ascetic extreme of the Gnostics.

Looking back from seven or eight centuries later, there seems to be a question not so much of *whether* the Knights Templar were at all influenced by the Muslims they met, as of *how much* they were influenced. Realize it or not at the time, Christian Europe itself was so influenced. Gothic architecture, with its characteristically pointed arches drawing the eye up to heaven, owes much to concepts of Islamic architecture brought back by Crusaders returning home.

The original 'uniform' of the Templars was a plain white mantle; the red cross was officially added in 1146 by Pope Eugenius III. Perhaps the colours were inspired by the Assassins; the Knights Templar had by then had close contact with them for nearly thirty years.

In 1129, for example, the Crusaders, including Templars, and the Assassins had hatched a plan together to take Damascus from the Muslims for the Christians, in exchange for the Assassins being given the stronghold of Tyre. The plan went disastrously wrong when it was discovered by the military commander of Damascus, and thousands were killed – but it shows clearly the willingness between supposed enemies to form mutually advantageous alliances.

Although some of the Templars, like many knights, were illiterate, they were not simple uneducated soldiers; many of them came from minor noble families. Some, like a number of Crusaders, had been born in Palestine, while others spent many years there, and so could speak Arabic – and the Arabs, like the Jews, were well ahead of most medieval Christians in learning. Christians were especially ignorant of Muslims and their religion, and were utterly intolerant of them; while Muslims saw Judaism and Christianity as early, incomplete but worthy attempts towards the true faith made perfect in Islam, Christians saw Muslims as evil, degenerate idol-worshippers. (This was partly medieval ignorance, but was also partly standard propaganda practice in war.)

It should be mentioned that the esoteric historian A.E. Waite is somewhat dismissive of the supposed links between the Knights Templar and the Assassins.

> Were it necessary to suppose that in the course of their long sojourn in Palestine a part of the Templars had become tinctured by the spirit of eastern lore, eastern theosophy, eastern hidden practices – all of which is part of the charge against them – there were sects enough in that region from whom they could have drawn and at whose questionable fountains they might have drunk deeply, without postulating the Assassins as a particular and only source. For the rest, it cannot be said that the Old Man of the Mountains and his votaries were desirable or decent neighbours; but it is to be questioned whether the Templars were a marked improvement on them.[23]

The Holy Land, sacred to the three Religions of the Book and influenced also by the lingering traces of Egyptian and Greek ideas, was a melting-pot of religious beliefs; as Waite says, 'there were sects enough in that region'. Already noted are the links between religion, philosophy, mysticism and magic. Whatever they had been taught at home in France or England by the Church, the Crusaders and the Templars inevitably encountered new and exciting beliefs and practices in Palestine. For those who want to learn, knowledge is always available.

It is more than likely, for example, that as the Cathars of the Languedoc were persecuted and eventually destroyed in the early thirteenth century, some joined the Knights Templar, taking their beliefs with them. According to one historian, 'numerous [Cathar] survivors found refuge in the Order of the Temple, and Cathars played a prominent part in the running of the Temple in the Languedoc region.'[24]

We are unlikely ever to know the full truth about the Templar beliefs, and how much truth, if any, there was in the accusations of blasphemy against them. It is possible that the great Templar heresy was simply the discovery that the Muslim God is the same as the Christian God. But it might have been more than that. Whatever the detail of their beliefs, the Templars, with their independence of the Church hierarchy, could perhaps have come to believe with the Assassins, with the Sufis, with the Cabalists, with the Cathars, with the mystics of all religions, that if God is worshipped from the individual's heart, the outward trappings of formal religion become irrelevant; and that, for any hierarchical religion, is rampant heresy.

CHAPTER TWO

FROM THE RENAISSANCE TO THE AGE OF REASON

IN THIS CHAPTER will be shown how some of the esoteric ideas discussed in the first chapter continued and developed from the late Middle Ages, through the Renaissance, to the Age of Reason. In most cases this was through an individual quest for knowledge or enlightenment; in a few cases like-minded individuals sought each other out. Some of the reasons for secrecy will be briefly looked at, after the religious and cultural background of late-medieval times has been discussed.

THE WITCH HUNT

Cathars were burned, Knights Templar were burned, and the Inquisition was in business. In the late Middle Ages Europe was in turmoil: the Black Death of 1347 to 1350 wiped out up to a third of the population of the entire continent, and the Hundred Years War (1337–1453) continued the depredation in France. When there was no 'official' war going on, out-of-work soldiers continued in action anyway, as brigands. Social order fell apart. The Church, in disorder itself and determined to maintain both spiritual and temporal order, came down heavily on anyone suspected of dissent or heresy. Civil authorities, especially local ones, added their support.

It was not a good time for anyone; it was especially not a good time for anyone of independent mind.

———

Estimates of the number of 'witches' burned throughout Europe over the centuries vary from several million down to 40,000–50,000. Although historical opinion today favours the lower number, this does not reduce the horror: tens of thousands of almost certainly innocent people, mainly women, were tortured, hanged or burned to death (though some were strangled in an act of mercy before being burned), often on no more 'evidence' than their confessions, or the confessions of others, extracted as often as not under torture. According to the most recent scholarship, however, most 'witches' were simply unpopular people turned in by their unfriendly neighbours.

Europe in the late Middle Ages was a superstitious place, and everyday life for country people was a perpetual struggle;[1] an accident or illness, or a stillborn child, or the death of a cow, or the blighting of a crop, was all too often blamed on someone known to harbour a grudge. In some cases, it seems, people confessed to witchcraft because they had wished ill of someone, who then suffered misfortune; a natural (if misplaced) feeling of guilt led to them accepting responsibility.

Most of the early witch-trials were actually for crimes against man rather than against God; but gradually the emphasis changed.

As society grew a little more sophisticated, the basis of morality as taught by the Church moved from the Seven Deadly Sins to the Ten Commandments. 'The effect,' says one historian, 'was to make sins against God – notably idolatry or the worship of false gods – the central offences, whereas the older system had given priority to sins against neighbours and the community.'[2] The guardian of morality and orthodoxy was of course the Church, and more specifically the Dominicans; and it was two Dominicans who, around 1486, wrote *Malleus Maleficarum*, the 'Hammer of the Witches', as a do-it-yourself Inquisitors' manual. Today it makes fascinating and horrifying reading. Now it can be seen as effectively a work of fiction, but it rapidly became the standard text on what witches believed and did, and the direct source, via a combination of common folklore and the inquisitors' leading questions during torture, of the lurid detail of witches' confessions.

From the surviving records, it appears that more than three-quarters of those killed as witches throughout Europe as a whole were women. Despite – or perhaps because of – the dissolute behaviour of all too many clerics, the Church disliked and distrusted women. Women enticed men, they led men into temptation and corruption; and yet they held the power and mystery of childbirth, of bringing new life into the world. Even when they had lost their sexual allure they still kept their power; midwives could not be kept under the control of the Church. It is no coincidence that in France, even today, the word for midwife is *sage-femme*, wise-woman. Whether true or not, it was thought by many that women had a wisdom, a secret knowledge, passed on from mother to daughter, from grandmother to granddaughter, from which men were excluded. Men feared women. It was an easy transition in both the Church's and the popular (male) imagination, from the village wise-woman, with her herbal lore, to the witch, with her evil powers.

The authors of the *Malleus Maleficarum* quite clearly feared women, and so hated them – though historian Robin Briggs insists that this is 'a peculiarly misogynistic text, many of whose assertions are very misleading as a guide to what happened in typical trials.'[3] Perhaps so, but all that this shows is that practice did not always follow theory; if common sense sometimes prevailed in trials, it was despite the official rubric of the Church, not because of it.

Jews, Romanies and Muslim travellers existed throughout Europe; but most medieval women and men, including convicted 'witches', were actually Christian, at least nominally; it was the *milieu* in which they lived, an inseparable part of society, of their very life. They might not have understood much theology, but everyone was Christian; there was really nothing else they could be. It is now considered extremely unlikely that, as historian Margaret Murray claimed in the 1920s and 1930s, country people still maintained the old Pagan beliefs. On the other hand, especially in small villages – and most of Europe was small villages – some small traces of the old beliefs probably lingered on; there was certainly a deep stratum of folk-belief and superstition. The Horned God, whether the Greek Pan or the Romano-Celtic Cernunnos, was almost certainly not believed in as God by anyone, but he was present in one form or another in country folklore as the male personification of nature, the generative force – perhaps, in a way, the popular equivalent of the philosophers' *dæmons*.

The Devil of the Bible does not have horns and hoofs. The well-known visual image of the Devil is entirely the creation of the medieval Church, taking the ancient folk-belief and turning it into the Christian Devil. By playing on superstition and credulity, the Church created a new weapon against dissidents: Devil-worship. (It will be demonstrated later how this imaginative stroke of the Church is still a powerful weapon today.)

Pan/Cernunnos, in the different mythologies, was a being who exemplified and celebrated the wildness and anarchic joy of life, the fecundity of nature – again, something from which the Church recoiled. In reality there might have been a few Spring dances, and the village youth might have got up to what youth traditionally get up to in the Spring, but the orgiastic sabbats of witches were again almost entirely the imaginative creation of the Church.

By demonizing the petty squabbles of already superstitious country people, the Church ratcheted up the level of persecution.

As Europe changed political, religious, intellectual and social shape over the centuries, so the trials continued, often ending in burning or hanging. So far as the people who were arrested and tortured were concerned, it probably made little difference that the Middle Ages passed into the Renaissance, and that the Renaissance itself then passed on. It made little difference whether the clerics condemning them were Roman Catholics, Lutherans or Calvinists; at different times and in different places these were all as vigilant as each other against the wiles of the Devil. The emphasis may have changed from punishing vindictive villagers to rooting out theologically divergent scholars, but the solution was the same.

The Church authorities – whether Dominicans and Jesuits, or Puritan Presbyterians – did not like 'difference'. Maintaining their power over society was difficult enough; toleration of deviant beliefs was not a luxury, it was a threat to stability. They feared the power of the individual. They did everything they could to stamp out personal choice. The burning of uneducated country women and the burning of highly educated heretical priests were two sides of the same coin.

Heresy simply means choice.

ASTROLOGY

At this point, a brief look can be taken at what astrology meant to those who believed in it and practised it for millennia.

Astronomers today dismiss astrology completely, and complain when people carelessly confuse astronomy and astrology. They appear annoyed that astrologers should even dare to trespass on their territory; the stars and planets belong to astronomy, which is a science, not to the hokum which is astrology.

It is necessary to rid ourselves of the present-day association of astrology with newspaper horoscopes, which have nothing to do with the astrology of the ancients, nor with that of the Renaissance philosophers. Like so much else in the esoteric realm, astrology has become meaningless; its content has been forgotten. Of course astrology *has* always been used for what could be called popular fortune-telling. But rather than foretelling fixed events in the future, serious astrologers would tell rulers the most propitious time for certain actions: a subtle but significant difference.

Astrology is an obvious application of the principle of 'As above, so below': the planets and stars affecting or reflecting our Earthly lives. But this is not a straightforward causal relationship. It is not the case that a planet, as seen from Earth, passing across a particular pattern of stars in the sky, *causes* anything. It is more the case that in the Cosmos created by God, everything is his handiwork, and everything is therefore linked to everything else.

Without the painstaking work of astrologers over more than two millennia, however, today's astronomers would not have the wealth of information they do have on past eclipses, comets and novas. Until really quite recent times, astronomers were astrologers; the two activities were not

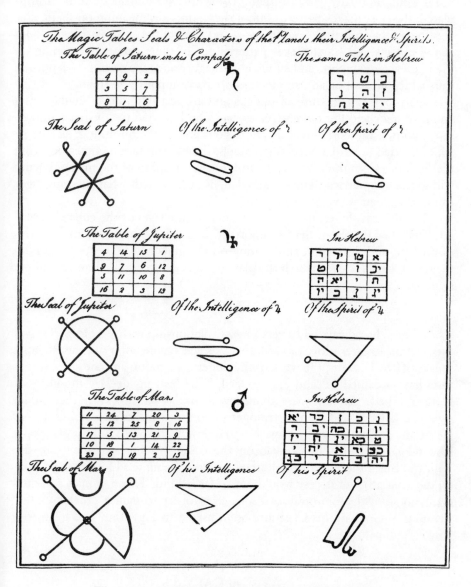

The magical tables, seals and characters of the planets
(Francis Barrett, *The Magus*, 1801)

separable. As an analogy, a poem is not the same as the words that make it up, but it would not exist without them. The words are units, data to be manipulated; the poet makes patterns out of them, imposes meaning on them, creates metaphor and simile and imagery and symbolism. The astrologer looks at the planets and stars, makes patterns out of them, imposes meaning on them, creates metaphor and simile and imagery and symbolism. It is not the stars which are important, so much as the pattern put upon them.

Astrology is a mixture of science and art and religion, of mathematics and metaphor and mythology. As anyone who has tried to construct a horoscope knows, the computations are tedious and time-consuming; as anyone who has tried to read a horoscope knows, the interpretation comes not from the lines but from the heart, from an intuitive grasping of the meaning lying within the geometrical figure - mingled, as always, with what the astrologer thinks the client wants to hear.

For the astrologer, it is not the planets or the stars or the constellations, but what they represent that is important. It is the accumulation of centuries of thought and discussion and writing on the gods and heroes – the fundamental archetypes – for which the planets, stars and constellations are simply symbols.

The Church has always had a very uneasy relationship with astrology. If it was used for the greater glory of God, that was acceptable; after all, the Psalmist speaks of 'thy heavens, the work of thy fingers, the moon and the stars, which thou hast ordained' (Psalm 8:3); indeed, 'The heavens declare the glory of God; and the firmament sheweth his handiwork' (Psalm 19:1). In the Middle Ages the Church had many astrologers among its priests and monks; it was by no means unknown for popes to consult them. (The Borgia pope, Alexander VI, had a full zodiac on the ceiling of his apartments in the Vatican.) But if there were any hint of astrology being used for other purposes, the accusation of heresy would not be far behind. Those monks, and others, who studied philosophy and science in order to gain a greater understanding of God and his Creation, often used astrology: they had to tread a very careful path.

ALCHEMY

Alchemy, 'the Royal Art', has always been a mixture of the scientific and the spiritual. Both the ancient Egyptian alchemists and their Renaissance descendants were actually chemists – and physicists, and astronomers, and mathematicians, physicians, botanists and biologists – all within the terms of their own day. Those who carelessly dismiss them as deluded or fraudulent magicians should remember that they were, in effect, the first scientists. They were the ones to discover that a polished lens of glass could focus the light of the Sun to a hot, burning point, or could magnify what is seen through it. They were the ones who studied physiology, and who worked out, sometimes rightly, sometimes wrongly, how the human body worked, and what the various parts of it were for. They were the ones who studied plants, and learned which were poisonous and which beneficial, and which lethal ones could, in tiny doses, heal.

If they also believed in the influence of the planets, and in the four elements, and in the humours, which cause modern scientists to smile condescendingly, such beliefs did not hold back their quest for scientific knowledge; indeed, there is plenty of evidence to show that they actually stimulated this pursuit of knowledge. If the alchemists used classification systems which today are seen as invalid, at least they were using classification systems – and, within their own terms, these worked.

In short, they studied the world within their current world-view, which is no different from what the great nineteenth-century chemists and physicists did, or what today's scientists do. A difference *does* exist, however, in that today's rigid professional stratification did not exist in medieval and Renaissance times, except in the craftsmen's guilds. Scientists then were also priests, monks, philosophers, poets, artists.

Two of the greatest teachers of the thirteenth century, Albertus Magnus (1193–1280) and Roger Bacon (1214–92) were both monks and scientists. Albertus was a Dominican who, despite his magical researches and his lifetime of studying Aristotle, rose to become a bishop. Bacon was a Franciscan, is credited with inventing eye-glasses and the 'scientific method' (i.e. personal observation of phenomena rather than simply accepting the received wisdom of authority), and spent the last fourteen years of his life in a dungeon for his supposed heresies. Depending on the source, both are credited with owning a speaking brazen head; Thomas Aquinas, who studied under Albertus, is said to have smashed the head because it disturbed his studies.

Another important name of the period is that of Ramón Lull (1232–1315), a Spanish philosopher who encountered both the Spanish Cabalists and the mystical Muslims of northern Spain. Lull drew together the teachings of the ninth-century Irish scholar John Scotus Erigena, the concept of the four elements (earth, water, fire and air) and their qualities (dry and cold, cold and moist, hot and dry, and hot and moist), the seven planets and twelve zodiacal signs of astrology, the three spheres (supercelestial, the realm of the angels; celestial, the realm of the stars; and material, the realm of man), the Jewish and Muslim emphasis on the Divine Names (or Attributes) of God, and much more besides, into one complex system known as Lullian Art, the basis of all arts and sciences, of philosophy and religion. He was also a proponent of the Art of Memory, or Theatre of Memory (see p. 72); his *Ars Memoria* was to be influential in the coming centuries.

Alchemy was regarded with suspicion partly because it involved non-Christian ideas. One of the most influential early alchemists was the Arab mathematician Jabir ibn Hayyan, or Geber (*c.* 721–*c.* 815), whose texts were so shrouded in allegorical symbolism that he has bequeathed to us the word 'gibberish'. The symbolism was used to mask the deeper meaning of the texts.

Although the early alchemists were chemists, who laid down many of the foundations of later practical chemistry, alchemy was never just to do with turning base metals into gold; that was always symbolic language for deeper psychological, philosophical and spiritual truths.

In a discussion on the meaning of initiation, the twentieth-century occultist Israel Regardie writes, 'The entire object of all magical and alchemical processes is the purification of the natural man, and by working upon his nature to extract the pure gold of spiritual attainment. This is initiation.'[4]

It is almost impossible to separate the physical and the spiritual in alchemical texts. Alchemists actually did spend years with their retorts and alembics; on one level the texts were genuine instruction manuals for their chemical experiments. On another, allegorical level, they gave instruction on the purification of the soul. And between these two, the physical and the spiritual, was the psychological level.

Even today's students of alchemy insist that the physical side of the work is important. To take an analogy, scrubbing a floor is a purely physical action; but a novice nun set to scrub a floor may also be learning important lessons of obedience, self-discipline and humility. She might also eventually learn the harder lesson that even scrubbing a floor can be dedicated to God; the physical effort, the repetitive motions, and the increasingly clean floor could even become aids to her contemplation.

Alchemists were searching for the Philosopher's Stone – probably not a stone at all, but a liquid, a tincture – which could turn a base metal into gold. It was the transformation which really mattered, not whatever gold might be created. The Stone was also known as the Elixir of Life, which could cure illnesses, and increase both the quality and the length of life; again, this is intended both physically and spiritually. The important word is transformation.

Descriptions of the alchemical process involve details of temperatures and timings and techniques of sublimation and distillation, with the colours that the chemicals and compounds will turn at each stage: to black, to white, sometimes to yellow, to red. But the instructions were never as clear as 'Put such an amount of sulphur into a retort and heat slowly to such a tempera-ture.' The processes, and the chemicals, are often described in astrological terms, or in terms of people or animals or birds; the king and queen, and their marriage, the dragon, the androgyne, were all part of the vocabulary of alchemy. Allegorical stories, along the lines of the *Chymical Wedding of Christian Rosenkreuz*, were often beautifully illustrated with woodcuts. There was symbolism within symbolism within symbolism. Winston Churchill's description of the action of Russia at the beginning of the Second World War as 'a riddle wrapped in a mystery inside an enigma', could as easily be applied to an alchemical text.

Alchemy, or the language of alchemy, or the hidden meanings of the language of alchemy, can be found in one way or another in all esoteric systems. Even within Freemasonry, which has never practised alchemy *per se*, the same sort of language has sometimes been used:

> 'There are celestial bodies and bodies terrestrial . . . and as we *have* borne the image of the earthly we also *shall* bear the image of the heavenly.' And the celestial body must be built up out of the sublimated properties of the terrestrial one. This is one of the secrets and mysteries of the process of regeneration and self-transmutation, to promote which the Craft was designed. This is the true temple-building that Masonry is concerned with.[5]

THE HERMETIC PHILOSOPHERS

As the Middle Ages moved into the Renaissance in the Christian West, the desire for learning, formerly almost entirely the province of monks, spread to the nobility as part of their fifteenth-century ethos of conspicuous display. The Florentine Cosimo de' Medici employed a monk and philosopher, Marsilio Ficino (1433–99), to track down interesting manuscripts; one of these was the collection known as the *Corpus Hermeticum*, which was mentioned in the last chapter. In 1471 it was translated into Latin and pub-lished, sparking off a whole new wave of esoteric study.

The *Corpus Hermeticum*, a fusion of Greek, Egyptian and other Mediterranean thought, was Gnostic and Neo-Platonist in nature; its texts covered religion, philosophy, mysticism, magic, alchemy and astrology.

The so-called Hermetic Philosophers of the next two centuries drew on its teachings and on the Neo-Platonist teachings of Ficino, and expanded on them in different ways. A few of the most significant people, and their influence, will now be looked at briefly.

In 1492, the year that, as we were all taught, Columbus sailed the ocean blue, something of perhaps equal significance in world affairs occurred: Spain and Portugal expelled their Jewish populations. The Jews, with their recently-developed mystical teachings, were forced to travel through Europe, settling in Germany and Poland, in Italy and France and (a little) in England. Scholars throughout Europe discovered the Cabala, and found in it an approach to the questions about God and his Creation which attracted them.

One of the foremost of these was the Florentine Giovanni Pico della Mirandola (1463–94), a pupil and friend of Ficino, who believed that Cabala 'proved' Christianity. He took the techniques of Cabala – the mysticism, the magic, the manipulation of letters, the concentration on the sacred names of God, the power of angels (or *dæmons*) – and created something new: Christian Cabala. Pico and later philosophers were adapting rather than adopting a Jewish system. Pico also wrote of a visionary trance in which the soul, separated from the body, is in communion with God.

Francesco Giorgi (1466–1540) was a Venetian, a Franciscan monk, and a Hebrew scholar. Influenced by Pico, he went on to show that the sacred, hidden name of God, the Tetragrammaton YHVH, could be manipulated into the name Jesus, thus proving that Jesus was the expected Jewish Messiah. Giorgi drew together Neo-Platonism, Neo-Pythagorianism, the teachings of Hermes Trismegistus, Cabala, angels, planets, harmony and number, and the architectural symbolism of Vitruvius (see p. 74ff) into a coherent system. His most significant work was *De Harmonia Mundi* (1525), which was translated into French in 1578, and which was well known to John Dee. If there could be said to be one founder of Hermetic Philosophy, it was Giorgi; yet his name is often forgotten by many of the modern commentaries on the Hermetic Philosophers, eclipsed by names such as Agrippa.

Although Henry Cornelius Agrippa von Nettesheim (1486–1535) wrote a draft of *De Occulta Philosophia Libri Tres* as early as 1510, the work was not published until three years before his death. It was a highly influential encyclopædia of magic which argued the importance of studying the texts of different religions.

Cornelius Agrippa was frequently condemned for mixing Christianity, Cabalism and Neo-Platonism. It is hardly surprising that he was regarded with suspicion, especially when he once argued – and successfully – that a supposed witch should be spared the fire. He lectured on Hermes Trismegistus, and wrote works on *The Nobility of the Female Sex* and *The Superiority of Women*, which again hardly endeared him to the Church, and also *On the Vanity of Arts and Sciences*, which attacked the worth of current scholarship. His *Occult Philosophy* argues that magic is a philosophical science, combining physics, mathematics (which included astrology) and theology.

Theophrastus Bombastus von Hohenheim, known as Paracelsus (1493–1541), was a physician and surgeon. He taught the theory behind homeopathy, pioneered the use of ether as an anæsthetic, and turned medicine into a proper science – again, in terms of his own day. His reforms of medicine were the most important since those of Galen (AD 131–210). A Swiss, he got into trouble for lecturing in German rather than Latin at the University of Basle, and for saying that physicians should throw away outmoded theories – he publicly burned Galen's work – and study 'The Book of Nature', i.e. the reality of God's creation. In his insistence on first-hand experience and experiment he echoed Roger Bacon (see p. 65).

Paracelsus argued that the effective physician must also be an astrologer, a theologian and a mystic, to understand all the influences on the body and soul. His teaching of harmony with one's true self, and that 'if the spirit suffers, the body suffers also', showed an understanding of what today we call psychosomatic illness. The fact that the medical teachings of Paracelsus were based on alchemical studies does not diminish the genuine effect that he had on medicine, particularly in the use of chemical and mineral cures for illnesses.

John Dee (1527–1608) was a true Renaissance Man: a doctor, astronomer, astrologer, cartographer, mathematician, philosopher, theologian, advisor to Elizabeth I, and probably spy. Enough books have been written on Dee that he needs only brief mention here. His donation of 4,000 of his own books to a new national library was later one of the starting points of the British Museum.

The Dee story is an excellent warning to all who become involved in esoteric studies, not to become obsessed with such a charismatic figure as Edward Kelley, who may well have been a genuine mystic but who was also undoubtedly a genuine charlatan. Under his influence, Dee became sidetracked from his proper studies for several years. Kelley was the medium; he dictated messages to Dee which he claimed to have received from angels, the equivalent of the *dæmons* of Neo-Platonism. In addition to giving him several significant occult texts, in 1583 the angels warned Dee of his impending murder, causing the two of them, with their families, to flee to Prague; Kelley was eventually imprisoned in Prague, where he died while trying to escape in 1595. Dee had returned to England in 1589, but his reputation had been destroyed, and he died in poverty aged 81.

But as historian Dame Frances Yates points out, 'The sensational angel-summoning side of Dee's activities was intimately related to his real success as a mathematician.'[6] He was a Christian Cabalist, following in the steps of Cornelius Agrippa and others. As far back as Pythagoras, number had been seen as the basis of all Creation; the Cabalists had borrowed and expanded on Pythagoras's ideas, and now the Hermetic Philosophers were doing the same.

Giordano Bruno (1548–1600) led a spiritually confusing life. He began as a Dominican monk (he had to flee when it was discovered that he had been hiding certain 'suspect' works by Erasmus in the monastery's privy), he spent some time as a Lutheran and as a Calvinist, and he ended up at odds with any form of orthodox Christianity. It was almost a question of which Church would take its revenge on him first. In fact, Bruno managed to annoy many people: his play *Il Candelaio* was a scathing attack on academic pedantry and hypocrisy.

Bruno's great mistake was that he loved to debate, and saw no bounds on what could be questioned. The Church thought otherwise. He was a daring thinker; he took Copernicus's heliocentric theory – that the Earth orbits the Sun, and not vice versa – and extended it: could it be that all the other stars were suns, each with planets around it? The accepted view was that the Earth was at the centre, circled by the Sun, Moon and planets, which in turn were circled by the stars, and God was beyond the circle of the stars. If the universe was full of faraway suns and planets, where then was God? Bruno argued that God pervaded every part of his creation, and also taught that man could effectively become a God, or at least a demiurge, by his own efforts; this was even more at variance with orthodox belief than was Pelagius's heretical doctrine.

Bruno was perhaps most greatly admired in his lifetime for his skill with the Art of Memory (see p. 72); he was often asked to teach its techniques. In 1591 he was invited to Venice to teach the Art to one Mocenigo – who then turned him over to the authorities with accusations of heresy. Bruno was imprisoned in Venice, then taken to Rome in 1593. After seven years of imprisonment and interrogation by the Inquisition he was burned at the stake in 1600.

Francis Bacon (1561–1626) was almost certainly neither an alchemist nor an early Rosicrucian nor an ur-Freemason, whatever the confident assertions of some of those of later centuries who wish to claim him for their own. He was a philosopher, and a scientist, and undoubtedly knew other philosopher-scientists of his day, many of whom were deeply engrossed in esoteric studies – but that is all. His significance to later 'historians' of the esoteric lies mainly in an unfinished late work, *New Atlantis*, an allegorical romance of a mythical Utopian society, published after his death. The society – in the wider sense of a community, not of an organization – is dedicated to the free pursuit of learning and the study of nature.

The book was informed at least as much by Bacon's extensive political experience as by his esoteric learning, but it was taken up as effectively an esoteric 'blueprint' by later secret societies.

A German Freemason, Christoph Friedrich Nicolai, argued in 1782 that the Solomon's House of *New Atlantis* was the precursor of the Freemasons. Dr Wynn Westcott, a Supreme Magus of the Masonic Order *Societas Rosicruciana in Anglia*, and one of the three founding members of the Hermetic Order of the Golden Dawn, claimed that Bacon 'became a Rosicrucian Adept', though according to esoteric historian A.E. Waite, 'he has neither evidence nor authority, good or bad, to offer for this statement.'[7]

Many modern esotericists, whether they know it or not, are strongly influenced by the teachings of the Theosophical Society (see p. 239 n. 33). According to the leading Theosophist Annie Besant (1847–1933), Bacon was one of the many incarnations of one of the Great White Brotherhood, the 'Brotherhood of Divine Men'; in an earlier life he was Christian Rozenkreutz, and in a later one, the Comte de Saint-Germain. The Church Universal and Triumphant, founded by Elizabeth Clare Prophet in 1974, takes the idea a little further. The Ascended Master Saint-Germain was formerly Francis Bacon, and before that was Christopher Columbus, Roger Bacon, Merlin, the Greek Neo-Platonist Proclus, Saint Alban, Joseph the husband of Mary, the prophet Samuel, and a high priest on Atlantis 13,000 years ago. At the age of twenty, they say, 'Bacon secretly founded the first Rosicrucian Brotherhood, the Rosicrosse Literary Society, and the first Lodge of the Free and Accepted or Speculative Masons.'[8]

The Los Angeles-based Philosophical Research Society, founded by Manly Palmer Hall (1901–90) and dedicated largely to publishing his 200-plus books, practically claims Bacon as the founder of the USA. It also persistently refers to him as 'Lord Bacon', although more correctly Sir Francis Bacon was Lord Verulam, Viscount of St Albans. A further look will be taken later (p.83 and p. 150) at the esoteric equivalent of the American Dream.

THE ART OF MEMORY

Today we can easily reach for a book to confirm a half-remembered fact; in the past this was not the case. Before the development of the printing press every book had to be hand-copied (which led, incidentally, to many variant texts because of both errors of transcription and scribes' attempts to 'correct' previous errors, real or imagined). In medieval times books were rare and valuable, and even a scholar might be proud of the six or ten he had accumulated during his lifetime. The thousands of books in the sixteenth-century John Dee's library would have been an unattainable dream not so very long before. Thus memory was far more important than it is today, for bards, druids, priests, monks, magicians, scholars – for anyone who had to know and be able to recall instantly a large body of material.

For anyone studying the esoteric arts a good memory was even more important; the slightest slip could spell disaster when preparing alchemical experiments or invoking *dæmons*. Gaining and retaining knowledge, by such means as Ramón Lull's *Ars Memoria*, was a complex art, almost a form of magic in itself. But like much else in the esoteric world, the term 'magic' is often a synonym for skill, and skill often depended upon mastering certain tricks.

The Art of Memory, Theatre of Memory or Memory Palace was such a means; versions of it are still used today by stage memory-men. One of several variant techniques is to imagine a building, and every room in it: to build a clear and detailed picture of it in the mind. Each room is ascribed a different branch of knowledge, and each part of it – by the door, window, or fireplace, or openly on the table, or hidden in a chest or behind a wall-hanging – is a subset of that branch. When a new piece of knowledge is learned, it is placed as a mnemonic image in the relevant place in the relevant room: a mental filing cabinet. Over time, an entire well-catalogued library is built up, with every individual piece of knowledge filed in its right place, and instantly retrievable.

Visualization is an important part of all esoteric work. It is worth noting that today's Rosicrucians and other schools of occult knowledge such as Builders of the Adytum all claim that through study of their teachings the initiate will improve his or her memory dramatically. The long and complex rituals and lectures in Freemasonry are all performed from memory.

SAFETY THROUGH SECRECY

Few of the ideas of the Hermetic Philosophers were 'safe'. The Roman Catholic Church's attitude to astrology, which was an essential part of the overall package, varied from pope to pope over the centuries; generally alchemy was held in deep suspicion by prelate and peasant alike. As for the summoning or raising of spirits or angels or demons, this was the blackest of sorcery. Catholics interested in the esoteric arts were suspected of dealing with the Devil; Protestants were accused of dabbling in the mumbo-jumbo of Rome. These two main branches of Christianity were in any case at loggerheads; most of the sixteenth- and seventeenth-century wars were actually about religion. It was not a safe time to hold unsafe beliefs. Many of the Philosophers had to do some quick talking to save their lives; several were forced to recant of their heresy; some, like Bruno, were killed for their beliefs.

If there were any chance of being accused of heresy, it was safer to keep quiet about what one believed, and to teach others only after they had been made keenly aware of the need for secrecy. The carefully-stepped progressive gradations of revealed knowledge in esoteric schools or secret societies today are partly because each level of knowledge rests on what has been learned previously, but there is also another reason, rooted in the past. New initiates would gain fairly innocuous knowledge at first; if the initiate decided to leave (or if he was a spy), he would not have learned much, and his teacher would not be threatened. But as someone climbed up the initiatory ladder, the teachings would become more suspect from an orthodox viewpoint, more dangerous if revealed. At some point, perhaps after several years but certainly several levels inwards, the initiate would realize that he had gradually become the possessor of a body of knowledge, and had perhaps taken part in rituals, that could send him to the stake.

It is tempting to think of the persecution of heretics and witches as a medieval barbarity, but it was a barbarity which continued right through the Renaissance – and beyond. The last person to be burnt at the stake for heresy was in Seville, as late as 1781. The Spanish Inquisition continued its search for heretics until 1834. In Britain, which likes to think itself tolerant, the anti-witchcraft law was not repealed until 1951. Today, Fundamentalists of all religions are demanding that whatever remnants of blasphemy laws still remain should be strengthened. The *fatwah* against author Salman Rushdie is a salutory reminder that it can still be dangerous to speak out too openly about religious beliefs. It is misleading to see this, from the haven of our Western liberal democracy, as a barbarism of Muslim extremism. The first screenings of Martin Scorsese's film *The Last Temptation of Christ*, based on Nikos Kazantzakis's novel, were met with demonstrations by Christian Fundamentalists; people going to see the film were spat on and called blasphemers. Even the writers and publishers of computer fantasy games have received death threats from Fundamentalist Christians in America.

ARCHITECTURE

When Constantinople was sacked by the Turks in 1453, scholars escaping (mainly to Italy) took away with them much of value in the way of ancient manuscripts, thus stimulating in the West the great Classical revival of the Renaissance; not only were Greek and Egyptian philosophy studied, but Greek and Roman architecture also provided models for Renaissance usage.

It is often wondered what real connection the modern 'speculative' Freemasons had with medieval stonemasons. One of the links is that the Hermetic Philosophers, who were among the predecessors of the Freemasons, rediscovered esoteric knowledge which, in its practical expressions, the architects and builders of the Middle Ages had never lost. Architecture was one of the many subjects which Cornelius Agrippa, John Dee and others studied and on which they wrote. The masons had kept their secrets of geometry and proportion for centuries. From the wealth of 'new' material which became available to them in the fifteenth century the Hermetic Philosophers discovered much the same knowledge; they also kept it, along with much else, secret – or at least, concealed.

The great Roman architectural writer of the first century BC was Vitruvius, who embodied philosophical ideas in his architecture. The Romans had absorbed Greek architectural ideas, though their slightly cruder approach to building shows they had lost some of the refinements.

Vitruvius's classic work *De Architectura Libri Decem* was certainly known in the twelfth century, but became lost for a while, being rediscovered in 1486. Both the medieval masons and the philosophers of the sixteenth and seventeenth centuries understood the symbolic truth of Vitruvius's architecture: proportion was all important. The proportion of buildings echoed the proportions of anatomy, for surely man was the pinnacle of God's design. The relation between the two can be found also in the preface to the notebook of the thirteenth-century French architect Villard de Honnecourt, which he hoped 'may be a great help in instructing the principles of masonry and carpentry. You will also find it contains methods of portraiture and line drawing as dictated by the laws of geometry.'[9]

Much of the knowledge of the basic laws of geometry, known to the Greeks, had been lost by medieval times – at least to scholars. Medieval architects and builders (i.e. masons), however, still had this knowledge. Some was undoubtedly passed down from master masons to their journeymen and apprentices, as with the secrets of any craft guild. In addition, much was learned, however directly or indirectly, from the Muslims of southern Europe. It has already been seen that their level of scholarship and their love of learning were way above those of Christians of their day. Muslim scholars collected and preserved knowledge from all sources, including the Greek philosophers, and taught it to whoever wanted to learn; Arab universities were reknowned seats of learning. All branches of mathematics, including algebra, geometry and trigonometry, were avidly studied. The route by which this knowledge came to Italian, French and English masons is no longer known, but those in contact with Muslims in the twelfth and thirteenth centuries certainly included both the Jewish Cabalists and the Knights Templar. From their geographical location and from their tolerance of others' beliefs, it is most likely that the Cathars had a similar contact.

It should be remembered that Gothic architecture was inspired by Arabic architecture.

According to the French historian Jean Gimpel, the secrecy associated with masonic knowledge dates from the end of the thirteenth century. There is documentary evidence from a century later that apprentices were told to keep certain things secret; the Regius Manuscript of 1390 says,

> He keeps and guards his master's teachings and those of his fellows. He tells no man what he learns in the privacy of his chamber, nor does he reveal anything which he sees or hears in the lodge or anything which happens there. Disclose to no man, no matter where you go, the discussions held in the hall or in the dormitory; keep them well, for your greatest honour, lest in being free with them you bring reproach upon yourself and great shame upon your profession.[10]

Gimpel argues that, rather than any esoteric knowledge, this simply referred to tricks of the trade – trade secrets – which should be kept within the profession.

What was it that was so special about architectural knowledge? One thing, of course, was the skill of the trade. There was a vast difference between building a labourer's home – little more than a hut – and building a vast cathedral. The building trade, then as now, would have had its 'cowboys', and professional masons didn't want the incompetence of such workers ruining a cathedral. Masonic handgrips and other recognition signals seem to have originated in Scotland, to distinguish true masons from 'cowans', labourers capable of building, say, a dry-stone wall. Some of the mystique surrounding the secrets of masons may have been allowed to develop to emphasize the difference between architect-craftsmen – often known as *magister*, *maître* or master of the works, and sometimes even as 'doctor of stonework' – and mere labourers.

It is likely that the new secrecy from the end of the thirteenth century in part simply reflected the increasing sophistication of society in the late Middle Ages. It is also quite possible that part of the reason for secrecy is that masons were worried about the Church's reaction if it discovered that they were acquiring architectural knowledge, directly or indirectly, from Muslims.

The mathematical knowledge itself needed to be protected. Pythagoras's right-angle theorem is known to every 14-year-old today, but seven hundred years ago few knew it, and fewer still knew its applications, such as how to construct a square with exactly half or twice the area of another square. Even how to measure an angle was unknown to most people. The Golden Section was even more esoteric, in the wider sense of the word. The complexity of mathematics – the 'magic' of mathematics, to ordinary people's eyes – led to it sometimes being referred to as a 'black art'.

Furthermore, buildings are constructed in three dimensions. Not just a conceptual leap is required, but various specific principles, in order to go from a drawing on parchment to a finished building – taking an elevation from a plan. This particular knowledge, acquired through years as an apprentice and a journeyman, would be jealously guarded by master masons.

Finally, architecture involves geometry, and geometry (and this Gimpel misses) involves symbolism. The relationship of circles and squares and tri-angles, the superimposition of two triangles to form Solomon's Seal or the Star of David, the significance of the number of points, sides and angles in different geometric figures – all had meaning.

Medieval and Renaissance cathedrals across Europe are full of symbol-ism, not just in their paintings, statues and carvings, which people were used to interpreting on one level or another, but in their very design. The con-gregations worshipping in them, the priests taking the services, even the bishops officiating at the most solemn ceremonies, century after century, have in the main been entirely unaware that the very stones around them had a message built into them by those who planned and designed and supervised their construction: the architects and master masons.

The Golden Section mentioned above, was a specific proportion known to ancient Greek and Roman builders; its discovery is attributed to Pythagoras. A line A–B is divided at roughly a third of its length at point Q, so that the ratio between the shorter part, A–Q, and the longer part, Q–B, is the same as the ratio between the longer part Q–B and the whole line, A–B. The exact ratio is 1:1.618.

This is a fundamental proportion in geometry. It can be found in the relationship between the lines of a regular five-pointed star (a pentacle) and a regular five-sided polygon (a pentagon) inscribed within the same circle. It is crucial in the construction of the *vesica piscis* or mandorla, the pointed oval often seen in religious paintings and stained-glass windows. It is also found in the proportions of the 'ideal' human figure. And it is found everywhere in esoteric architecture.

Generations of schoolchildren tormented by 'the square on the hypotenuse' would probably have cursed Pythagoras for this further geometrical constant. Generations of worshippers in and visitors to cathedrals are awed by the majesty of the huge enclosed space towering heavenwards, testifying to the skill of the architects and builders; but they also feel a holy peace, a *rightness*, and this testifies to the *art* of the architects and builders – their knowledge and understanding of the use of proportion, developed over centuries, traceable back through the Muslims to the Romans and Greeks, and dependent on the esoteric significance of geometry and number. The Greek word for 'art', it should be recalled, gives the word 'magic'.

It is only fair to mention here that at least one historian of architecture sees the original link the other way around. Speaking of the ancient Greeks, Peter Kidson says, 'However they came by it, the architects' experience of applied geometry may well have supplied the philosophers with the raw material of their theorems.'[11] This may or may not be so; in any case it makes no difference to the mutual interdependence of architectural and philosophical geometry.

What is clear, however, is that the medieval architects and builders had not lost this ancient knowledge, for it to be miraculously rediscovered in the fifteenth century. The architects kept designing and the builders building, long before Cornelius Agrippa and John Dee began studying the philosophy inherent in 'the queen of the sciences'.

At this point, a brief glance can be taken at the symbolism of geometry and architecture.

Churches built in the form of a cross are clearly symbolic, as is the placing of the altar at the East end, while spires direct the eye heavenward; so much is obvious. But there is much more to it than this. The mason takes lumps of raw stone (in Freemasonry, 'rough ashlar'), trims them into shape, polishes and carves them, and makes a glorious cathedral out of them to the glory of God; this is symbolic of the spiritual building, remaking or renewal of the shaped and polished soul from within the rough raw material of the physical body.

The Pythagorian idea of the spiritual qualities of numbers comes through clearly in the symbolism of the geometry underlying much of architectural design, from the smallest decorative carving to the structural layout of the largest cathedral.

Three is the number of God, both in the Christian Trinity and triple Gods in other religions, and in the idea of perpetuity or eternity, of past, present and future. In sexual symbolism, a triangle pointing upwards is male, a triangle pointing downwards is female. In terms of the elements, an upward triangle is fire, a downward triangle water. Four is the number of matter, and also of completion: the four elements, the four seasons, the four evangelists, the four cardinal points of the compass. The square, and hence the cube, is firm, solid, dependable, four-square authority. (The Emperor, in the Masonic Tarot, sits on a solid cube.) Five is the number of man: the head and four limbs in a five-pointed star, as in the well-known drawing of a human figure in a circle and a square. It also represents the five senses, and so the sensual world. It is also traditionally the number of esoteric spirituality, perhaps because (as in the dots on a die or a domino) the Unity of One (i.e. God) is within the Four of matter.

The numeral zero is not numerologically significant, but the shape of the circle is. The circle represents perfection, God's whole Creation, the entire cosmos. It also reminds us of the ever-rolling seasons, and of the continuance of life through death to life, and so eternity, and infinity – and, of course, the 'heresy' of reincarnation, believed in by many early Christians, and central to most esoteric beliefs. In astrology it represents the sun, but also the circle of the zodiac, the heavens in which the stars and planets move. The fifth-century BC Greek philosopher Empedocles wrote, 'God is a circle whose centre is everywhere and whose circumference is nowhere.'

The sphere is both the soul and the universe, and again the zodiac. It is the most perfect geometric figure.

The egg is something like the sphere, but also contains the mystery of birth, creation and fertility; it symbolizes life and latency.

The *vesica piscis*, the rounded lozenge or almond shape made from two overlapping circles, shows the meeting and joining of two forces or two worlds: male and female, matter and spirit, earth and heaven, man and God. It is often seen within stained-glass windows, sometimes enclosing the figure of Christ, the mediator between man and God. It also represents both virginity and female sexuality, because of its vulva shape. The almond symbolizes the sweet fruit within the husk, the hidden secret, and Christ's divine nature within his human form. (See pp. 122–23.)

This is just a selection of shapes and numbers and their spiritual significance and symbolism. One further design, sometimes seen in continental cathedrals, will be mentioned: mazes and labyrinths symbolize the soul trapped and tangled in matter – a Gnostic idea – and its arduous journey to God. Few of these labyrinths remain undamaged and on open view; later Church authorities either didn't understand their symbolic message, and so built over them – or did, and so deliberately obscured them.[12]

THE ROSICRUCIANS

Dame Frances Yates puts forward a convincing case for the birth of the Rosicrucians having been directly inspired by John Dee, who studied the works of Cornelius Agrippa and Francesco Giorgi, and who in turn informed Edmund Spenser's *The Faerie Queene*, one of whose characters is the Red Cross Knight.

The Rosicrucians, as a body, sprang out of nowhere. The first the world heard of them was with the publication of the *Fama Fraternitatis* in 1614, the *Confessio Fraternitatis* in 1615, and *Chymische Hockzeit* or *The Chymical Wedding of Christian Rosenkreuz* in 1616. These works, between them, contained the story of Christian Rosy Cross himself, a religious manifesto, and an allegorical fable. None named an author. The three works together are generally known as the Rosicrucian Manifestos.

The *Fama* (variously translated as *Echoes* [or *A Discovery*] *of the Fraternity of the Most Praiseworthy* [or *Laudable*] *Order of Rosicrucians* [or *the Rosy Cross*]) tells the story of the discovery, 120 years after his death, of the tomb of Christian Rosy Cross, who was born in Germany in 1378, travelled to the Holy Land, Turkey and Arabia as a young man, learned many things, founded the Brotherhood of the Rosy Cross, and died in 1484 aged 106. His tomb was discovered by one of the Brothers; it was seven-sided and contained an altar and the uncorrupted body of the Founder, who had instructed the Brotherhood to keep itself secret for a hundred years. The tomb was resealed, but now the Brotherhood could come into the open.[13]

The *Confessio* says, briefly, that there is a hidden brotherhood of men, skilled in learning and in medicine, who will bring good to the world through their teachings and their subtle influence. It condemns the Papacy, and it also condemns those charlatans who bring alchemy, astrology and the other occult arts into disrepute.

The *Chymical* [or *Alchemical*] *Wedding* [or *Marriage*] is a strange and complex fable of Christian as a young man on a journey, who has to face numerous tests to prove his worthiness; it is clearly a spiritual journey of discovery and self-discovery, and his travels and trials are also clearly symbolic. In one way it could be compared to John Bunyan's *Pilgrim's Progress*; in another way it could be compared to the journey of the Fool through the Tarot (see p. 148); in another, it is an alchemical allegory.

Most authorities see 'the Illuminated Father and Brother CRC' as an allegorical invention himself. The ideas and ideals within the three documents echo closely those of the Hermetic Philosophers of the day, but it cannot be claimed with any certainty who wrote each one. The *Fama* was published alongside another text, *The Reformation of the World*, a German translation of a chapter of a book by an Italian, Trajano Boccalini. The *Confessio* was published alongside a rewriting of part of a work by John Dee, *Monas Hieroglyphica*. (There is no suggestion here that the authors of these two Manifestos were Boccalini and Dee; only that the distributors, and presumably the authors, of the Manifestos were aware of the work of these writers.)

The *Chymical Marriage* is widely attributed to Johann Valentin Andreae (1586–1654); Andreae claimed in his autobiography (undiscovered until 1799) that he had written it at the age of 17, but he put a great deal of effort during his life into distancing himself from accusations that he had written any of the three documents. As a Lutheran minister, he had to be careful to dispel any tinge of heresy. He is the most likely candidate for authorship of the *Chymical Marriage*; many believe that he also wrote the *Fama*, possibly along with other scholars.

The Rosicrucian Manifestos all spoke of a secret brotherhood, working for the good of mankind. Those adepts who wished might join it; but the documents contained no membership address, no application form. Magical philosophers all over Europe were running around making themselves known, in the hope that they would be contacted and invited to join.

The symbol of the Rosicrucians was a superimposed rose and cross. This in itself wasn't new; both Andreae and Martin Luther had similar combinations of rose and cross in their family arms. The cross is usually assumed to be the straightforward Christian cross, though it should be remembered that Christianity did not invent the cross as a religious symbol. Indeed, the cross predates Christianity by millennia; it has long been a symbol of the meeting of heaven and earth, of God and man; alchemically it represented the joining of the active, male principle (the vertical line) and the passive, female principle (the horizontal line); numerologically it represents both the solidity of Four and the God-in-man idea of Five, the centre being taken as a point (see p. 78). A cross within a circle was an early symbol for a solar deity. However, the very name of Christian Rosenkreuz suggests that Rosicrucianism is based on the Christian religion – though not necessarily on orthodox, exoteric Christianity.

The rose is also an age-old symbol. It too can represent the Sun, and so divine light or spiritual illumination. The rose was a symbol of love, both sensual and divine. With the petals seen as the unfolding labia, it can represent female sexuality; it can also symbolize purity and virginity, and is thus one of the symbols of the Blessed Virgin Mary. The rose, long before the Rosicrucians and Freemasons emphasized this meaning, was a symbol for secrecy; *sub rosa* refers to the custom of having a rose on or above a dining table, so that whatever might incautiously be said after too much wine was 'under the rose', and not to be spoken of outside. (Some Roman Catholic confessionals have a rose carved above the grille; to go from the sublime to the profane, some brothels have roses on the ceiling, with exactly the same significance.) A few centuries before the Rosicrucian manifestos the rose was used as a symbol of the Holy Grail. The rose is beauty surrounded by suffering (its thorns), and thus could represent the passion of Christ, or the difficult life-path of a believer. The usual five-petalled rose of Rosicrucianism is also a Cabalistic symbol from the Zohar.[14]

There is a school of thought, however, which claims that the rose of the Rosicrucian symbol, while referring to any or all of the above, was also deliberate misdirection; and that the 'Ros' of Rosicrucian derives not from the Latin *rosa* meaning 'rose', but from the Latin *ros*, meaning 'dew'. This would tie in the Rosicrucians with the alchemists, for whom dew was itself a powerful symbol of regeneration; in alchemical symbolism dew was the universal alkahest, the most powerful solvent of gold.

Was there actually a body called the Rosicrucians? It seems very unlikely. The life-story of their founder and leader, Christian Rosy Cross, was very obviously allegorical. It has even been suggested that the *Fama* could have been nothing more than a *ludibrium*, a standard academic jest that then got completely out of hand. And yet there were people all over Europe who were – individually and without the name – already Rosicrucians: the Hermetic Philosophers.

What seems most likely is that one or more of these – perhaps Andreae, perhaps someone else – issued what was effectively a call to arms, as if to say, 'We shouldn't be sitting around pursuing our own individual studies for our own personal benefit, be it intellectual or spiritual. With the knowledge that we have we could, and should, be out there doing something useful.'

In other words, that Rosicrucians created themselves out of a desire to exist.

Attacks on and defences of the Rosicrucians began immediately. One of the first open defenders of Rosicrucianism was Robert Fludd (1574–1637), who wrote *Tractatus apologeticus integritatem societatis Rosae Crucis defendens* in 1616. A dramatically innovative thinker, and like Dee and others a philosopher scientist, Fludd was a Fellow of the Royal College of Physicians, though initially it looked as if his Paracelsian views would bar his admittance. His contribution to esoteric thought was somewhat unusual: Fludd taught that there were specific demons for specific illnesses – actually a mystical Jewish idea – and that prayer and spells were as efficacious as medicinal treatment. He also had a new approach to the age-old theological problem of good and evil; rather than the dualism of Gnosticism, Fludd taught that the bright sun of Apollo and the Prince of Darkness Dionysus, one the maker and mender, the other the breaker and spoiler, were effectively two sides of the same coin: both were God. Much Hermetic, Christian Cabalist and Rosicrucian thought was strongly influenced by Neo-Platonism and Neo-Pythagoreanism (as, to a lesser extent, is orthodox, exoteric Christianity); Fludd drew links with that other great Greek philosopher, Aristotle, identifying Aristotle's ten spheres with the ten *sephiroth* of the Cabalist Tree of Life.

Several other well-known names soon became associated with the Rosicrucian movement. These included the alchemist and physician Michael Maier (1566–1622), who wrote a defence, *Silentium post clamorem* (*The Silence after the Shouting*), in 1617. He was better known for two other works, *The Secret of Secrets* (1614) and *Atalanta Fugitiva* (1618), in which he drew links between mythology and alchemical symbolism. Somewhat later the mathematician and Jesuit Athanasius Kircher (1602–80) also wrote about mythology, particularly the Egyptian myth of Isis and Osiris. In attempting to draw in comparisons with other mythologies, including Mexican and Japanese, he was a forerunner of the more recent idea that similar truths lie behind all mythologies and religions. The work of Maier and Kircher on mythology also anticipated the much later work of Carl Gustav Jung.

Others whom the present-day Orders claim to have been early Rosicrucians, and who were certainly associated with the ideas of the movement, include the mystic Thomas Vaughan (1621–65); the astrologer William Lilly (1602–81); Sir Kenelm Digby (1603–65), as much a chemist as an alchemist; and the historian Elias Ashmole (1617–92), founder of the Ashmolean Museum in Oxford, and a founding fellow of the Royal Society, which held to some of the Rosicrucian ideals and is said to have been a realization of the concept of the Invisible College of the Rosicrucian Brotherhood.

The word 'claim' is used deliberately. Many nineteenth- and twentieth-century Rosicrucians believed that the Fraternity did exist as such long before the publication of the *Fama Fraternitatis* in 1614; John Dee, who died in 1608, has been described as a Rosicrucian Grand Master. Scholars, however, generally accept that whatever links there might have been between alchemists, Hermetic Philosophers and other esotericists before 1614, the term Rosicrucian dates from then, and Rosicrucian Orders date from later.

There may not have been a Rosicrucian Fraternity at the time the three documents were published, but soon there were many. Their aims were spiritual reform, both of individuals and of religion itself; and social reform, making the world a better place. Not surprisingly they were seen as heretics and revolutionaries. When, in 1623, word spread that there were several important Rosicrucians in Paris, both visibly and invisibly, a leaflet rapidly appeared, denouncing the 'Invisibles' as having made a pact with the devil.

By the 1640s there were Rosicrucian lodges throughout Europe; one founded by Ashmole and Lilly in London in 1646 is thought by some to be the origin of the Freemasons.

The original fervour died down within a few decades. In 1710 Sigmund Richter, under the name of Sincerus Renatus, published the laws of the alchemical Brotherhood of the Golden and Rosy Cross (this will be taken up again later), but in general the early decades of the eighteenth century – the Age of Reason – saw little overt esoteric activity. What it did see, though, was the emergence of the largest secret society of them all, Freemasonry, and two major revolutions, in France and in America. There is a strong argument that the esoteric spiritual ideas of the Rosicrucians were transformed for a while into revolutionary social and political ideals and actions.

Further discussion of the Rosicrucians in their later and current manifestations follows examination of the Freemasons in some detail in the next chapter. First, however, a brief look at the influence of the Freemasons, and perhaps the Rosicrucians, on the birth of the USA.

THE FOUNDING
OF THE UNITED STATES

Freemasonry arrived in North America around 1730, though individual Masons had been there for some years previously. Benjamin Franklin became a Freemason in 1731; by 1734 he was Provincial Grand Master in the State of Pennsylvania. According to the *Fraternitas Rosae Crucis*, based in Pennsylvania, in 1774 he was also one of the 'Council of Three' of the Rosicrucians then in America. On his visits to England it seems he was also involved in Sir Francis Dashwood's Hell Fire Club, which appears to have mixed serious esoteric study with revived Pagan worship and with drunken orgies.

George Washington was also a Freemason, having been initiated in 1752. A quarter of a century later there was a suggestion that there should be a Grand Lodge of all America, and Washington was proposed as Grand Master. He declined the honour, though in fact the Grand Lodge never got off the ground. He was, however, Master of an individual Lodge at the time he became the first President of the United States of America in 1789.

There is more than a suspicion that Freemasons were responsible for the Boston Tea Party in 1773; certainly Paul Revere was a Mason, later becoming a Grand Master of Massachusetts. Admiral John Paul Jones and General Andrew Jackson were also Freemasons, as were many others who played a significant role in the Revolution.

Masonic apron presented to General Washington by Mme Lafayette
(Robert Macoy, *General History, Cyclopedia and*
Dictionary of Freemasonry, 1850)

For many years both conspiracy theorists and patriotic American Freemasons have claimed that the American Revolution was largely inspired and organized by Freemasons. According to the Masonic scholar John Hamill, this has been vastly overstated. 'Modern American Masonic historians, in preparation for the bicentennial of the United States, carried out a great deal of research into the revolutionary period and junked many cherished legends.'[15] For example, according to the generally sound author Michael Howard, of the fifty-six signatories of the Declaration of Independence, 'only six were not members of the Masonic Order';[16] according to Hamill, however, 'only eight . . . can be positively identified as

Freemasons.' Thomas Jefferson, who actually drafted the wording of the Declaration, was not a Freemason.

Much of the argument for Masonic, Rosicrucian or other esoteric influence in the birth of the United States rests on the Great Seal of the country. This was several years in the formulation. The decision to design a Great Seal was made in 1776, on the day that the Declaration of Independence was signed; several successive committees and artists came up with ideas, but it was not until June 1782 that designs were finally approved. The obverse shows the bald-headed American eagle; above its head, in a cloud of glory, are thirteen five-pointed stars in the shape of Solomon's Seal, representing the thirteen original states; in its talons it clutches a thirteen-berried olive branch and a bunch of thirteen arrows, symbolizing peace and war; a banner reads 'E Pluribus Unum', 'out of many, one', which clearly refers to the thirteen states

The truncated pyramid and the Eye of God,
in the Great Seal of the USA

85

becoming one nation, but is also thought to mean that all Gods are one.

The reverse of the Great Seal is more obviously esoteric. The thirteen levels of the truncated pyramid again refer to the thirteen states, but the truncated pyramid itself is supposed to represent the loss of ancient wisdom. Floating above the pyramid, instead of a capstone, is a frequent esoteric symbol, the All-Seeing Eye of God in a triangle, surrounded by rays of light. On the bottom course of masonry is the date 1776. This obviously refers to the date of independence; the often-found suggestion that it also refers to the founding of the Illuminati is a clear case of making conspiracy out of coincidence. The two inscriptions on this side read 'Annuit Cœptis', 'He favours our undertakings', and 'Novus Ordo Seclorum', 'New Order of the Ages'.

The New Order, according to some Rosicrucians today, was a real-life application of Francis Bacon's fictional *New Atlantis*; the USA, they say, was designed from the start to be a real Utopia.

'We hold these truths to be self-evident, that all men are created equal, that they are endowed by their Creator with certain unalienable rights, that among these are life, liberty and the pursuit of happiness';[17] these are sentiments which would be equally at home in the mouth of a Rosicrucian or a Freemason.

THE ILLUMINATI

In the same year as the American Declaration of Independence, the Order of Perfectibilists was founded in Bavaria in 1776 by Adam Weishaupt; it soon became known as the Enlightened, or the Illuminati. It was quite deliberately modelled on the strict order of the Jesuits, but was opposed to what the Jesuits stood for in almost every respect. It was more overtly political than most Rosicrucian or Masonic groups; its declared aim was to abolish monarchies, abolish the clergy, abolish private ownership, and set up a Utopian state where all men were equal and free, and lived by something similar to Rosicrucian ideals, i.e. individual spiritual wisdom. Social reform had always been seen as a natural and desired outcome of esoteric spiritual development; with the Illuminati it came centre stage. Membership was by invitation only. Branches of the Illuminati sprang up throughout Europe, sometimes based on existing Masonic Lodges; Weishaupt joined the Masons in 1777.

They were too revolutionary for the authorities; within ten years both the Illuminati and Freemasonry had been banned in Bavaria, and Weishaupt, a university professor, had been sacked. It is commonly asserted by conspiracy theorists, though as so often with no hard evidence, that the Illuminati went underground, that they resurfaced from time to time under assorted names, or as the hidden power behind other groups, and that they continued to have political influence throughout the next two centuries.

It has been said that whether or not the Illuminati actually *have* exercised such influence through the years, the *belief* that they have means that in reality they have.

A CONSPIRACY THEORY

Do the Illuminati, or anything resembling them, still exist? Some have suggested so.

In the 1960s, the British prime minister Harold Wilson was able to fight many opponents, but against the 'Gnomes of Zurich' he had no defences. This was his phrase for the international bankers and financiers who, he believed, *really* ran things. They were shadowy figures; often they could not actually be identified at all. Behind those who were known by name seemed to lurk others. A handful of people in Switzerland, in Germany, in France, in Italy, held the strings which made all of Europe dance.

It has been suggested by conspiracy theorists that these people, Harold Wilson's Gnomes of Zurich, were the mid-20th century equivalent of the Illuminati. They were powerful; they controlled money, banks, financial institutions, business, industry - and ultimately, because it cannot be separated from all of these, politics.

Some take the theory a step further. The original Illuminati wanted what was effectively a United States of Europe. It has always been historically inevitable that the Common Market, the European Economic Community, would move towards the European Union – a complete political union – whatever the wishes of the people.

Joining the Common Market in 1973 meant that Britain had to leave EFTA, the European Free Trade Association, which was the rival trading bloc; EFTA, without its strongest member, crumbled. It meant throwing away trading agreements with, in particular, Australia and New Zealand, which turned those countries economically towards the Pacific Rim countries, and politically against Britain. Britain lost both power and respect in her own Commonwealth.

With these consequences, why did successive British governments of both major parties feel they had to join? What clout did the EEC have that was greater than the very powerful trading links Britain already possessed? Who was really pushing for Britain's entry? And who is now pushing for a single European currency?

The answer, of course, is the bankers, the financiers... Harold Wilson's Gnomes of Zurich. In other words, the successors to the Illuminati. Perhaps they are P2 (see p. 198). Perhaps they are the *Prieuré de Sion* (see p. 99). Perhaps they are some other, even more shadowy group. But it is they, and not our elected governments, who are the ones with *real* power. Even if they are illuminated with secret wisdom, few would believe that such a benevolent dictatorship, ruling from behind the scenes, could be a good thing.[18]

Such a conspiracy theory is not in any way being seriously proposed here; it is merely being given as an example of how far such theories can be taken. Whether it has any validity whatsoever, who can say? There is absolutely no real evidence to support it – but neither, of course, can it be disproved.

Although a present-day Illuminati conspiracy theory can be treated lightly, it should be emphasized that there is a darker side to be considered. There are numerous small secret societies in Europe, North and South America, and elsewhere, which have powerful and influential people among their members. Some have Masonic connections, though Freemasonry would disown them. The Italian-based Masonic offshoot P2, discussed later in this book, is probably the best-known, but it is not alone. What is particularly disturbing for anyone living in one form or another of a liberal democracy, is that many of these groups are extremely right-wing; some are white-supremacist and anti-Semitic.

There are, beyond any doubt, 'odd intrigues between secret services, more or less "deviant" clandestine Lodges and Templar organisations in recent neo-templar history.'[19] Sceptics are probably right to scoff at the more inventive conspiracy theories; but the reason people believe in them is that they often have at least some basis in fact.

CHAPTER THREE

FREEMASONRY

FREEMASONRY often says that it is not so much a secret society as a society with secrets; with about 600,000 members throughout Great Britain, tens of thousands on the continent and maybe three and a half million in North America, classing it with small, secret cabals of a few dozen is laughable. Nevertheless Freemasonry prefers to keep its rituals secret; even though most of them have been published, Freemasonry still officially restricts them to initiates only.

Membership is currently rising by about one and a half per cent a year. It is only in the last three years that, with computerized records, the number of individual members has been known accurately. Previous estimates of 600,000 Masons in England and Wales alone were based on Lodge membership, and many Masons are members of more than one Lodge. It is not particularly expensive to be a member of the Craft, though costs rise as one joins additional Lodges, and additional Orders. For an ordinary Mason in the UK who is a member of one Provincial Lodge (i.e. outside London), including his annual dues to United Grand Lodge, his own Lodge subscriptions, and the cost of dining after Lodge meetings, the total annual cost in 1996 was probably only around £60–£80.

Contrary to the claims of critics, very few current British MPs or Lords are Freemasons; the heyday for Masonic MPs was from the 1860s till the First World War. After that, says John Hamill, Librarian and Curator at Freemasons' Hall, London, both society and politics changed considerably; politics became a full-time job, and few politicians could find the time for active Freemasonry. Only two British prime ministers have ever been Masons: George Canning in the early nineteenth century, and Winston Churchill early in the twentieth century.

So much has been written on Freemasonry, both for and against, and much of it either obscure, misleading or biased, that a moderately interested reader coming upon any one book on the subject is most unlikely to find anything approaching a useful and balanced account. It will thus be useful to mention in this chapter a number of books, and their merits and faults.

Freemasons used to be quite open about their membership of the Craft, and Freemasonry as a body was publicly visible; there would be Masonic services in churches, Masonic processions through high streets and Masonic ceremonies at the laying of foundation stones of major new buildings. Then at some time between the two world wars, for no reason that anyone can now think of, Freemasonry drew in its horns, closed in on itself, and became profoundly secretive. When attacks were made on it, this secrecy only served to reinforce the suspicions of outsiders.

Stephen Knight's *The Brotherhood*, poorly argued as it was, came as something of a bombshell in 1983. Suddenly Freemasonry was in the news, and stayed in the news. Knight's book had one beneficial result: the following year the governing bodies of British Freemasonry officially dropped the closed-mouth attitude. Senior Freemasons were now prepared to talk to the press, even – in the case of Commander Michael Higham, the Grand Secretary of United Grand Lodge – appearing on radio phone-in programmes. Freemasons' Hall on Great Queen Street in London set up a permanent public exhibition of many Masonic treasures, and allowed non-Masons, both male and female, to visit its Temple. At least two public relations videos have appeared about Freemasonry, one of them showing the ceremony at Earls Court in 1992 for the 275th anniversary of the founding of the Grand Lodge. Several classic works of Freemasonry have been reissued by the Aquarian Press, under the general editorship of John Hamill. And senior Freemasons such as Hamill have written books about Freemasonry, officially laying to rest many of the more outlandish theories, some of which had been propounded by Freemasons themselves in the past.

The Freemasons may have left it just too late. Knight's book was followed by Martin Short's far better written, but far more vicious *Inside the Brotherhood* (1989). Both had a devastating effect on the reputation of Freemasonry. According to Hamill, Freemasonry is beginning to recover from this damage, but it's a long, slow process. 'It's the old cliché: it takes fifty years to make a reputation, it takes thirty seconds to lose it – and it takes seventy years to rebuild it.'[1]

Before moving on to an examination of Freemasonry in the context of this book, it is therefore necessary to look briefly at this perennial topic.

IS FREEMASONRY CORRUPT?

According to *The Brotherhood* and *Inside the Brotherhood*, Freemasonry is absolutely riddled with corruption. Masonic policemen, barristers, judges, MPs and Lords, all trade favours with each other, give preferment to each other, find the guilty innocent, and so on. Masonic town councillors give lucrative contracts to businessmen who are in the same Lodge. It is said that the country is run by people who recognize each other by funny handshakes.

There is undoubtedly an element of truth in such accusations. The detailed case histories in Knight's and Short's books – even those based on hearsay and circumstantial evidence – might well be entirely accurate; each reader must judge how much weight can be placed on often undocumented anecdotes. But whether they are true or not, what is at fault is the inferences the authors draw from these cases. Their reasoning appears to be that because there have been 'proven' instances of corrupt conduct involving Freemasons, then Freemasonry itself is responsible: the organization itself is corrupt.

The logical lacuna here is obvious. Does discovery of one dishonest policeman result in suspicion being cast on the whole of the police force; or does one Catholic priest's fathering of a love-child destroy the moral reputation of the Roman Catholic Church?

There will of course be corrupt Freemasons. There are corrupt businessmen, policemen and lawyers who are Freemasons, and others who are not. Knight and Short ignore the simple fact that if two members of the same Lodge trade commercial favours to their mutual advantage, what this actually shows is that there are two corrupt individuals, who happen to be Freemasons, working together. What it *doesn't* show is that Freemasonry is a corrupt organization.

One of the most common accusations is that, with the large number of judges who are Freemasons, favour is shown when sentencing brother Masons. It is quite possible that on some occasions this might have happened, but at least one High Court judge who is a Freemason has stated publicly that if he were to see a defendant making Masonic signs in court, his personal inclination would be to sentence him more harshly for abusing his Masonic membership in attempting to secure a miscarriage of justice.

It is often said that Freemasons are pledged to keep each others' secrets except in cases of murder or treason. On this point it is worth looking at the actual wording of the Obligation made on becoming a Master Mason:

> that my breast shall be the sacred repository of his secrets when entrusted to my care – murder, treason, felony, and *all other offences* contrary to the laws of God and the ordinances of the realm being at all times most especially excepted.[2]

ORIGINS OF FREEMASONRY

The origins of Freemasonry are astonishingly blurred, considering how relatively young the movement is. We can look back to the sixteenth, seventeenth or eighteenth centuries and say with some degree of certainty that, for example, the Calvinist movement or the Bank of England or dictionaries of the English language began because certain specific people said or did or wrote certain specific things at certain specific times, and we can then trace their development. In the case of Freemasonry we cannot do this. There are indications and clues, but they often seem to be pieces from different jigsaw puzzles.

Even John Hamill, the Librarian and Curator of the United Grand Lodge of England, the Centenary Master of the research Lodge Quatuor Coronati No. 2076, and one of the most respected Masonic scholars in Britain today, says, 'We don't know enough about how Freemasonry evolved, and we don't know enough about the early development of rituals; the earliest ritual fragments we have date from the mid-1690s onwards. We don't know what went on before then.'

The one clear, undisputed fact in the early history of Freemasonry is the getting together of four London Lodges at the Goose and Gridiron alehouse in St Paul's churchyard on 24th June 1717 to form a Grand Lodge. The first Grand Master was Anthony Sayer, a gentleman; the first noble Grand Master, the Duke of Montagu, was appointed four years later. It is certain that there were some Lodges in existence before then, but details are sketchy. Elias Ashmole noted in his diary in 1646 that he was initiated into a Lodge in Warrington; other Lodges were founded in Chester around 1670, and in Scarborough in 1705, and no doubt there were others.

By 1730 there were over a hundred English Lodges under the Grand Lodge. An Irish Grand Lodge was established by the mid-1720s, and a Scottish one in 1736. Then complications set in, with the establishment of various rival Grand Lodges.

The most serious rift was between the 'Antients', founded in 1751, and the 'Moderns', the original 1717 Grand Lodge. The confusing names occur because a group of five Lodges came together with the 'desire to revive the Ancient Craft upon true Masonical principles', accusing the original Grand Lodge of modernizing rituals.

After decades of often bitter infighting among Masons, the two rival Grand Lodges, each with a royal prince as its Grand Master, were eventually reconciled in December 1813; the United Grand Lodge of England was born nearly a century after the first Grand Lodge.

Those years of dispute produced much of the ritual of today's Freemasonry – and also much of the confusion of fact and fiction, history and legend, that bedevils Masonic historians today.

Just one example will suffice to show how Masons created a rod for their own back. William Preston's highly influential *Illustrations of Masonry* was first published in 1772, and went through many expanded editions over the following fifty years. It includes at face value a letter and annotated pamphlet now known to be a forgery; the letter, dated 1696, purports to be from the philosopher John Locke to Thomas, Earl of Pembroke, and accompanies a supposed copy of a copy of an 'original faid to be the hand-writing of K. Henry VI', which is a set of questions and answers about 'the Myftery of Maçonrye'.

QUEST. What dothe the maçonnes concele and hyde?
ANSW. Thay concelethe the arte of ffyndinge neue artes, and thatt ys for here own proffytte, and preife: they concelethe the arte of kepynge fecrettes, that foe the worlde mayeth nothinge concele from them. Thay concelethe the arte of wunderwerkynge, and of forefayinge thynges to comme, that fo thay fame artes may not be ufedde of the wyckedde to an euyell ende. Thay alfo concelethe the arte of chaunges, the wey of wynnynge the facultye of Abrac, the fkylle of becommynge gude and parfyghte wythouten the holpynges of fere and hope; and the univerfelle longage of maçonnes.

This wonderful document certainly dates back as far as 1753, but who wrote it, and when, and why, are all unknown. Preston, one of the leading lights of Freemasonry in his day, quoted it as genuine, and it was clearly believed so by many other Masons. Preston's *Illustrations* makes fascinating reading, claiming as it does that 'From the commencement of the world, we may trace the foundation of Mafonry. Ever fince fymmetry began, and harmony difplayed her charms, our Order has had a being.'[3] Disentangling the fact from the fantasy, here as elsewhere, has caused problems ever since.

Masonic legends trace the history of Freemasonry as far back as King Solomon, and some early Masonic historians stated this as fact. Most present-day writers, whether Freemasons or not, distinguish between such legends and more likely factual origins. In general they see two main starting points: the medieval stonemasons' guilds, and the seventeenth-century interest in esoteric philosophy – or, loosely, Rosicrucianism. Others, more controversially, insist that the Freemasons are the descendants of the Knights Templar.

THE TEMPLAR CONNECTION

According to John Hamill and R.A. Gilbert,

> there is not the slightest evidence that the Order of the Temple survived
> in any form even for four decades, let alone for four centuries. There is,
> indeed, not the slightest historical support for the Templar theory of
> origin. But no matter: for those with a vision of chivalry, such difficul-
> ties were minor problems to be glossed over. They wished Freemasonry
> to be derived from Templarism; *ergo*, it *was* so.[4]

That seems dismissive enough – but we have already seen that their first
assertion is not entirely accurate; Portugal's Knights of Christ were, initially,
more or less Portugal's Knights Templar under a new name, even retaining
the same banner, the Templar Cross. The pope may have officially disbanded the Templars in March 1312, but the overwhelming majority of knights
survived, some to join other Orders, some to join mercenary armies, and
others to go whither they willed.

The evidence suggests, however, that the rest of Hamill and Gilbert's
dismissal is probably a fair statement of the truth.

The bonds between Scotland and France in the eighteenth century were far
closer than those between Scotland and England; thus many of the Rites and
Orders which developed then, and which are still present in Freemasonry
today, had a Scots–French origin.

The first reference to Masonic Templars in Scotland is in 1769, but the
origins can be traced back further. The introduction of chivalric Orders to
Freemasonry, with their higher, more esoteric Degrees, took place very early
on in actual Masonic history – and occurred, as might be expected, in France.

A Jacobite, the Chevalier Andrew Michael Ramsay, was initiated a
Freemason in England in 1730; moving to France, he delivered a lecture to
the nascent French Masons in 1736, in which he spoke of the brotherhood,
symbolism and secret signs between Crusading knights, 'religious and warrior princes', though he didn't mention the Templars by name. The Saracens
infiltrated the Crusaders' organization;

> the knights, having discovered the existence of these spies, became more
> careful in the future, and instituted certain signs and words for the
> purpose of guarding against them; and, as many of their workmen were
> new converts to Christianity, they adopted certain symbolic ceremonies,
> in order more readily to instruct their proselytes in the new religion.[5]

When these knights returned to their home countries, Ramsay said, they established Lodges in which to preserve, study and teach the esoteric architecture they had learned in Palestine, particularly with regard to rebuilding the Temple in Jerusalem.

For good or for bad, Ramsay's Oration was directly responsible for the proliferation of chivalric Rites within Freemasonry in the eighteenth century; they particularly appealed to the nobility, and caught the imagination of many influential Masons. It might also have been indirectly responsible, at least in part, for the later upsurge in Romanticism and interest in chivalry, Arthuriana, etc. of the nineteenth century.

The effects on Masonry were far-reaching. The Ancient and Accepted Scottish Rite of Freemasonry, widely practised by American Masons today, is effectively *Écossaise*, a 'Scottish' Rite developed in France, and inspired by Ramsay's Oration. (The English equivalent, usually known as the *Rose Croix*, is a later development, not being officially accepted until 1845.)

The specific introduction of the Knights Templar to Freemasonry occurred about thirty years after Ramsay's Oration, in Germany. A French prisoner and a German priest together created the story that after Jacques de Molay's execution in 1314, a number of Templar knights sailed to Scotland with their treasures and their secrets. Other Masons, including a self-proclaimed Scottish nobleman, George Frederick Johnson, added to the Templar myth. Johnson claimed to be Knight of the Great Lion of the High Order of the Lords of the Temple at Jerusalem, and also Provost-General of the Templar Order of the Scottish Lords.

The person who really sparked off the Templar degrees within Freemasonry, however, was Baron Karl Gotthelf von Hund (or Johann Gottlieb von Hund, according to A.E. Waite), who established around 1754 a complex system of degrees known as the Strict Observance because of its vows of absolute obedience to Unknown Superiors.

Baron von Hund claimed that he had been initiated into an Order of the Temple in 1742, though no such Order is known to have existed at that time; further, he claimed mistakenly that Charles Edward Stuart – Bonnie Prince Charlie – was present at his initiation. (Interestingly, the Chevalier Andrew Ramsay had been the Young Pretender's tutor in the mid-1720s.) Von Hund also claimed that he had been commanded and empowered by Unknown Superiors to develop a new Rite. (There is, perhaps, a similarity to be found with the hidden leaders of the Hermetic Order of the Golden Dawn; see p. 164). Having commissioned him to do the job, the Unknown Superiors never contacted him again. How much of this has any factual validity is unclear. However, the Baron did as he was told, and established the Rite, with all its ritual.

The central legend of the Rite was that Jacques de Molay was succeeded as Grand Master by Pierre d'Aumont, the Templar Prior of Auvergne, who took the Order to Scotland. He was succeeded by an unbroken line of Grand Masters, who kept their identity secret: the Unknown Superiors.

Baron von Hund's Rite of the Strict Observance died with him, in 1776, largely because he was never able to produce his Unknown Superiors. But many of von Hund's ideas were picked up by the Lodge of the Rite of the Philalethes at Lyons, and (quite understandably) by the Provincial Grand Prior of Auvergne, and were adapted into a Rite which today is still practised by the Grand Priory of Helvetia. According to Pick and Knight's officially approved and very detailed *Pocket History of Freemasonry*, in Switzerland:

> the Great Priory of England is in communion with the Grand Priory of
> the Rectified Scottish Rite, more often referred to as the Knights
> Beneficent of the Holy City. This is, in effect, the old Rite of Strict
> Observance of Baron von Hund. It is regarded as an exalted pinnacle of
> Freemasonry and its Swiss members have the privilege of attending
> meetings of the 33° of the Scottish Rite.[6]

The Great Priory of England is the governing body of today's Masonic Knights Templar or, to give them their full name, The United Religious, Military and Masonic Orders of the Temple and of St John of Jerusalem, Palestine, Rhodes and Malta in England and Wales and Provinces Overseas, under whose control comes the English Great Priory of the Holy Order of Knights Beneficent of the Holy City, or *les Chevaliers Bienfaisants de la Cité Sainte*, which apparently meets very rarely.

Brief mention must also be made of the Clerical Chapter of Knights Templar invented around 1770 by Johann August von Starck, self-styled '*fils et frère des pères de la famille de Sçavans l'Ordre des Sages par tous les générations de l'univers* (son and brother of the fathers of the family of Savants of the Order of Wise Men throughout all generations of the Universe)'.[7] He claimed:

> that the original Knights Templar were divided into two classes,
> military and sacerdotal; that the Clerical branch possessed the inner
> knowledge of the Order; that it had been perpetuated in secret; that
> Starck was its present ambassador; that it was superior to the Secular
> Branch; and that if recognised by Baron von Hund, the treasures of its
> knowledge should be opened to him and his Rite.[8]

Supposedly descendants of the Essenes, the Clerical Chapter appears to bear some similarity to the *Prieuré de Sion* (see p. 99). When the Templars were dissolved, the clerks of the Clerical Chapter, including the Knight John

Eures, reputedly rescued the secret documents and treasures, and kept them safe through to Starck's time.

Pick and Knight, like Hamill, stress that 'it is important to discount at once any theories (and there have been several) which claim an historical or ritual connexion with the medieval Military Orders with similar titles.'[9]

The connection was more likely to have been between Freemasonry and the French and Scottish Jacobites of the early eighteenth century. This was a romantic, idealized cause, whose romanticism and idealism were strengthened by the idea that the Freemasons were the more or less direct descendants of the Knights Templar. There may well be some truth in the belief that a number of Templars sailed to Scotland. It is also possible that some of those who arrived in Scotland kept some vestige of their chivalric tradition alive for a while. However, the period between the death of Jacques de Molay in 1314 and the formal establishment of the Freemasons' Grand Lodge in 1717 is rather too long – twelve generations – for such a secret tradition to be passed down from father to son, from initiator to initiated. Even if, somehow, it had been, there is little chance that it could have remained secret for so long.

John Hamill's assessment is probably nearest to the truth. 'There was a liking – rather stronger than a liking – for the ideals of chivalry, the ideals of Christian knighthood.' It is from this romantic liking of *ideals* that the chivalric elements of Freemasonry developed, and almost certainly not from any direct continuation of tradition.

The Chevalier Ramsay, Baron von Hund and the others blended enough history into their created mythologies for them to be accepted by the French and Scottish Freemasons of their day – and for them to be further embellished by a number of present-day writers who often do not distinguish between established fact and unsubstantiated fable.[10] They build a convincing enough case for the casual reader – but most of their arguments and assertions were dismissed by, among others, A.E. Waite, some seventy years ago.

Waite lists several different 'Legends of Perpetuation', among which are Ramsay's Oration; the Charter of Larmenius, dated 1324, of the French Order of the Temple, of which Waite says,

> It began to be heard of in Paris about 1804 and was founded wholly on imposture. The only question concerning it which remains for criticism to determine is whether its chief document was forged in 1705 or at a much later period.

97

In 1861 the French occultist Éliphas Lévi claimed that:

> Prior to his death, the Chief of the Temple – that is, Jacques de Molay
> – organised and instituted Occult Masonry. From the purlieus of his
> dungeon the Grand Master erected four Metropolitan Lodges, at
> Naples for the East, at Edinburgh for the West, at Stockholm for the
> North and at Paris for the South.

Waite's only comment on Lévi's assertion is 'but it will not detain us long.'
    Lévi also claimed that the secret aim of the Templars was the rebuilding
of Solomon's Temple in Jerusalem – whose foundations, it should be recalled,
according to tradition lay under the Templars' original quarters. The
Templars were supposed to be connected to the 'Brethren of the Thebaid'
who, from almost the time of Christ, had preserved the mystical measure-
ments of the Temple. When the Templars were disbanded, they took their
secret knowledge to the lodges of operative masons – hence accounting for
the symbolic elements of architecture in Freemasonry. Waite comments that
'the secret conspiracy had no other local habitation than the brain of the
French occultist who put it forward in 1862.'[11]

And yet, and yet. There is still a lurking suspicion that somewhere in the
background of the Freemasons is a link to the Knights Templar. John J.
Robinson's *Born in Blood* argues such a direct link while at the same time
admitting that 'All this is speculative, no matter how much sense it may
make, because there is absolutely no historical evidence of the existence of
a secret society specifically based on fugitive Templars.'[12] Robinson does,
however, raise some interesting questions, one being about the origin of
the blood-curdling oaths which Masons were, until recently, required to
make at their initiations. There is no way, he says, that such penalties as
having your tongue torn out by the roots or your heart ripped out would
have been required, say, for revealing an ingenious new way to hold a chis-
el; but they would make sense as a penalty for one fugitive Templar betray-
ing another.
    True, but all the evidence seems to point to the gory penalties being a
late seventeenth- or early eighteenth-century invention, like so much else in
Freemasonry.

Another recent theory links the Templars and the Freemasons through a
more shadowy organization. Baigent, Leigh and Lincoln, in their controversial bestseller *The Holy Blood and the Holy Grail*, say,

There was a secret order behind the Knights Templar, which created the Templars as its military and administrative arm. This order, which has functioned under a variety of names, is most frequently known as the Prieuré de Sion ('Priory of Sion'). The Prieuré de Sion has been directed by a sequence of Grand Masters whose names are among the most illustrious in Western history and culture. Although the Knights Templar were destroyed and dissolved between 1307 and 1314, the Prieuré de Sion remained unscathed.[13]

Michael Howard's *The Occult Conspiracy: The secret history of mystics, Templars, Masons and occult societies* is a much sounder book than most on this general subject; in the few places where he mentions the *Prieuré de Sion* he is careful to use phrasing like 'The foundation of the Priory can be traced back allegedly to the Gnostic adept Ormus who lived in the first century CE' and 'the Priory of Sion, which we are led to believe promoted the heresy that Jesus survived the crucifixion'.[14]

Lionel Fanthorpe, one of the few science fiction authors in holy orders, is even more wary about the *Prieuré de Sion*:

> The Priory of Sion may be one of the most ancient, powerful, and remarkable secret societies in the world; or it may be the last vestigial trace of an inner group of Knights Templars; or it could be a perfectly innocent, respectable, and prosaic 'friendly society'; or it may not exist at all.[15]

It is perhaps worth noting that *none* of the more serious historical works on the Templars[16] mentions the *Prieuré de Sion* even in passing. As a top Masonic historian, John Hamill's comment is worth noting:

> As far as I am aware the *Prieuré de Sion* was never referred to before the appearance of *The Holy Blood and the Holy Grail*. With certainty I can say there is no reference to it in any Masonic literature.[17]

Just because we know, or strongly suspect, that most of the 'ancient' Templar-type Orders and Rites were created out of whole cloth in the eighteenth century, does not, of course, necessarily mean that there could *not* have been a very secret society, completely hidden from view, from the time of the Templars (or even from the time of Christ) to the present day. But we should beware of any complex theory which is largely based, as is the case with Baigent, Leigh and Lincoln, on lists of Grand Masters through the ages. The eighteenth century was awash with such. We should, perhaps, be even more suspicious when these lists include such luminaries as Léonardo da Vinci, Isaac Newton, Victor Hugo and Claude Debussy.[18]

Too frequently, books on secret societies throw so many disparate elements into the melting pot of theories that some of them are bound to adhere to each other. Statisticians have long been aware that you can find links between almost anything if you try hard enough – and if you select only the data which support your case. This book, which includes many of these same elements, is trying to tread a careful line between credulousness and scepticism. It cannot really be doubted that there *are* some such links – but the conclusions drawn from them ought not to be flights of fancy.

It is not just the Templar-type Orders within Freemasonry which are clouded with such confusion; as Waite says,

> The Roll of Templar Grand Masters – which no one has seen in
> England – is no worse than the fraudulent charter of Craft succession
> produced by James Anderson; the general Templar claim of the Strict
> Observance is a colourable romance of history when placed side by side
> with the ineffable mendacities which passed for literal Craft history in
> England during the eighteenth century, not to speak of forged
> documents, like the Charter of Cologne *et hoc genus omne.*[19]

The *Quatuor Coronati* Lodge is the section of Freemasonry specifically dedicated to historical research of all matters Masonic 'actual and traditional';[20] its *Transactions*, known as *Ars Quatuor Coronatorum*, are very highly regarded. It freely admits the difficulty of sorting out the facts from the fictions. It is largely due to the present-day work of *Quatuor Coronati* that many of the wilder claims of the eighteenth and nineteenth centuries have now been dismissed.

THE ROSICRUCIAN CONNECTION

The question of the origins of Freemasonry has not been helped by writers over the years – both opponents of Freemasonry and Masonic 'historians' – spouting wild theories, accepting dubious connections, and believing (or creating) fake documents.

John Hamill and his co-author R.A. Gilbert, in their *World Freemasonry: An Illustrated History* – a model of clarity and common sense – are determined, however, to separate Freemasonry from Rosicrucianism. They accept that the two movements share some ideals, 'and it is also not inherently improbable that some aspects of Rosicrucian thought may have inspired those who created the first speculative Masonic Lodges,'[21] but they describe any closer connection than that as 'nonsense'.

The general thesis of the present book is that the links between the different movements and organizations covered are, in most cases, links of ideas and ideals rather than of a direct lineage; which is much the same as what Hamill and Gilbert say of Rosicrucianism influencing Freemasonry. But in the case of these two movements one suspects that they are perhaps being a little disingenuous.

First, a glance at the list of the many higher degrees, or more correctly 'side degrees' of Freemasonry, shows a vast range of high-sounding chivalric and historically resonant names, many of which show a connection with Rosicrucianism or earlier esoteric movements: the Knights Templar and Knights of Malta, the Red Cross of Constantine, and the Knights of the Holy Sepulchre and St John the Evangelist; the fifth degree of the *Societas Rosicruciana in Anglia* is a qualification for membership of the Order of Eri, which includes the grades of Man-at-Arms, Esquire and Knight, under the leadership of the Enlightened Knight Commander; while a member of the Royal Order of Scotland progresses from being a Brother of Harodim to being a Knight of the Rosy Cross. The best-known sequence of side degrees, the Ancient and Accepted Rite, is generally known as the *Rose Croix*.

Today's Masonic historians say that these side degrees, and their high-sounding names and titles, were simply the attempts of enthusiastic but perhaps misguided late eighteenth- or nineteenth-century Masonic luminaries to add mystique to the whole business. This is certainly quite possible, but if they were simply choosing mysterious names, why *these particular* mysterious names?

In passing, it should be noted that these chivalric titles, like all Masonic titles, have no force outside their particular Orders. According to Hamill,

> A senior rank in the Ancient and Accepted Rite confers no seniority or rank in the Craft or any of the other Orders. Masonic ranks have no relevance outside the particular Order of Freemasonry which has conferred them. They certainly have no status outside Freemasonry, and anyone using their Masonic ranks in non-Masonic circumstances could lay themselves open to charges of advertising their membership for improper reasons.[22]

Second, many of the leading lights in either Freemasonry or Rosicrucianism in the early years were also in the other. It is of course possible that there was no more link here, for some people, than there is in someone belonging to, for example, both the Methodist Church and the Labour Party. In that example, though, a Christian Socialist might find that each body complemented the other, that one aimed to put the spiritual ideals of the other into social action. Perhaps the same could be said of Rosicrucianism and Freemasonry.

Third, and perhaps most compelling, is the *Societas Rosicruciana in Anglia*, the Rosicrucian Society of Freemasons, which will be examined in the next chapter.

It is worth looking at how a few other Masonic historians treat the possibility of a link with the Rosicrucians. Douglas Knoop and G.P. Jones don't even mention Rosicrucianism, or anything in the slightest esoteric, in their *Genesis of Freemasonry* (1947); for them, everything is traced back to the operative masons. Haywood and Craig, in *A History of Freemasonry* (1927), spend only two pages on 'the obscure and troublesome problem of the Rosicrucians and kindred occult societies'. They mention that 'there are survivals in the modern Masonic ritual which strongly suggest hermetic influence', and suggest that it would have been 'rather curious' if someone involved in one were not also involved in the other – and then drop the whole subject.

Haywood and Craig do, however, point out that those involved in 'Kabalism, astrology, alchemy, and various mystical philosophies . . . were the scientists of their day, and to their labours may be traced the beginnings of modern chemistry, physics and astronomy.'[23] This is in stark contrast to the views of Bernard E. Jones, another extremely respected Masonic historian, who states that the seventeenth-century Rosicrucians:

> were now 'scientific' dabblers, whatever else they were. As to their
> 'philosophy' and 'science', it must be said frankly that much of what
> passed under these names in the minds of many men – even educated
> men – in the sixteenth and seventeenth centuries would to-day be
> regarded as nonsense. Chemical philosophers, alchemists, astrologers,
> hermetic philosophers – all at some time or other regarded themselves
> as Rosicrucians, and apparently any educated person with a gift for
> words could find a place under the Rosicrucian banner.[24]

Jones's stance is a product of the mechanistic world-view of the nineteenth century, which although quite brilliant in some ways, was utterly blinkered in others. Much the same can be said of the views of anti-Masonic writer Walton Hannah, who complains that 'Freemasonry is frankly humanist in tone, and yet at the same time includes a great deal of mystical and symbolic nonsense about geometry and astronomy which no educated Mason in this enlightened age would dream of taking seriously.'[25]

It cannot be seriously doubted that there was *some* form of causative link, direct or indirect, between the Rosicrucians and the early speculative Freemasons.

Freemasonry appeared shortly after the Rosicrucians, who grew out of the Hermetic Philosophers of the Renaissance. Could it be that Freemasonry began as a socially acceptable 'outer court' for the 'inner court' of the Rosicrucians, safe from accusations of heresy? This is, of course, only a hypothesis, but it would explain both the very definite connection, and Freemasonry's usual determination to deny any such connection. Freemasonry was, on the whole, publicly acceptable; it was a cross between a gentlemen's club, a mutual benefit society, and a charitable institution. It had religious ideals, and some semi-religious rituals and teachings, but these could be interpreted in many different ways. For many – perhaps most – members, all of Freemasonry's symbolism and allegory was simply interesting dramatic spectacle. But for those who looked more deeply into it, and who wanted to look still more deeply into it, Freemasonry could introduce them to people who, after a suitable period of 'vetting', might initiate them into another society with more overtly esoteric teachings. It should be noted that membership of most of the side degrees is by invitation only.

A 1777 document from a German Rosicrucian Order, the Brotherhood of the Golden and Rosy Cross, might add considerable weight to this thesis. In its 'traditional history' it is stated:

> That the better to conceal their real purpose the Superiors of the Order
> established those lower Degrees which pass under the name of
> Freemasonry. That they served, moreover, as a seminary or preparation
> for the higher curriculum of the Rosicrucian Order and as a kind of
> spiritual prolegomenon . . . it [Freemasonry] remains the preparatory
> school of the Rosy Cross . . . [26]

The counter-argument, of course, is that the Brotherhood of the Golden and Rosy Cross in actuality might have been no more than an early side degree itself, equivalent to the *Rose Croix* (see p. 112): in other words, that it was a minor extension of Freemasonry, rather than Freemasonry having been created as its 'preparatory school'.

The direction of the cause-and-effect arrow cannot any longer readily be determined.

But if there is anything at all in this Outer Court hypothesis, it could be that as Freemasonry developed over the years, and lost touch with its origins, the founders of the *Societas Rosicruciana in Anglia*, among others, determined to restore some of the lost esoteric spiritual content. Two quotations will suffice to show that there are some Masons who believe that such a restoration is not only necessary, but essential, if Freemasonry is to have any meaning at all today.

Foster Bailey (died 1977) is best known as the co-founder with his wife Alice Bailey of the Arcane School and the Lucis Trust publishing house. He was both a Theosophist and a 32° Freemason, albeit in a Co-Masonic Order; this is a form of Freemasonry open to both sexes, and not acknowledged by United Grand Lodge. However, his book *The Spirit of Masonry* is on sale in the Masonic bookshops across the road from Freemasons' Hall in London. In it he writes:

> All mankind of every race and creed are the children of the one God. This Masonry from time immemorial has always known and taught its members . . . Masonry has oft been proclaimed as a spiritual quest. If it is not so understood, it is an ancient but empty shell.[27]

Another senior Freemason said in 1962,

> It may be that we Freemasons of the twentieth century are the modern representatives of the ancient Magi, or Wise Men of the East, though sadly shrunken in stature from those great and gifted men. The secrets and mysteries which they knew and understood have become for us a formula of words, of which the inner, esoteric meaning is seldom even suspected.[28]

This theme will be taken up again later in the book.

THE MASONIC CONNECTION

Medieval masons differed from workers in most other professions in that many of them travelled from place to place, from job to job, from working on a cathedral in one city to working on a cathedral in another city. Some, of course, stayed still – a *magister* or *maître* might remain in charge of a major construction for most of his life – but many went where the work was. Understandably proud of their skills, if they heard of a beautiful new cathedral being built in some other city, with vacancies for skilled masons, they might well move on, lured by the opportunity. They might learn new skills there; and they could pass on some design feature, or some trick of the trade, which they had learned in their previous positions. So masons, and their knowledge, spread around Europe.

Masons worked together, and they usually slept together in dormitories near their work. Their lodge – sometimes little more than a lean-to against a cathedral wall – was where they kept their tools, ate, met to discuss problems, sheltered from the weather, and sometimes did work which didn't have to be performed *in situ*, such as stone carvings.

It was inevitable that they would become a close-knit fraternity. When new masons arrived from elsewhere they would be accepted into the group, but they would have to prove in one way or another that they were fit people to be accepted, perhaps by a letter of introduction and recommendation from their previous lodge, or perhaps by knowing the answers to questions asked and answered only within a lodge, or perhaps by a special grip of the hand.

It would, of course, be necessary for such questions and answers, and such recognition signals, to be kept secret.

The term 'freemason' referred to the type of work and the type of stone; it is usually believed to be a contraction of 'freestone mason', freestone being a soft stone which could be carved. A freemason, then, was a craftsman with stone, rather than just a hewer of stone. When the new speculative Freemasonry moved to France in the early eighteenth century, the name was translated as *franc-maçon*, and the idea developed that they were in some way free.

John J. Robinson puts forward an inverse derivation of the name Freemason, which might or might not have any validity: French Masons would call their brother Masons '*frère maçon*' ('brother mason'), which was corrupted by English Masons into Freemason. This seems unlikely, if only because most educated Englishmen of the time would have understood at least basic French.

As mentioned in the previous chapter (p. 75), it is thought that hand-grips and passwords developed in Scotland to distinguish true masons from 'cowans', unskilled labourers capable of only basic building work. In the initiation of an Entered Apprentice, the Junior Warden tells the Worshipful Master that the Tyler is outside the door of the Lodge, 'being armed with a drawn sword, to keep off all intruders and Cowans to Masonry'.[29]

Joseph Fort Newton quotes a delightful Masonic story of how the stone-masons used to deal with cowans:

> Legend says that the old-time Masons punished such prying persons, who sought to learn their signs and secrets, by holding them under the eaves until the water ran in at the neck and out at the heels. What penalty was inflicted in dry weather, we are not informed. At any rate, they had contempt for a man who tried to make use of the signs of the craft without knowing its art and ethics.[30]

This treatment makes far more sense than the blood-curdling oaths which eighteenth-century Freemasons tried to ascribe to the early stonemasons.

Freemasonry abounds with symbolism, and much of it is architectural (see pp. 76–78). For example, the three great types of Greek column, Doric, Ionian and Corinthian, have particular symbolic significance. The reason that Freemasons concentrate on the classic Greek columns rather than on the glories of Gothic architecture has little to do with aesthetic appreciation of different periods of architecture. It is much more likely that, while operative masons built in a wide variety of styles over the centuries, speculative Freemasonry took its architectural symbolism not from operative masons – stoneworkers – but from the seventeenth-century esoteric philosophers; and they took it, largely, from Vitruvius who, in the first century BC, wrote about Classical Greek architecture rather than about a style which was not to come into existence for another twelve or thirteen centuries.

WHY FREEMASONRY?

Where, then, lie the origins of Freemasonry? Although romantically tempting, the hidden Templar theory is probably the least likely. The Rosicrucian theory satisfies many questions, though not that of proven historicity. The most mundane theory, that of the medieval stonemasons, ought perhaps by Occam's Razor to be the most acceptable; but it is the least satisfying.

If there is indeed one origin, it may never be known. More likely, perhaps, is the suggestion that all three theories, in whatever variant forms, along with others not discussed here, have had some part in the formation and development of the Freemasons.

John J. Robinson asks why the Freemasons, assuming they already existed in secret, waited until 1717 before 'coming out'; his answer is that before that date there was still a chance of the Roman Catholic Church coming back to power in Britain, and that Freemasonry and Rome had always been opposed to each other, going right back to the days when the Church wiped out the Cathars and Templars. The Act of Settlement in 1701 ensured that from then on no Catholic could sit on England's throne; the Act of Union in 1707, in creating Great Britain, ensured that no Catholic could sit on Scotland's throne either. The Hanoverian (and hence Protestant) succession was confirmed when the German George I was crowned after Queen Anne's death in 1714. At the end of 1715 the Jacobite Rebellion met with very little support, emphasizing the fact that the days of a Catholic monarchy in Britain were gone for good. The establishment enemy of the Cathars/Templars/Freemasons was no more, in Britain at least; the Freemasons were now safe; they could announce themselves.[31]

It's an interesting theory, but it falls down on two counts. First, the Roman Catholic Church made no comment of any kind on Freemasonry

*The tools of stonemasons and the symbols of architecture combine in this
eighteenth-century trestle board, a Masonic teaching aid*
(Robert Macoy, *General History, Cyclopedia and
Dictionary of Freemasonry*, 1850)

until the Papal Bull *In Eminenti Apostolatus Specula* in 1738. Secondly, it fails to take into consideration the fact that Freemasonry spread rapidly – and openly – in France, which could hardly be called a Protestant country. (On the other hand it could be argued that France was building up to its Revolution, in which Freemasons were probably involved; and that their involvement in the Revolution was at least in part in order to reduce the power of the Roman Catholic Church.)

The same background, however, suggests a possible different reason, not for the Freemasons announcing their existence, but for their formation at around this time.

Protestantism may have many things in its favour, but mystery is not one of them. The Church of England was originally simply the Catholic Church without the Pope; but the further it removed itself from Rome, the more it divested itself of ritual and symbolism. The Presbyterians were essentially a dour bunch in their worship. Puritanism did not welcome glorious clerical vestments, candles, incense, paintings and statues; it roundly condemned 'idolatry'; it shrank in horror from what it saw as the barbaric heresy of transubstantiation in the mass. Evangelicalism, in contrast with Rome, was rational and straightforward.

All the mystery had gone out of religion. There was something almost magical about a service with a physical impossibility at its heart, conducted in a tongue few of the congregation understood, with robes and ritual and complex ceremonial (see pp. 138–40). Even the most rational of people need mystery in their lives. It was not to be found in Protestant churches. But the semi-comprehensible rituals of Freemasonry could supply that need. To quote Waite, 'Greatest among all the Instituted Mysteries working in the open world are those of the Greek and Latin Rites; but there are Secret Orders which convey their Divine Message under less heavy veils.'[32]

The USA was settled by Protestants: Puritans of various persuasions, Presbyterians, Baptists, Quakers and Unitarians. Americans took to Freemasonry more than did any other nation. There were Masons among its Founding Fathers, those who drew up the Declaration of Independence, and those who approved the design of the Great Seal.

But what of France, that great Catholic country? Why should Freemasonry take such strong hold there in its early years? One possible reason is that France, above all countries, was at the forefront of the eighteenth-century Age of Reason; those intellectuals who embraced Reason with the mind still needed mystery for their heart – and found it, in Freemasonry.

Even today, when hard-headed businessmen don their aprons and jewels and walk in prescribed steps around their tiled (and tyled) halls, calling out ritual challenges and making ritual responses, at its most basic level

Freemasonry supplies an element of play-acting to their citified lives. It can supply much more besides, for those who want to look further.

Masons love their rituals; they love all the traditional aspects of Freemasonry. Some have objected to two fairly recent changes, which have been seen by outsiders as being at least in part a response to external criticism: the down-playing of the bloodthirsty oaths (since 1986 initiates have been told of 'the danger which traditionally would have awaited you . . . the physical penalty at one time associated with the obligation of a mason, that of having your throat cut across', etc.), and the dropping of the word Jahbulon (see p. 117ff). One of their arguments was simply this: what right do outsiders have to criticize the Masons' internal rituals? It's a good question. But also, there is something to be said for archaic, rolling phrases, as in the ringing splendour and the solemn but welcoming atmosphere of a traditional Church of England service of thirty-odd years ago; why change for the sake of change? (For example, the wording of the new Anglican Confession might be simpler, but it lacks the sonorous beauty of 'Thou, O Lord, have mercy upon us, miserable offenders', and is completely devoid of any sense of moment. See p. 138.)

Freemasons have good reason to want to keep to their old rituals, however archaic and (to outsiders) outlandish they may be.

To return to both influences *on* Freemasonry, and the influence *of* Freemasonry, Martin Short spends pages showing how much Freemasons had infiltrated nineteenth-century society; it was Masons, for example, who 'succeeded in erecting Cleopatra's Needle' on Victoria Embankment in London in 1878; when its twin was raised in New York in 1880, the celebration was 'a brazenly Masonic affair'; while the Washington monument 'was dedicated in another dose of fraternal self-congratulation.'[33] It may well be that Freemasons had a particular interest in Egyptology at the time, and were involved in the erection of the monuments; but this was more likely because, first, they simply reflected one of the intellectual fascinations of their age and, second, at that time many men of importance were Freemasons – again, a societal reflection. Like many similar critics, however, Short is confusing cause and effect.

The words spoken in 1992 by Edgar Darling, Grand Master of the Grand Lodge of the Commonwealth of Massachusetts, apply even more strongly to the Masons of the eighteenth and nineteenth centuries: 'Masons are movers and shakers, dreamers and builders, and above all we are free-thinkers.'[34]

It is clearly the implications of these last words which upset so many Christian critics. There is certainly an overlap between the early Freemason ideology and the Deist beliefs of many intellectuals of the early eighteenth century. Deism is defined by David Christie-Murray thus:

> Deism could be either a Christian heresy or a creed with nothing of Christianity in it . . . All Deists would agree that one God exists who created the universe and the natural laws which control it; that he does not capriciously interfere with human affairs by miracles; that religious observances are for the most part at best symbolic acts and at worst mumbo-jumbo; that man can by exercising his will choose good and reject evil, and that his choice in this life will determine his rewards and punishments in the next.[35]

Other 'free-thinking' religious philosophies strong in the eighteenth century included Unitarianism – related to Arianism – and Universalism, which also doubted the Trinitarian definition of God, and which believed, like the Brethren of the Free Spirit (see p. 46), that all men will be saved.

Whatever beliefs individual Freemasons today might hold, there is no doubting that from the start Deists and other free-thinkers had a major influence on Freemasonry in Britain, in France, and in North America; among the great luminaries of American history, Thomas Paine, Benjamin Franklin and Thomas Jefferson were all Deists, although of these three, only Franklin is known to have been a Freemason.

One further point should be made. The Craft is now open to men of all religions, so long as they believe in a Supreme Being. But almost certainly this was not the case in the beginning, according to Hamill.

> I have a feeling, from the evidence that I have studied, that Freemasonry initially was a Christian organization – largely because when it was evolving you were either a Christian or you were a heathen. Deism had a part to play in it; the intellectual debates in the eighteenth century on Deism and Theism must have had some form of effect. Or it could be simply that they changed in the early Grand Lodge days, because of this business of wanting to bring people together; there was sufficient intolerance between the branches of Christianity, let alone when you start to look at relations with the Jewish community, and then with the Muslim community, and then as India started to be opened up, with Hinduism and the Sikhs and the Parsees . . . But it is a very difficult one to trace; it's the whole problem with the early period of Freemasonry, there just isn't sufficient information to work from.

Why should that be, when so much else from that period is fairly well documented? Hamill continues:

> It doesn't surprise me, because if you look at the context of the times in which Freemasonry was developing, which the preponderance of Masonic scholars today think is the late 1500s to early 1600s, it was a time of enormous political and religious turmoil. Politics and religion were inextricably linked. If you've got a group of people who are looking to forget politics and religion and find out what people have in common, it's a fairly radical if not revolutionary idea, and certainly a rather dangerous one in the context of the times, so they're going to meet privately, they're not going to keep records of what they're doing; until 1717 there's no central governing body so there's nobody to report to – which is why, certainly for the English evidence, much of the evidence that we have for the pre-1717 period comes from private papers and diaries and odd diary references.

The origins of Freemasonry, then, are clouded in the murk of undocumented history. We can guess at some of the general influences on the early movement, but it is unwise to speculate on direct causative influences, because we simply don't know. One thing we can say is that if Freemasonry was a true child of its times, then it would have reflected the concerns and the fascinations of the intelligent and cultured men who were its early members.

ORDERS AND DEGREES

There is little point in spending pages repeating the initiation rituals for an Entered Apprentice, Fellow Craft and Master Mason. For any non-Mason who has seriously wanted to know them, they have not been a secret for the last two centuries. Today most public libraries will have a number of books setting out the rituals in great (and reasonably accurate) detail; if they are not available on the shelves, a request at the Enquiries desk will bring them out of store. Three which are likely still to be available are Walton Hannah's *Darkness Visible* and James Dewar's *The Unlocked Secret*, which are both by non-Masons, and *A Ritual and Illustrations of Freemasonry* which comes from a Masonic publisher.

A few words on the structure of Masonic degrees might, however, be useful. At its simplest, Freemasonry consists of the three degrees of the Craft: Entered Apprentice, Fellow Craft and Master Mason. These should not be confused with the many offices found within a Lodge, such as Worshipful Master, Senior Deacon, Junior Deacon, Senior Warden, Junior Warden,

Tyler, Inner Guard, and so on; these are positions – jobs – which Masons take on during their career. Most Masons will go on to become Master Masons, simply because the first two grades are introductory, apprenticeship levels; a normal 'full' Mason is a Master Mason.

For most Masons this is sufficient. Freemasonry takes time, and costs money; most are content to be full members, and aren't interested in the extra time, money and considerable effort of going further. A lot depends on how much of one's life one wants to devote to Freemasonry.

The Holy Royal Arch, for complex historical reasons, is not regarded officially as an additional degree, but as the completion or fulfilment of the 3rd degree. Roughly a third of Master Masons progress to the Holy Royal Arch. The entrance requirements are slightly different in England, Ireland and Scotland; most American Orders follow the Scottish rule, by which entrants to the Royal Arch must first be Mark Masons.

In the three degrees of the Craft, initiates are taught hand grips and signs of recognition, and are given secret words; for the Entered Apprentice this is 'Boaz'; the password between the first two degrees is 'Shibboleth'; for the Fellow Craft the word is 'Jachin'; the password to the Third Degree is 'Tubal Cain'; and the secret word of the Master Mason is 'Machaben', 'Machbinna' or 'Mahabone'.

Most of these words come from the Old Testament. Boaz and Jachin, for example, were inscribed on the two pillars of the porch of Solomon's Temple (I Kings 7:21); they are now sometimes found, as B and J, on the pillars on either side of the Papess or High Priestess in Tarot packs such as the popular Rider-Waite pack.

In the Holy Royal Arch, the password is 'Ammi Ruhamah', meaning 'My people have found mercy', and initiates were until recently given the words 'Jehovah' and 'Jahbulon'. This last word will be examined later (see p. 117).

Mark Masonry is based on the identifying marks that stonemasons would often use to 'sign' their work; it is also linked, as is much else in Freemasonry, to legends about the Temple of King Solomon. There are around 60,000 Mark Masons in Britain.

The 'higher degrees' – or, more correctly, side degrees – include the Ancient and Accepted Rite, often known as the *Rose Croix*, from the title of the 18th degree, 'the Knight of the Pelican and Eagle and Sovereign Prince Rose Croix of Heredom'; candidates are admitted straight to that degree, being granted the 4th to 17th degrees automatically on the way (the 1st, 2nd and 3rd are the same as in the Craft). Similarly, the next step, to the 30th degree of 'Grand Elected Knight Kadosh, Knight of the Black and White Eagle', includes the 19th to 29th degrees.

Unlike that of the Craft, membership of the Ancient and Accepted Rite at any level is by invitation only. Despite that apparent restriction, the *Rose*

Sanctuary of the Temple: the ceremony for the 4th degree of the
Rose Croix, *Secret Master*
(Robert Macoy, *General History, Cyclopedia and*
Dictionary of Freemasonry, 1850)

Croix has around 35,000 members in some 860 Chapters, mostly in England and Wales; it is certainly an attainable and honourable goal for the ordinary Mason. The Knight Kadosh is more ambitious to aim for, and less easily attainable; a candidate must have been in the *Rose Croix* for at least three years, and have been installed as Most Wise Sovereign of his Chapter, the equivalent of being Worshipful Master of a Craft Lodge. After the 30th degree, numbers are strictly limited: in England there are 400 members of the 31st degree, 180 of the 32nd, and only 75 of the 33rd degree, the Grand Inspector General.

These, then, are the main Orders of Freemasonry: the Craft, with its three degrees; the Holy Royal Arch; Mark Masonry; and the *Rose Croix*, the Ancient and Accepted Rite. Besides these there are many, many other Orders, each containing numerous degrees. Most are independent Orders, technically quite independent of the United Grand Lodge; but as their membership is restricted to Master Masons (and often to Mark Masons and/or Royal Arch Masons), they can quite fairly be reckoned as part of Freemasonry. Membership in many of them, including the Ancient and Accepted Rite, is also restricted only to Christians, in contrast to membership in the Craft.[36]

The fact that many of the most advanced and most prestigious Orders are exclusively Christian, incidentally, makes all the allegations about Freemasonry being a front for polytheism, Deism or even Satanism look rather silly. The *Rose Croix* ceremony, for example, is 'consistent with the Christian faith. In a series of highly mystical experiences, it expresses the figurative passage of man through the darkest vale, accompanied and sustained by the three theological virtues.'[37]

One of the smallest of these additional Orders is the *Societas Rosicruciana in Anglia*, commonly known as the Soc Ros, which will be looked at in more detail in the next chapter. Others include the Royal Order of Scotland, the 31 degrees of the Holy Royal Arch Knight Templar Priest, the Knights Templar and Knights of Malta, and the Red Cross of Constantine, the Holy Sepulchre and St John the Evangelist. There are around 16,000 Masonic Knights Templar in Britain.

Each of these Orders or Rites has its own rituals, and its own symbolism within the rituals. Each also has its own robes and regalia, which can be quite expensive, but the membership dues per year usually work out to less than those in the Craft, as most of them only meet two or three times a year.

It's tempting for an outsider to suppose that, as these Orders are self-selecting in their membership, they would be more exclusive in social terms. A butcher, a baker or a candlestick-maker can easily become a Master Mason; but one might think that small businessmen, and the lower ranks of the civil

The importance of study in Freemasonry: a 1774 Masonic medal
(Robert Macoy, *General History, Cyclopedia and*
Dictionary of Freemasonry, 1850)

service, local government, the police, armed forces and clergy are unlikely ever to become a Knight of this or an Eminent Preceptor of that. Not so, says John Hamill: 'The social mix is the same as in the Craft – I know that from experience having been a member of all the various side degrees at one time.'[38]

However, conspiracy theorists looking for the 'Secret Masters of the Universe' mentioned in the Introduction might be tempted by, for example, the Supreme Magus of the *Societas Rosicruciana in Anglia*; or by the one person who holds the positions of Provincial Prior of the Knights of St John and Knights Templar, Grand Inspector General of the Knights of the Rose Croix, and Grand Superintendent of the Rite of Baldwyn; or even by the Most Reverend Great Prior (a lifetime appointment) of the Holy Order of Knights Beneficent of the Holy City (usually known as *les Chevaliers Bienfaisants de la Cité Sainte*), the direct descendant today of Baron von Hund's Strict Observance Rite.

True conspiracy theorists would say that these people are most likely 'fronts' for the *real* Secret Masters. Cynics would say that they are a handful of late-middle-aged, upper-middle-class men who like dressing up in gloriously patterned costumes.

There is much more to it than that, of course. The side degrees may abound in complex and colourful ritual, but several of them are also serious academic study groups. Members of the Soc Ros are expected to present papers on philosophy, science and theosophy. Candidates for the August Order of

Light, which specializes in 'the old world religions and notable mythologies of India, with sidelights from the cults of ancient Egypt, Greece and Rome', have to present a paper before their application for membership can even be considered. The ceremonies of the Order of Eri 'are couched in Bardic Verse and include much ancient Irish lore'.[39]

John Hamill distinguishes between the Craft and the side degrees thus: 'In general terms, they take a principle or a precept which you would find in basic Freemasonry anyway, and concentrate on that, and expand on it in a dramatic way.' He gives a few examples: the basic message of the Mark degree is 'not rejecting something simply because it's unknown'; the basic ideal of the Order of the Secret Monitor is the value and the responsibilities of friendship; in the Christian degrees there is a specifically Christian slant on the message or ideal.

Shortly the esoteric depths of Freemasonry will be discussed. On the question on whether an esoteric or liberal theology has passed into Freemasonry, Hamill responds:

> I think it is different for different people. Taking basic Freemasonry, Craft Freemasonry, the three ceremonies that are worked in Lodge – no. But a lot of the additional degrees which grew up in the eighteenth and nineteenth centuries, I think have overlaid ideas from other traditions onto Masonic ceremonies. If we take the Masonic Knights Templar, I think that grew out of an enormous interest in the idea of chivalry, which was going around Europe in the 1740s and 1750s, and I think initially it was, if you like, a harking back to the ideals of the Templars, the ideals of a pilgrim and of protecting the holy places; and then in the late eighteenth century and early nineteenth century they got overlaid with other slightly more esoteric ideas . . .
>
> The attraction of Egypt, Egypt as the cradle of knowledge and civilization, allied with the cradle of religion and mysticism, and esoteric ideas, certainly had a very strong impact, particularly in Europe from about the 1760s onwards . . . There were a number of people, like Cagliostro, in the eighteenth century, who built up a system which didn't proliferate very far, of what he called Egyptian Masonry. You then get in the nineteenth century the Ancient and Primitive Rite, the Rite of Memphis and Misraim, again harking back to this idea of Egypt being the cradle of everything . . .
>
> I think in terms of mainstream Freemasonry, other than as an archæological exercise, it didn't have a very great impact; in some of the additional degrees, yes, you get the influence – but it was more in what I would call the fringe Masonic areas that there was a very heavy interest and an attempt to build something on it.

The side degrees, then, do tend to cater more for those Freemasons who wish to explore the esoteric side of Freemasonry in more depth. But they cater for other needs and interests too. Hamill, again:

> For some there is the idea of belonging to something which is slightly more exclusive than the Craft; for a lot there is a very deep love of ritu-al and ceremonial; right through the full gamut to those who think they're going to find the answers to all questions – which they may find for themselves. I would argue that that's not why they're there; it's a way of extending your Masonic acquaintance, of extending your like of ritual and ceremonial and pageantry. Some people may see it as a part of their personal search – and some people just like to belong to things.

THE WORD 'JAHBULON'

Until 1989, when a Mason was initiated into the Holy Royal Arch he was given the secret word 'Jahbulon'. This one word is responsible for much of the religious controversy about Freemasonry – and for a vast amount of mis-understanding and misdirection. Since Stephen Knight's *The Brotherhood* has received such a high profile over the last dozen years, and is still being quot-ed as gospel, it seems necessary to note in passing certain of its claims and suggestions.

Knight, quite correctly, breaks Jahbulon down into three syllables revealing, quite incorrectly, 'a precise designation that describes a specific supernatural being – a compound deity composed of three separate personal-ities fused in one.' These are, in Knight's words:

YAH = Yahweh, the God of the Hebrews.
BUL = Baal, the ancient Canaanite fertility god associated with
    'licentious rites of imitative magic'.
ON = Osiris, the Ancient Egyptian god of the underworld.[40]

Note the pejorative slant of the description of the second syllable; more subtly, note that Yahweh is 'God', while Baal and Osiris are 'god' (see p. 13). Knight then goes on to discuss Baal:

> the 'false god' with whom Yahweh competed for the allegiance of the Israelites . . . the sixteenth-century demonologist John Weir identified Baal as a devil. This grotesque manifestation of evil had the body of a spider and three heads – those of a man, a toad and a cat. A description of Baal to be found in de Plancy's *Dictionary of Witchcraft* is particularly

apposite when considered in the light of the secretive and deceptive nature of Freemasonry: his voice was raucous, and he taught his followers guile, cunning and the ability to become invisible.[41]

This passage reveals a number of unexamined assumptions. First, and most simply, medieval and Renaissance demonologists, following the lead of Sprenger and Kramer in *Malleus Maleficarum* (1486), used their imagination to paint demons as terrifyingly as possible. Second, it is standard practice for one religion to demonize the Gods of another; it is equivalent to the malign propaganda that politicians of different parties spread about each other today. Third, is Baal being seen as a Canaanite God, or as a demon, or as a devil, or, by the next page, as *the* Devil? As a logical progression it is fallacious, but it slips by very easily on the emotive level, allowing Knight to say a few pages further on, 'The implication was clear: if Christ was an acceptable part of Freemasonry even to a non-Christian, why not the devil as well?'

Instead of blithely accepting the colourful fictions of medieval demonology as fact, it is worth looking at Baal more closely.

The word *ba'al* is simply Hebrew for 'lord, master, possessor or husband'; with different suffixes, it appears several times in the Old Testament in personal names and place names. It came to be applied as a title (not a name) for the God of the Canaanites, but in itself it is a neutral descriptive term, not a name. The plural word *baalim* used in the Old Testament refers to different local deities, the 'masters' or 'owners' of different peoples. It should be remembered that we are talking about a time when every 'nation' was basically a tribe, and every tribe had its own God or Gods.

The situation is further muddied by the name 'Beelzebub'. However one views Beelzebub – as the Devil (theologically unlikely), or a devil, or a *dæmon* (the word translated 'devils' in Mark 3:22), or as its original meaning, the title *Ba'al-zbub*, meaning Lord or Master of the Flies, which was simply the Israelites insulting their neighbouring tribe's God – it doesn't affect the fact that *ba'al* merely means 'master'.

The fact that the word *ba'al* is not regarded by Jews with the righteous horror given to it by Knight and others is borne out by its use in the title *Baal Shem Tov* meaning 'master of the Good Name' or 'good master of the Name', given to the highly respected Israel ben Eliezer (1700–60), the Polish founder of Hasidic Judaism.

Interestingly, in the 'Ugaritic' Canaanite myths, Baal is the son of the High God, El. S.H. Hooke, Professor of Old Testament Studies at the University of London, points out 'how much of the Baal myth was taken over by the Hebrews and transferred to Yahweh when they settled in Canaan,'[42] emphasizing still more the great care that needs to be taken (and rarely is) when in the late twentieth century one discusses the origins of belief, some three to four thousand years ago, in what is now known as the Judæo–Christian God. Neither Christian nor Jewish theology arrived fully formed out of nowhere.

Far from being the Devil, then, Baal means 'master', and usually, but not always, refers to one particular early tribal God at a time when, to be historically factual, Yahweh was simply another particular early tribal God.

Rather than relying on Knight's exposition, it is worth quoting what the Freemasons themselves say about Jahbulon, in the lecture immediately following the revelation of the word to the Holy Royal Arch initiate:

It is a compound word, and the combination forms the word Jahbulon. It is in four languages, Chaldee, Hebrew, Syriac and Egyptian. Jah is the Chaldee name of God, signifying His Essence and Majesty Incomprehensible. It is also a Hebrew word, signifying I am and shall be, thereby expressing the actual, future, and eternal existence of the Most High. Bul is a Syriac word denoting Lord or Powerful, it is in itself a compound word, being formed from the preposition Beth, in or on, and Ul, Heaven, or on High; therefore the meaning of the word is Lord in Heaven, or on High. On is an Egyptian word, signifying Father of All, thereby expressing the omnipotence of the Father of All, as in that well-known prayer, Our Father, which art in Heaven. The various significations of the words may be thus collected: I am and shall be; Lord in Heaven or on High:
> Father of All: In every age,
> In every clime adored
> By saint, by savage, and by sage,
> Jehovah, Jove or Lord.[43]

Whatever the validity of this etymology, the sentiment is somewhat different from Knight's interpretation. Is there not a case for accepting what the Freemasons themselves say they intend the word Jahbulon to represent?

Walton Hannah calls the word 'blasphemous', yet makes no comment on the main text of the Holy Royal Arch lecture, which he reproduces in full, and which describes the fall of Adam, the need to be humble before God, the need for the right frame of mind in order for our prayers and praises to be acceptable to God, the frailty of man and his need for Divine favour, and the necessity to 'throw ourselves on the mercy of our Divine Creator and Judge' in the sure hope of salvation.[44] There is nothing in that which is contrary to even the most orthodox of Christian teaching.

So far as the origin of Jahbulon is concerned, the word seems to have been concocted in 1834 by a committee which revised the Holy Royal Arch ritual; they were attempting to recreate how the three original Grand Masters of legend would each have said the name of God. It was assumed that King Solomon would have spoken in Hebrew, King Hiram of Tyre in Syrian, and Hiram Abiff, the murdered mason at the centre of the Third Degree ritual, in Egyptian. In retrospect, they would no doubt have been horrified at the consequences of their creative use of etymology.

According to Hamill, when the word was dropped in 1989, to be replaced by the tetragrammaton YHVH, it was not as a result of external pressure from such critics as Hannah and Knight; the entire Holy Royal Arch ritual had been under debate within the Order since the early 1970s. He also points out that there has been much confusion among non-Masons about 'names' and 'words'. The word Jahbulon, which he is still obliged to call 'the tri-syllable word',

> was erroneously referred to by outsiders as being an alternative name for God. It wasn't. It was the word for the Royal Arch; it was used as a test word if you went to a Chapter where you weren't known, in the same way as the words, the passwords in the Craft were used. In the rituals, a very strong differentiation was made between the Name and the word – and it was word with a small 'w', not with a capital, which was another accusation which went around.

The debate over this word, which has been briefly covered here, appears to have been blown out of all proportion, and to have taken on a significance it never merited.

IS FREEMASONRY SATANIC?

It is unfortunately necessary to spend a little more time on the charge that Freemasonry is a front for Satanism. The charge keeps being raised, always with much the same 'evidence'; it seems irrelevant to the critics that this has long been discredited.

Martin Short's book, for example, contains a chapter entitled 'The Devil in Disguise?' in which he uses several arguments to suggest that Freemasonry is satanic. He begins with some anecdotes of Masons who suffered problems. 'From such personal testaments two strands emerge: the psychic and psychiatric distress which Freemasonry can cause in certain personalities; and the idea that, somewhere in all this, the devil is making himself manifest.'[45]

The first 'strand' may be true, inasmuch as 'certain personalities' can be tipped over the edge by anything, no doubt including Freemasonry. The second 'strand' is actually unsupported by the anecdotes, except for a couple of born-again Evangelical Christians saying 'I believe it is of the devil' – a phrase which one hears just as frequently applied to pubs, dances, rock music, short skirts, long hair, television plays, advertising and any other such wicked temptations which the fervent convert now believes kept him away from God. Such claims, though commonplace, have no objective validity.

Short then turns his attention to Albert Pike, Grand Commander of the Supreme Council of the Scottish Rite in America.

> On 14 July 1889 Pike allegedly issued these instructions . . . 'Lucifer is
> God, and unfortunately Adonay is also god . . . the true and pure
> philosophical religion is the belief in Lucifer, the equal of Adonay; but
> Lucifer, God of Light and God of Good is struggling against Adonay,
> the God of Darkness and Evil.'[46]

This is, of course, a restatement of the extreme Dualist position in Gnosticism (see p. 31), though it is by no means the belief of all Gnostics. Whether it is the belief of Pike remains to be demonstrated. Having quoted Pike's 'alleged' instruction, Short says,

> There are problems with this quotation: its meaning is not immediately
> clear and its authenticity is in doubt. It was first attributed to Pike in
> 1894 by a French authoress who detested Freemasonry, yet no original
> text seems to exist.

One might wonder, then, why Short felt it worth while quoting it. But then he continues: 'Yet the quote sounds authentic . . . If genuine, it indicates there is a Satanic – or Luciferian – strain in American Masonry.'

This is simply guilt by innuendo: Freemasonry, it seems, must be Satanic.

Here are the facts about the 'alleged' quotation and the 'French authoress'. It is a story of immense embarrassment to both sides of the conflict, and is widely known and fully documented.

A French Mason, Gabriel Jogand Pagès, under the pseudonym Leo Taxil, was the scourge of the Catholic Church with 'scandalous stories concerning ecclesiastics' – until, in 1885, he was thrown out of the Masons, changed sides, and began attacking Freemasonry in a similar vein; according to Waite he was 'a writer of pornographic romances'. In 1891 he wrote *Y a-*

t-il des femmes dans la Franc-Maçonnerie? ('Are There Women in Free-masonry?'), which described a rite supposedly invented by Pike called New and Reformed Palladium, which was a Masonic Order for both men and women and included both Satanism and sex-magic. This was followed by a pamphlet entitled 'Are there Lodges for Women?' which, says Waite, 'contained a forged instruction of Albert Pike, advocating the worship of Lucifer as the true God, licence in sexual intercourse, and other enormities and follies.' Next, in 1893, came *Le Diable au Dix-Neuvième Siècle* ('The Devil in the Nineteenth Century') under another pseudonym, Dr Henri Bataille. This made Pike 'Sovereign Pontiff of Universal Freemasonry', and said there was 'another and most secret Masonry' behind the public face of Freemasonry, which was devoted to Lucifer and the occult in general, and was both anti-Christian and politically revolutionary. Then, in 1895, came Taxil's *pièce de résistance*, a serial magazine entitled *Mémoires d'une Ex-Palladiste* ('Memoirs of an Ex-Palladist'), supposedly written by a Miss Diana Vaughan who, now a good Catholic girl, was confessing to her part in sexual and Satanic rituals as 'the wealthy, beautiful and highly placed Palladian Grand Mistress'.

In 1896 A.E. Waite exposed all of this as a complete fabrication, and in 1897 Taxil owned up: he and some co-writers had done the whole thing, he claimed, to further discredit the Catholic Church by exploiting the 'known credulity and unknown idiocy of the Catholics'. (He had even taken in Pope Leo XIII, who had granted him a private audience.)

> Leo Taxil avowed that the whole transaction had been an imposition from beginning to end, that he had never been a genuine convert to the Catholic Faith, and that his life had been devoted to the invention of literary rascalities and hoaxes. As to Diana Vaughan, she was a typist in his employment.[47]

This was the source of the text which Short quotes. It is not the case that 'its authenticity is in doubt'; its authenticity is provably false.

Whatever his motives might have been, Taxil was not the first, and has certainly not been the last, to use deceit to blacken the name of Freemasonry. He was, however, one of the most influential; his fictions are still being quoted a century later.

Short is also disturbed by the symbolism in Freemasonry. 'Occult symbols are often also sexual symbols, and in these Freemasonry abounds.'[48] Among these are the *vesica piscis* or mandorla, the pointed oval shape made by two over-lapping circles, which can symbolize female sexuality but which has been used for centuries in religious art to enclose portraits of Christ as Redeemer, uniting heaven and earth; the *tau*-cross, which Short finds phallic, but which was the symbol of, among others, St Antony of the Desert; and the dot in the centre of a circle, which he sees as the penis in a vagina, but which has for millennia symbolized the manifest God.

Symbolism has to be interpreted, and it can often be interpreted in many different ways. This doesn't invalidate symbolism in the slightest, but it does mean that one has to be extremely careful when seeking to prove a point by referring to symbols. As the singer-songwriter Melanie says in her song 'Psychotherapy', 'A thing's a phallic symbol if it's longer than it's wide.'[49]

When critics can use such arguments to lead up to the rhetorical question, 'Are Masons today inadvertently worshipping the devil instead of a benign God?'[50] it is hardly surprising that the Masonic scholars John Hamill and R.A. Gilbert are upset by Knight's book and by

> Martin Short's more recent and immeasurably more venomous attack, *Inside the Brotherhood*. Both of these works – allegedly 'researched' in depth – abound in mistakes, distortions, illogical arguments, and the repetition of old and long exposed fables and lies, and yet they have been publicized and promoted by press and television alike as sound and scholarly productions that reflect a true state of affairs.[51]

Almost any book written by a Mason will contain ample evidence that such critics, for whatever reasons of their own, are deliberately muddying the water. The following quotation is taken almost at random:

> A man who does not believe in the existence of God, and in the doctrine of a future state, in which is implied that of a judgment to come, is declared by one of the ancient landmarks [of Freemasonry] to be incapable of admission into the Order; a profession of belief in these simple first principles of religion being required of every candidate. That more than this is desired, evidently appears from the reverence shown to the Word of God, and the place assigned to it in all Masonic solemnities . . . However simple and few the absolute requirements of religious profession, purposely made so that all may be admitted to the benefits of Freemasonry except those who have no religion, yet it must be considered that the greatest perfection in religious knowledge and faith is deemed desirable, as indeed Freemasonry aims at nothing short of perfection in all that it cultivates, or incites the members of the brotherhood to cultivate.[52]

These are hardly the sentiments of a Satanist.

SHOULD CHRISTIANS BE FREEMASONS?

There have been several books arguing that Freemasonry and Christianity are incompatible, partly because of the blood-curdling oaths that initiates had to make until recently, but mainly on theological grounds. Much of the argument rests on definitions. Is Freemasonry simply a society with religious connections, like the Mothers' Union or the Scouts, or is it a religion in itself? If Freemasons actually mean all the things they say in their rituals, argue the Christian critics from as far back as the great Evangelical preacher Charles Finney in 1869, they're blaspheming, but if it's simply theatrical mumbo-jumbo, then they're trivializing spiritual matters. Damned if you do, damned if you don't.

Some of these books are written by traditionalists, some by Evangelical Christians. In both cases their authors often confuse the issue in their en-thusiasm for the purity of their belief, by redefining terms without saying so. For example, both Walton Hannah in *Darkness Visible* and Robert Morey in *The Truth about Masons* condemn everything which isn't Christian as pagan (note the lower-case 'p'). This is factually incorrect. The word pagan was originally applied by Roman city-sophisticates to the ways and customs of unsophisticated country-folk ('pagan' means 'of the country', just as 'heathen' means 'of the heath'). With a capital letter, Pagan refers to the old religious beliefs of a people before the benefits of Western civilization and a state religion are brought to them.

The many localized early forms of Hinduism could be called Pagan; so can the Celtic beliefs of northern Europe – but not Judaism and Islam.

Hannah asks 'whether it is lawful for the Christian to join in common worship with the Muslim of a common-denominator God specifically of neither faith, whom each in his heart worships as his own God,'[53] forgetting that the Muslim God is in fact the same being as the Christian God, the Jewish God and, for that matter, the Bahá'í God. The Religions of the Book (which can arguably now be taken to include the Bahá'í Faith) all worship the same God by definition; Yahweh is God-the-Father is Allah. The names, the theology and the means of approach might be different, but it is the same One Creator God in each of these religions.

Many will not like this assertion; some will doubt its accuracy. A moment's reflection will show that it is true. The Christian God the Father of Jesus is undeniably the God of the Old Testament, the Jewish or Israelite God, 'the God of Abraham, Isaac and Jacob'. The Koran contains many references to Old Testament figures, including Adam, Moses, Aaron, Noah, Joseph, Jonah, Solomon, David and Goliath, and Abraham, Isaac and Jacob – and also to New Testament figures including Jesus, Mary, John the Baptist and the apostles. The God of all these people in the Old and New Testaments is also the God of these same people in the Koran, and hence the God of the Muslims, Allah – which, in any case, is simply the Arabic word for God, or 'the God'; it is probably etymologically related to El, one of the several Hebrew words or titles for God.

It is often not realized just how many different terms were used by the people who became the Israelites to describe their own God: *El, Eloah*, meaning 'a God'; *Elyon, El Elyon* meaning 'the most high God'; *Elohim* meaning 'Gods'; *Yahweh*, from the verb 'to be' ('I am that I am', Exodus 3:14); *Yahweh Elohim*; *Yahweh sebaot* meaning 'the Lord of hosts'; *Qedos Yisrael* meaning 'the Holy One of Israel'; and other titles. In English Bibles the sacred tetragrammaton *YHWH (Yahweh)* is usually changed to 'LORD' or 'Jehovah', though the name Jehovah is not Biblical at all; it is a medieval composite of *YHWH* and the vowels of the word *adonai*, which means 'lord'.[54]

One might also look at it another way: Judaism, Christianity and Islam all believe in the One Creator God, and there is only room for one such, whatever the various names and attributes given to him by man.

Freemasonry insists on a belief in the One Creator God. From the details of the Craft rituals, it is clear that this is the God of the Old Testament, who is common to Judaism, Christianity and Islam. A favourite hymn in Masonic meetings is:

Immortal, invisible, God only wise,
In light inaccessible hid from our eyes,
Most blessèd, most glorious, the Ancient of Days,
Almighty, victorious, thy great name we praise ...

Great Father of Glory, pure Father of Light,
Thine Angels adore thee, all veiling their sight;
All laud we would render: O help us to see
'Tis only the splendour of light hideth thee.[55]

This is a glorious hymn in praise of the majesty and power of God. It is sung in Christian churches around the world, though it nowhere mentions Jesus. Theologically it could just as easily be sung in Jewish and Muslim services. Christians, Jews and Muslims could stand side by side singing this hymn in praise of the One Creator God, without any of them compromising their faith. Indeed, they do – in Masonic Lodges.

As Freemasonry doesn't teach any specific theology, doctrine or dogma, but simply requires a belief in God, many of the complaints of Hannah, Morey and others vanish away, because Jewish, Christian and Muslim

125

Freemasons are acknowledging the *same* God. The charges that Christian and non-Christian Freemasons are worshipping different Gods alongside each other, or are worshipping a composite God, are simply wrong.

Some Christian critics, like Hannah, accuse Freemasonry of going for the lowest common denominator among religions. He mentions several times that Christianity is an exclusive religion, and that membership of Freemasonry cannot be compatible with this. Theologically, in one sense Hannah is right. Mainstream Christianity states that God became man, that Jesus was God, that God died to save us; Jews and Muslims don't believe this. Judaism and Islam, on the other hand, while accepting that Jesus might well have been a prophet, find the assertion that he was God blasphemous. The two positions *are* mutually exclusive.

But Freemasonry doesn't require people of different faiths to accept each other's beliefs as true; in fact, it categorically forbids discussion of variant religious beliefs in the Lodge. The only religious requirement is a belief in God. The mutual exclusivity of different religions is irrelevant to the Craft.

Christianity may well be, as Hannah says, an exclusive religion; but a lot depends on the definition of Christianity. For many Christians, it is not only Christianity which is exclusive, but their own particular brand of Christianity. For many Roman Catholics, until very recently, the word 'Christian' meant 'Roman Catholic'; anyone else was beyond the pale. Similarly, for many Evangelical Christians, any other variety of Christianity *isn't* Christian: High Church Anglicans are in league with Rome, and Rome is the Whore of Babylon, while liberals are treated with more suspicion and horror than were communists at the height of McCarthyism. Some Fundamentalist Evangelicals, such as the Exclusive Brethren, will not even eat a meal with anyone who is not one of their own number – or even with one of their own who has committed such an act.

There seem to be more varieties of exclusivity within Christianity than in most other religions. The word 'Christian' means different things to each of them. This clearly affects how they view any religious practice which is not their own.

The practice of Freemasonry, that Christian, Muslim and Jew – and indeed, anyone who believes in One Creator God – may pray and sing hymns to that God side by side, *would* be seen as dangerous liberal heresy both by those who believe in the authority of the Apostolic Succession in the Church, and by those who would cry 'Idolator!' if they saw a priest bobbing his head at the cross on an altar.

Those for whom Christianity, or their branch of Christianity, is exclusive might well find difficulty in accepting the open approach of Freemasonry.

Those who are less inclined to believe that they alone have the truth find this less of a problem; indeed many, like John Hamill, find within Freemasonry a confirmation and strengthening of their beliefs:

> Freemasonry reinforces my religion. The ceremonies made me think again, and took me back into my religion . . . Freemasonry expects its members to have a religion; how they practise it, how they progress through it, is entirely up to the individual, and Freemasonry will not either guide or direct them. It lays out that it's there, and it's up to them then to follow.

However, the religious thrust of Freemasonry *is* liberal, if only in that it accepts that the Truth is not to be found exclusively in Evangelical Christianity, establishment Roman Catholicism, or any other subset of the huge diversity of Christianity. Moreover, it accepts the findings of comparative religious studies and of Biblical criticism that there is much of value in earlier religions, and that, whatever the historicity of the Jesus myth, there is little in Christian doctrine or practice which is original. This is anathema to devout Christians of many persuasions, and particularly – but not only – to Evangelicals.

Walton Hannah, a High-Church Anglican priest who later joined the Roman Catholic Church, raises the issue in *Darkness Visible*, saying that Masons will argue:

> Is not Christianity also full of pagan customs and ceremonies, is not Easter a time-immemorial festival of new life in the Spring, and the reverence paid to the Mother of God but an echo of the Magna Mater of imperial Rome? Did not other religions have as a saviour a virgin-born demi-god who died and rose again?[56]

The answer to all these questions, and to many others of a similar nature, is of course 'yes.' Hannah admits 'the possibility of a substratum of truth in these assertions,' but then goes on:

> Before that supreme and final revelation of truth in the Incarnation of our Lord there had of course been partial glimpses and foreshadowings of it, purely human and not revealed, by no means entirely limited to the Jewish nation. There were anti-types [*sic* Presumably he means 'ante-types'] indeed of our Saviour in the pagan world . . . whatsoever truth, however partial, had been before guessed or discovered by man's intellect was naturally included [in Christianity] . . . Many customs, symbols, and ceremonies which were of value were adopted.

They were indeed, in large number, along with many beliefs and many standard religious myths, such as the Virgin Birth. But by defining such 'borrowings' as ante-types, Hannah is simply echoing the second-century Justin Martyr, who claimed that 'whatever things were rightly said by any man, belong to us Christians'. The argument is as strong or as weak now as it was 1800 years ago.

If a time-traveller were to visit first-century Palestine and ask one of the twelve disciples about the Trinity he would be met with a blank look; if he asked about the Virgin Birth, he would probably get the response, 'Which one?' The hundreds of small Fundamentalist Christian denominations which claim to go back to the pure beliefs of the New Testament Church generally forget that the fundamentals of Christian theology were not developed until some considerable time later – in some cases with 'retro-fitting' of proof texts into the New Testament itself; one example is '. . . baptising them in the name of the Father, and of the Son, and of the Holy Ghost' (Matthew 28:19), which the authoritative *Peake's Commentary* accepts is 'a late doctrinal expansion'[57] rather than Jesus' own words.

One point missed by most critics of Freemasonry, whether writing from a Christian viewpoint or not, is that the ritual stories enacted in Freemasonry are not intended to be taken literally. They are stories, fables, allegories, not history. Robert Morey and others get hot under the collar about the central legend of the murder of the builder Hiram Abiff not being scriptural; Masons never claim it is. It is a teaching story, a morality play – a parable.

The Great Architect of the Universe; a 1655 Masonic medal
(Robert Macoy, *General History, Cyclopedia and
Dictionary of Freemasonry*, 1850)

But Morey has a strange attitude to such stories in any case: 'Legends, myths ... and traditions are so unreliable that they are worthless.'[58] In fact myths – and legends, traditions and even folklore – are at the heart of all religions. Whether one accepts that they have any *factual* basis must be an individual decision; it is their *meaning* which is of importance.

Books such as Morey's *The Truth About Masons* are not always reliable themselves. For example, he asserts that 'Waite... took over the Order of the Golden Dawn... after Crowley died.'[59] In fact Waite died in 1942, five years before Crowley. Then he says, 'Aleister Crowley... was the previous leader of the Golden Dawn.' Crowley was never leader, and was actually only involved in the movement for a short time (See p. 167).

Morey complains that in Freemasonry:

> while all other religions can pray in the name of their deity such as
> Allah, Buddha, Shiva, or Krishna, Christians are the only ones who are
> forbidden to pray in the name of their deity, Jesus Christ! If the
> Muslims can use the name of Allah, why can't the Christians use the
> name of Jesus?[60]

This is incorrect. As a Fundamentalist, Morey is understandably rejecting the fact that Allah is the same deity as Yahweh, Jehovah or the LORD, who is the same deity as God the Father of Jesus. But in fact Christians are not 'the only ones who are forbidden to pray in the name of their deity.' Muslims are not allowed to use the name of Allah in the Lodge; even in a totally Muslim Lodge they would use the terms Great Architect of the Universe, Grand Geometrician, and Most High, just as in any other Lodge.

Morey is not alone in propagating such errors, as Hamill explains.

> There's a whole similar literature in America, where the Fundamentalist
> Evangelicals now have got to the level where they run programmes on
> cable television and on local radio, which are basically anti-Masonic
> programmes. A couple of American Masonic scholars have looked at the
> booklets and pamphlets they put out, and quite a lot of it is just blatant
> lies. If you actually look at the sources they're quoting, they're either
> misquoted or taken completely out of context – or, in a number of
> cases, the quotations which they produce don't exist in the books they
> claim they come from.

There is an interesting example of this in Morey's book. In a chapter on 'The Legacy of Albert Pike' (see pp. 121–22), Morey sets out both to damn Pike fairly comprehensively, and also to show how widely respected he is, at least in American Freemasonry, thus also damning Freemasonry by its approbation of Pike. Among the other plaudits is one which appears to be from Waite: 'In 1970, the occultist A.E. Waite did not hesitate to call Pike, "a master genius of Masonry."'[61]

Apart from the fact that Waite's *New Encyclopaedia of Freemasonry*, from which this quotation comes, was first published around 1920, and that Waite had been 28 years dead by the time of the 1970 reprint, what Waite actually says is that Pike 'has been characterised as "a master-genius of Masonry"'; he is quoting *other people's* opinion. Waite's own opinion of Pike is not at all as Morey paints it:

> as a critical scholar of Masonry, a historian and a writer on the ethical and philosophical side of the subject he is not to be taken as a guide. No man had a greater opportunity and no one a freer hand when he undertook to revise the Rituals of the Scottish Rite, and he scored only failure.[62]

One can only speculate as to why Morey found it necessary to misrepresent Waite's judgement so comprehensively. Perhaps it was to give support to his entirely unsubstantiated assertion that Waite, who was actually a devout mystical Christian, was a Luciferian.[63]

In the last few decades traditional church-going in Britain as elsewhere has been on the wane, but the Evangelical wing of Christianity has been growing rapidly. Although most mainstream Christians would be reluctant to say that all Jews, Muslims and members of other religions are unbelievers who are going to hell, Fundamentalist Evangelicals, by definition, do believe this. The liberal religious aspects of Freemasonry would certainly not be acceptable to them.

Hamill agrees that there are difficulties for Masons who are fervent Evangelicals. 'Fundamentalists in any religion, not just Christianity, have to my mind tunnel vision, and the one thing that they don't like about Freemasonry is the fact that we teach tolerance.'

Earlier, Pelagianism was referred to as 'a very British heresy'. A lot of British people would say they were Christian simply because they were born in Britain, which is 'a Christian country'. If asked exactly what they do believe, many might become embarrassed. If pressed for an answer, few would come out with a doctrinally sound summary of orthodox Christian beliefs. Many would find difficulty with the Trinity, the Virgin Birth, and even the resurrection. And a fair number would say that salvation depended as much on leading a good life – i.e. by doing 'good works' – as on faith.

Both Pelagianism and Arianism – loosely, the belief that Jesus is not equal to the Father in a Triune Godhead – lurk within many a traditional British pew-sitter on a Sunday morning. Both 'heresies' would be entirely comfortable within the undefined theology of Craft Freemasonry. Both hark back to the early centuries of Christianity, before today's standard Christian doctrine was hammered out in councils and synods between bishops whose decisions were as often politically as spiritually motivated.[64]

Part of the reason for the strength of Freemasonry in Britain is that the Church of England has traditionally prided itself on being a broad Church. Any denomination that can include within itself the bells 'n' smells of High Anglicanism, the guitars and speaking in tongues of Evangelicalism and the Charismatic Movement, and the liberalism of the 1960s Bishop of Woolwich and the 1990s Bishop of Durham, can put up with the generalized theological approach of Freemasonry. Much the same applies in the USA, with the Episcopalian Church. But such broad tolerance is clearly changing, with the rise of Fundamentalism.

The compatibility or otherwise of Freemasonry and Christianity is thus even more of an issue today than it was when Hannah wrote *Darkness Visible*.

THE SECRET DOCTRINE

Many of the religious critics of Freemasonry quote Joseph Fort Newton's statement that 'It is true that Masonry is not *a* religion, but it is Religion, a worship in which all good men may unite, that each may share the faith of all.' The critics see this as non-Christian, even anti-Christian. It is a shame that in their determination to attack and condemn they don't read on to see what Newton was actually talking about. It is worth quoting at length.

All this confusion results from a misunderstanding of what religion is. Religions are many; religion is one – perhaps we may say one thing, but that one thing includes everything – the life of God in the soul of mine, which finds expression in all the forms which life and love and duty take. This conception of religion shakes the poison out of all our wild flowers, and shows us that it is the inspiration of all scientific enquiry, all striving for liberty, all virtue and charity; the spirit of all thought, the *motif* of all great music, the soul of all sublime literature. The Church has no monopoly of religion, nor did the Bible create it. Instead, it was religion – the natural and simple trust of the soul in a Power above and within it, and its quest of a right relation to that Power – that created the Bible and the Church, and, indeed, all our higher human life. The soul of man is greater than all books, deeper than all dogmas, and more enduring than all institutions. Masonry seeks to free men from a limiting conception of religion, and thus to remove one of the chief causes of sectarianism. It is itself one of the forms of beauty wrought by the human soul under the inspiration of the Eternal Beauty, and as such is religious.'[65]

The religion within Freemasonry does not deny God's revelation in Jesus Christ, as Christian critics claim; but it also doesn't, as many Evangelical Christians appear to, refuse to acknowledge the importance of people's quest for God since the beginning of time. A relationship has to work in both directions. To suggest that people's longing for God before the advent of Christ 2,000 years ago was met only with a stony indifference by God, is surely a far greater heresy than the suggestion that there might be some truth in all religions, an idea which Fundamentalists condemn outright.

Over the last few years there has been considerable confusion both within and without Freemasonry not just as to whether or not it is a religion, but even whether it is in any way religious – or, more to the point, whether it has any right to be. Some say it is, and should be; others that it is, and shouldn't; some deny that, at least for them, it has any religious content at all.

Critics such as Martin Short say that Freemasonry is trying to be all things to all men; he seems to find it incomprehensible that some Freemasons derive deep spiritual satisfaction from the Craft, while others say they have little religious belief and enjoy it purely as a social club.

> In court [Grand Lodge] claimed that Freemasonry is dedicated to advancing religion, but outside it was saying the Craft has no dogma and bans religious discussion. This must be a nonsense. How can Freemasonry 'advance' religion, and educate its members in spirituality, if they are not allowed to discuss the meaning of the ritual's religious elements? . . . each Mason, it seems, must fumble his own way through the ritual's labyrinth of ideas from all manner of primitive and mystical cults, some pre-dating even Judaism.[66]

But there is nothing incompatible here at all. What Short fails to grasp is that Freemasonry, through its rituals and their explanatory lectures, provides its members with a body of symbolism; and that whatever the members choose to do with this is entirely up to them. Some will grudgingly put up with all the ritual for the sake of the social side; others will enjoy the play-acting simply as spectacle; but some will let the symbolism of the ritual wash through them, leading them further on in their *individual* quest for the Divine.

This, surely, is the whole point of the spiritual side of Freemasonry: in contrast to the set dogmas of the established Church, Freemasonry teaches that it is for each individual member to establish his own relationship with God, in his own way. Freemasonry may provide signposts along the path, but the path has to be walked by each man alone.

So Freemasonry can at one and the same time be 'dedicated to advancing religion' and have 'no dogma'. There is no contradiction; it certainly is not 'a nonsense'. As for banning religious discussion, this makes perfect sense. The moment people start to discuss their own individual, personal spiritual quests and experiences, arguments begin; there is dissension. Factions form – 'My path is better than your path' – which is precisely what Freemasonry has been against from the start. It is not just a Christian–Jew–Muslim problem; when Freemasonry began in an organized way, it was a Roman Catholic–Church of England–Methodist–Baptist–Congregationalist–Presbyterian–Quaker–Unitarian–Deist (and the rest) problem. Most of these were quite happy to tear out each other's throats (at least metaphorically) in argument.

Through the rose-tinted spectacles we turn on history, we see the Pilgrim Fathers and others crossing the Atlantic to escape persecution, and going to a Promised Land of religious tolerance. It wasn't so. They were just as bigoted as those they left behind. The Congregationalists who settled in New England in the early seventeenth century initially outlawed all other denominations. Eventually, reluctantly, they allowed Baptists and Episcopalians. In Massachusetts Congregationalists imprisoned and whipped Quakers. Three Quakers were executed there in 1659, for the crime of being Quakers.

It made sense in the late seventeenth and early eighteenth centuries to ban discussion of religion, and also discussion of politics, within the Lodge; it still makes sense now. And there is no dogma, no clear, specific teaching of the meaning of it all, because this would be forcing just one interpretation onto the symbolism, and insisting that just one spiritual path is correct. This is expressed exquisitely by Joseph Fort Newton:

> With the subtleties of speculation concerning those truths, and the unworldly envies growing out of them, it [Freemasonry] has not to do. There divisions begin, and Masonry was not made to divide men, but to unite them, leaving each man free to think his own thought and fashion his own system of ultimate truth. All its emphasis rests upon two extremely simple and profound principles – love of God and love of man. Therefore, all through the ages it has been, and is to-day, a meeting-place of differing minds, and a prophecy of the final union of all reverent and devout souls.

133

Time was when one man framed a dogma and declared it to be the eternal truth. Another man did the same thing, with a different dogma; then the two began to hate each other with an unholy hatred, each seeking to impose his dogma upon the other – and that is an epitome of some of the blackest pages of history. Against those old sectarians who substituted intolerance for charity, persecution for friendship, and did not love God because they hated their neighbours, Masonry made eloquent protest, putting their bigotry to shame by its simple insight and the dignity of its golden voice.[67]

Newton is, however, too optimistic. He writes that 'a vast change of heart is now taking place in the religious world' as different religious movements begin talking to each other. Perhaps that was so in 1914 when he wrote these words; sadly, sectarianism and competing Fundamentalism seem stronger today than ever before. The need for 'a meeting-place of differing minds' is greater than ever. From this point of view, if none other, writers such as Walton Hannah, Robert Morey, Stephen Knight and Martin Short have made their own contribution to increasing the disharmony. Freemasonry's 'simple insight and the dignity of its golden voice' (if this was not an over-idealized view to begin with) have become buried under a mass of unpleasant-ness; some might indeed be of its own making, but most is the fault of its critics.

What is the secret at the heart of Freemasonry? According to many Masons there isn't one. For perhaps most Masons the rituals express dramatically certain moral ideas, and that's that. But for the more mystically-inclined Masons, what is the great secret they find within Freemasonry?

Critics sneer at the answer that it is a secret that can never be revealed because it is a secret which cannot be formulated or communicated. But this is the essence of an individual mystical experience, a personal spiritual quest, an apprehension or realization of God within and without: a gnosis. By defi-nition it cannot be communicated, because for each man it is personal and different. In this it is like the *latihan* or spiritual exercise and experience of the Subud movement:

> the latihan of two people can never be the same, because everyone is different from everyone else. It is clear, then, that there cannot be a theory or a spiritual teaching in Subud because each person is different . . . Every person will find for himself the right way towards God, and what may be the right way for one may be completely wrong for another.[68]

Subud, like Freemasonry, is open to members of all religions, and for the same reason.

The Secret Doctrine can be described in different terms. For Waite, 'it concerns the essential life of religion behind the externals of dogma and the translation of the cosmic Christhood into the personal life of each individual soul.' He explains how it can be found within Freemasonry:

> a soul passes the threshold and so enters upon grades of real experience, which are shadowed forth in the secret Orders by revelation in symbols. They are thus suggested to the prepared heart in following the path of initiation, or the heart – independently of initiation – suggests them to itself, and is thus its own initiator. Mystical experience of this order may be defined provisionally as a substantial realisation of Divinity by means of loving intuition.[69]

Newton states it more simply:

> Here lies the great secret of Masonry – that it makes a man aware of that divinity within him, wherefrom his whole life takes its beauty and meaning, and inspires him to follow and obey it.[70]

And here, ironically, a mystical Freemason and an Evangelical Christian might be closer than was suggested above. They share a common emphasis on the individual's response to and relationship with God, rather than the traditional teaching that God can only be approached through the hierarchy of the Church. An open-minded Evangelical who is not automatically condemnatory of those who don't share his beliefs, might actually find something both familiar and of great spiritual value within Freemasonry. An Evangelical with a mystical bent might well find the Inner Mysteries at the heart of Freemasonry more acceptable than he thinks.

———

It should be mentioned again that I am neither a Freemason nor in any way an apologist for Freemasonry. During the research and writing of this chapter it became apparent that many of the popular books opposed to Freemasonry, which claim to be fair, balanced and honest accounts, are riddled not only with misleading arguments but also with factual errors, whether by carelessness or by deliberate deceit. I felt it necessary to try to set the record straight, even though doing so has caused this to become rather a long chapter. Even so, it has barely skimmed the surface of the fallacious arguments propounded by such anti-Masonic authors, and the popular misconceptions reinforced by them.

CHAPTER FOUR

THE RESURGENCE OF ESOTERIC SOCIETIES

BEFORE RETURNING to the development of Rosicrucian ideas, and the more recent spread of Rosicrucian and other esoteric societies, a look in some depth at the whole concept of the esoteric would be worthwhile.

The connection, however major or however slight, between secret societies and the esoteric – or worse, 'the occult' – is enough for many to condemn such societies out of hand. But the word 'occult' simply means 'hidden', and any initiatory society, by definition, keeps some things hidden from outsiders.

It should be stressed at this point that this book is not implying that Freemasonry is an occult society in the usual sense of the term. A number of books have claimed this, and it is hardly surprising that the United Grand Lodge becomes vastly irritated at such accusations, whatever the esoteric beliefs of many early Freemasons, the connections between later Freemasons and various 'occult' groups, or the deeply mystical beliefs of a minority of Freemasons today.

In its usual sense, though, the word 'occult' is equated with magic, and worse, with the powers of darkness. It is to be hoped that this chapter will, at least for some, dispel the belief that anything occult, or magic itself, is necessarily evil.

WHAT IS 'MAGIC'?

According to science fiction and popular science author Arthur C. Clarke's 'Third Law', 'Any sufficiently advanced technology is indistinguishable from magic.'[1] As Tom Shippey and Peter Nicholls point out in *The Encyclopedia of Science Fiction*,

This echoes the observation by Roger Bacon (*c.* 1214–92) 700 years
before that 'many secrets of art and nature are thought by the
unlearned to be magical'; the irony whereby Bacon, a pioneer of
experimental science, gained a posthumous reputation for sorcery goes
far to confirm Clarke's 'Law', and is at the heart of James Blish's novel
of the history of science, *Doctor Mirabilis* (1964).[2]

Doctor Mirabilis is the story of Roger Bacon's life. While clearly fiction, it is
an excellent exploration of the immense difficulties which confronted a late-
medieval scholar who had to face suspicion from the Church at every step of
the way.

Magic is in the eye of the beholder. As Alice's Humpty Dumpty might have
said, it's a word which means whatever the user of the word wants it to mean
– and it means many things. It is no coincidence that the same word is used
of esoteric religious rituals and of stage conjurors; as was noted earlier (p. 26),
a good religious ritual often benefits from skilled showmanship.

There have been many definitions of magic. Most include either trickery
or (usually the dark side of) the supernatural. The following is an attempt to
avoid both, and to be morally neutral rather than pejorative:

Magic could be said to be the artistic application of skills unknown or
unavailable to other people, usually for a spiritual purpose.

It can be argued that ritual in itself is magical, at least in its effects. Ritual is
the set, formalized repetition of certain words, often with certain movements.

Certainly in many religions, old and new, certain sounds are sacred;
believers chant the names or attributes of God, and bring themselves to a
state of enlightenment. In some religions, and in some secret societies,
there is a tradition of a lost tongue, perhaps the language of the angels, or
the language of Eden, a language in which God and man could once speak
to each other, and man could speak of God, and men could speak with each
other, without misunderstanding; this partly underlies the myth of the
Tower of Babel. It is, indeed, a mythical, Golden Age language. Those who
have argued for keeping services in Latin are, perhaps unknowingly, following a version of this belief, this longing. So are those who treat the
King James Bible as if it in itself is sacred; it's partly the validation which
comes from familiarity and tradition, but it's also partly the beauty of the
phrasing, compared to most modern translations; the language contains a
power in itself. For some, Hebrew is the sacred tongue; it is significant that
all the 'occult' orders which study Cabala teach their members to read and

speak certain Hebrew words and phrases. Even in Freemasonry, most of the passwords are Hebrew. Freemasonry also has the tradition of 'the lost word'.[3]

Often, with sacred sounds and sacred words, the meaning of the word is unimportant compared to the sound of it; this is especially so with mantras used in meditation. The argument over the *Book of Common Prayer* and the *Alternative Service Book* of the Church of England, for instance, illustrates this perfectly; it is a matter of heart versus mind, of 'what feels right' rather than the precise sense of the words. So far as the language of these two books is concerned, one has power; the other hasn't.[4]

Those who use ritual magic are very careful over the words they use, and the sounds of the words. Very often, in its transmission over the centuries, the wording of a barely-understood ritual has become garbled; the attempts of occultists to repair the damage and restore the original sense and sound often make things worse. Today's Schools of Occult Science take very great care when restoring rituals.

The Roman Catholic Church has long held the position that the efficacy of the sacraments does not depend on how pure-of-heart the priest is as he performs the ritual, so long as he says the right words; it is the ritual itself which makes the sacrament valid. Article XXVI of the Thirty-Nine Articles of the Church of England (found at the back of the *Book of Common Prayer*) makes much the same point.

The central ritual of mainstream Christianity is the communion service. The following discussion should be considered in the context of this section; the communion service is a particularly holy ceremony for devout Christians, and no offence to them is in the least intended.

In a Roman Catholic, Eastern Orthodox or High Anglican (or Episcopalian) service, the vestments, music, candles, processional, and set forms of prayer and worship all add to the overall effect. In a traditional Eucharist in a traditional church, consider the relative spiritual positions of the celebrant and the congregation, and their relative physical positions. The people are in the nave, separated from the priest and his assistants (including the choir) by the chancel steps or arch, or in older churches by the rood screen. When they come up to receive communion, the people are allowed to come this far, into the chancel, up to the communion rail, where they kneel; on the other side of the rail are the altar, and the priest, and the bread and wine.

Even without considering the mysteries of transubstantiation or consubstantiation, that moment of coming to the rail, after the build-up of both the emotional and the spiritual 'atmosphere' through music and formal prayers, can be very powerful. In convent schools, first communicants have

Magical implements prepared for a particular ritual
(Francis Barrett, *The Magus*, 1801)

been known to faint at this point. Very few ordinary parishioners would feel 'right' about stepping beyond the rail into the sanctuary (holy place) or presbytery (priest's place). It's sacred; it's as if God is on the other side of the rail.

The words *sacred*, *holy*, *powerful*, and *mysteries* could as easily be replaced by the words *magical* and *magic*.

Physically, the whole ceremony is a ritualized, symbolic enactment of the separation of man from God, of man being able to come thus far and no further – and then of God reaching across to man through the bread and wine in the hands of the priest.

Without going too far into the complexities of the different attitudes and beliefs about the Mass, the Eucharist, Holy Communion, or the Breaking of Bread, whether one accepts the Real Presence, or the symbolic presence, or the commemoration and remembrance, the moment itself can clearly be viewed as the magical climax of a religious ritual. The 'higher' the ritual, the more magical, mysterious, mystical is the moment. Through this ritual, the priest has brought God into the presence of the people. (Anthropologically, of course, the symbolical ritual eating of the body of the God to partake of his power, long pre-dates Christianity.)

This interpretation is being worded in this way quite deliberately in order to make a point. Christians of all persuasions may well recoil from it; it is not my intention to give offence to those with deeply held beliefs. Others have made the same point in the past, often far more strongly; one has only to read extreme Protestants of the last few hundred years inveighing against 'popery' to realize that this was precisely the interpretation they were placing on it, and part of the reason they hated the Roman Catholic Church so much.

Indeed, the separation of Protestantism from Catholicism can be seen in terms of separating faith from religion, or religion from magic. This whole argument, it must be stressed, is a matter of interpretation and perception, not a bald statement of fact.

Ritual, then, can be viewed as a form of magic. Ritual and elaborate ceremonial play a large role in secret societies. This could be one reason for the antagonism of organized religions to secret societies: for the Eastern Orthodox and Roman Catholic Churches, because secret societies are appropriating 'techniques' which they see as rightfully theirs; and for the Protestant Churches, because ritual implies magic, and magic is 'by definition' evil.

Usually when Christians use the word 'magic', they give it a pejorative meaning. But an examination of the Old Testament – and even of the New Testament – actually reveals very little difference between magic and miracles. What is magic when performed by an idol-worshipping Pagan is a miracle when performed by a Jewish prophet or a Christian apostle. (Religious polemic rarely bothers to be fair; Pagans no more worship idols than Christians worship the cross on an altar.) The same principle applies to war and to religion: if the enemy do the same thing we do, then call it by another name to make it sound bad. The visitor from Mars would see little difference between an incantation and a prayer.

As for the evil power of magic: for those who believe in it magic is undoubtedly powerful, but there is no reason why power should equate with evil. Electrical power is part of the essential infrastructure of twentieth-century life; yet if it is used carelessly or maliciously, it can kill. The same applies to the motor car. For a chef, a wood-carver or someone living out of doors, strong sharp knives are essential. In the hands of a thug they are lethal weapons.

There is no doubt that of those who have practised magic through the ages, including today, there have always been some who have abused its power. That no more makes magic itself evil than thousands of drunken drivers make motor cars evil. In fact, practitioners of magic would argue that its main purpose is healing and regeneration – physical, spiritual and moral – and hence it is considerably more beneficial than the motor car, with its daily contributions to pollution, stress, injuries and violent death.

Mainstream Christianity through the centuries has regarded magic in three quite different ways. At times it has said that magic is all tricks and delusions: effectively stage-magic used by unscrupulous religious charlatans with a taste for power over others. There have undoubtedly been some examples of that; Helena P. Blavatsky, founder of the Theosophy Movement, is known to have used tricks in her séances. The first approach, then, is that magic does not exist.

The problem with this stance – which has probably been the main view for the last two hundred years or so, until the rise of Fundamentalism – is that it flies in the face of the evidence. However magic be *explained* (and there are plenty of thoroughly good psychological explanations which don't involve the supernatural at all), few who have really thought about it would dismiss it out of hand as non-existent. The second approach, then, which has been the practice if not the formal policy of the Church for centuries, is that magic *does* exist, but that one needs to be very careful to distinguish between natural magic and sorcerous magic, or perhaps between the permissible Christian *study* of magic, and the forbidden *practice* of it; James Blish's novel shows Roger Bacon treading this tightrope. Sometimes it has depended on who is using it, and for what purpose. A fair number of monks and priests over the centuries have practised alchemy; while if astrology is counted as part of the occult, then quite a few popes have dabbled in occult matters.

The third approach is a natural consequence of poor logic applied to the exclusivist beliefs of Christianity. If magical power is real, and if it doesn't come from God – which, as its users clearly have beliefs which are not orthodox Christian, must be taken as a given – then the only place such power can come from is the Devil.

Like most either/or arguments, this one falls at the first post, by its various pre-assumptions, including that such power can only come from God or from the Devil, and its definition of what is acceptable Christian belief – the latter raising the common and invidious assumption that 'if we are right, you must be wrong'.

It is this attitude which led to several centuries of killing witches and heretics, and which today leads to a person who has a natural healing ability being branded a Satanist because he or she doesn't use the Trinitarian formula when taking away someone's headache. Regarding the extreme Protestant position around 1600, historian Robin Briggs points out, 'It was actually better to die a pious death than to obtain healing by magic' – as he adds wryly, 'a position more notable for its logic than its persuasiveness.'[5]

Today it is handy for upholders of orthodoxy to lump all esoteric beliefs together as either 'occult' or 'New Age', condemning them all as the Devil's deceptions. A common sign of those so 'deceived' is their use of Tarot cards.

TAROT: HISTORY, DESIGN, SYMBOLISM

Secret societies, schools of occult science, movements and individuals studying magic: all lay a great emphasis on symbolism. By far the most widespread and well-known esoteric symbolism is that found in Tarot; millions of people around the world are familiar with it. It is significant that many esoteric movements use Tarot, and that several have designed their own Tarot pack to express pictorially their own particular teachings.

Today there are dozens, if not hundreds, of different Tarot packs available. Many of them derive, in one way or another, from either the Rider–Waite Tarot (1910) or the somewhat older Marseille Tarot (c. 1700). Most of the symbolic meanings of the cards, so painstakingly learned by thousands of people using Tarot for divination today, go back only a century.

Tarot is much older than that, but nowhere near as old as some authorities would have us believe. Its origin in early China or ancient Egypt may safely be dismissed as fantasy. As esoteric authority Fred Gettings says so succinctly, 'Any history of the Tarot cards can be little other than an extended commentary on human credulity, duplicity, inventiveness, ignorance and superstition.[6]

There is some disagreement between authorities as to whether today's playing cards developed out of Tarot, or vice versa. It is likely, however, that the idea of playing games with cards came to Western Europe from the Islamic world in the early- to mid-fourteenth century, some decades after the Crusades were over.

We often know about heresies from the attacks written against them; the first we hear of playing cards is in edicts forbidding their being played with – in Berne in 1367 and Florence in 1376. If they were widespread and popular enough to be banned in 1367, they must have been around for some years before that.

In 1392 King Charles VI of France paid 56 sous to Jacquemin Gringonneur for three packs of cards, hand-painted and gilded, but it is not known whether these were Tarot cards. One of the earliest Tarot packs still surviving, and the one most complete (only four cards are missing) was made for the ruling Visconti-Sforza family in Milan, around 1450.

Early packs are sometimes known by the name of their presumed artist (e.g. Bembo), sometimes by the family they were made for (Visconti-Sforza), sometimes by the name of a later owner (Brambilla), and sometimes by the university museum which now holds them (Cary–Yale).

The order of the trumps (now known as the Major Arcana) quite often varied between these early packs. In Italy, three different styles and orders developed, in Ferrara, Milan and Bologna. The well-known Tarot de Marseille is descended from the Milanese version of the early Tarot packs. In Florence in the early sixteenth century the Papess was dropped, and twenty additional picture cards joined the pack, illustrating the twelve signs of the zodiac, the four elements, and the four virtues of Faith, Hope, Charity and Prudence (in addition to Temperance, Fortitude and Justice); such packs became known as *minchiate*. At different times in different countries, some cards have been redesigned and renamed for political or religious reasons: one pack has both seated and standing Emperors and Popes; others replaced the Pope and Papess with Jupiter and Juno.

Although all these were recognizable as Tarot packs, and usually had more similarities with each other than differences, it should be kept in mind that the twenty-two cards of the Major Arcana were not absolutely fixed as we know them today through Waite and others.

Initially Tarot cards were only for the nobility; they were essentially beautiful miniature works of art. Printing changed that. From woodcuts, the outline designs could be printed in sheets; some would still be hand-coloured, but usually they were coloured, a sheet at a time, through cut-out masks. Compared with modern printed cards they were crude. Compared with the beautifully-executed cards made for the nobility they were crude. But they were cheap, they were affordable by people somewhat lower down the social scale, and they caught on rapidly – as a card game. There is no evidence that they were ever used for divination, for predicting the future.

That changed, with Antoine Court de Gébelin in 1781. He was a member of a short-lived reform movement within French Freemasonry, the Rite of the Philalethes, which had interests in, among other things, alchemy, Swedenborgianism, magic, chivalry and the esoteric Christian tradition, and which had been strongly influenced by Baron von Hund's Strict Observance Rite (see previous chapter p. 95). In volume 8 of his *Le Monde Primitif* – which Tarot writer Brian Innes describes as a 'vast pot-pourri of uninformed speculation on the survival of ancient myths, symbols and fragments of primitive tongues',[7] an opinion shared by most authorities – Court de Gébelin launches into a flight of fancy about Tarot being an ancient Egyptian work, miraculously preserved, and containing in symbolic form all the wisdom of the ancients.

His ideas, unsubstantiated as they were, were picked up by others. A Paris wigmaker, Alliette, turned to fortune-telling, reversed his name, and as Etteilla in 1783 built a shaky edifice on Court de Gébelin's unsteady foundations: Tarot was actually the Book of Thoth, planned by Hermes Trismegistus; it had taken 17 mages four years to create it. He also noted that there were 22 cards, and 22 paths between the Sephiroth of the Tree of Life. Etteilla backed up his theory with his own design of Tarot cards, and the bandwagon was rolling.

Next came Éliphas Lévi Zahed, the pseudonym of Alphonse Louis Constant, who in 1855 and 1856 published *Dogme et Rituel de la Haute Magie*. Each of these writers sought to outdo his predecessor; 'the marvellous Book of the Tarot,' according to Lévi, is:

> of all books the most primitive, the key of prophecies and dogmas, in a
> word, the inspiration of inspired works, a fact that has remained
> unperceived, not only by the science of Court de Gébelin but by the
> extraordinary intuitions of Etteilla or Alliette.[8]

Lévi drew precise correspondences between the cards, the paths of the Sephiroth, and the 22 letters of the Hebrew alphabet. His ideas lie behind the symbolism of the Tarot pack designed by Oswald Wirth in 1889, which is otherwise based on the Marseille Tarot.

After Lévi came the physician Gérard Encausse, whose *Tarot of the Bohemians* was published in 1896 under the pseudonym Papus. He also builds on the work of his predecessors, though he says 'The *Tarot of Etteilla* is of no symbolic value, it is a bad mutilation of the real Tarot.'[9] Papus, though highly influential in the development of the occult significance of Tarot, cannot wholly be trusted; he describes Court de Gébelin as 'an illustrious scholar, who discovered the Egyptian origin of the Tarot'.[10] Looking at the symbols on the cards, Papus says, 'They at once prove that the Tarot of Marseille is really the exact representation of the primitive Egyptian Tarot, slightly altered to the epoch denoted by the costumes.'[11]

The late eighteenth- and nineteenth-century fascination with Egyptology has a lot to answer for.

So far most of the esoteric 'authorities' on Tarot have been French; attention now turns to the Hermetic Order of the Golden Dawn (see p. 162), and its leader, Samuel Liddell 'MacGregor' Mathers, of whom Papus is fairly dismissive: 'Mathers, an English author, has recently published a short account of the Tarot, which contains nothing very original . . . It is chiefly written as an aid to *fortune-telling by cards*.'[12] Mathers's wife Moina drew a Tarot pack under his instruction; members of the HOGD made their own copies of this, from which several of the esoteric packs of the twentieth century have derived. The best-known is the Rider–Waite pack, painted by Pamela Colman Smith to the instructions of Arthur Edward Waite, and initially published by Rider in 1910. Waite, an intelligent man who should perhaps have known better, based both the esoteric elements of his designs, and the divinatory meanings, on the HOGD's development of the pseudo-Cabalistic interpretations which had developed during the previous century.

Although the Rider–Waite pack is not well drawn, and is very crudely coloured, it has become the most popular pack of the twentieth century; this is largely because it was the first modern pack to be widely available in the UK and North America, but also because it had picture cards for the Minor Arcana, rather than simply numbers of Cups, Coins, Staves or Swords, as in the pip cards of normal playing-card packs. Most new packs, consciously or unconsciously, take elements of their design, and their divinatory meanings, almost direct from Waite. Whatever its merits and demerits, it has become the standard.[13]

The HOGD caused confusion to all later users of Tarot by swapping the order of two cards, Justice (originally 8) and Fortitude (11) to 11 and 8. This was to make the cards fit better into their Cabalistic interpretation. As has been noted, the very earliest packs had the Trumps in slightly different orders; either the order was unimportant, or it could be varied to suit the need. Yet generations of Tarot users have learned the order (whether pre- or post-HOGD) as gospel.

A former member of the HOGD, the self-styled 'Beast' Aleister Crowley, designed a radically different esoteric Tarot, strangely and stunningly painted by Lady Frieda Harris and exhibited in 1942, though not published as a pack until 1969. Crowley added yet more reinforcement to Court de Gébelin's Egyptian idea by calling his pack the *Book of Thoth*.

There are many more Tarot packs, many of them mythological in basis, and a fair number carrying within their designs Cabalistic, alchemical and astrological symbols. One, instead of pictorial representation, shows only the Sephirothic paths of the Tree of Life. No one today claims to be 'recovering' the original designs, though several claim to be returning to the lost truths of what Tarot was originally about. Most, however, are content to use the Tarot archetypes, while adapting their symbolical representation to whatever milieu concerns them.

That, briefly, is the history of Tarot, since the cards first appeared.

Although, once cheap printed cards became available, Tarot or *tarocci* was quite definitely a card game – probably very similar to the *jeu de Tarot* still available in France today – it seems unlikely that the earlier hand-painted cards would have been used in such a way by the nobility of Italy. For one thing, they were expensive little works of art, not only hand-painted, but illuminated with gold and silver. For another, they were too large to be used in a card game: 7 by 3½ inches (about 180 by 90 mm). So what was their original purpose? Where did the *idea* for the cards, and for their designs, come from?

There are many theories. The name Tarot is the French version of the Italian *tarocco*, plural *tarocci*, which was first recorded in 1516; its etymology is uncertain. Before that, the cards were known as *trionfi*, or triumphs, from which comes the English word 'trumps'. There is evidence that a card game called Triomphe was played in France in 1482.

Many of the original images bear a resemblance to characters and themes in the *Triumphs* of Petrarch, a series of poems written between 1340 and 1374: the Triumph of Love, the Triumph of Chastity, then of Death, of Fame, of Time and of Eternity. The poems became very popular for their spiritual and moral teaching over the next century or so, and were often illustrated with paintings, woodcuts and engravings; some of these are similar to some of the early Tarot cards. It is well within the realms of possibility that the original Tarot packs (*trionfi*) were nothing more nor less than a means of illustrating Petrarch's *Triumphs*. (Although this theory was first propounded by Gertrude Moakley as far back as 1956, it is still unknown by most Tarot users, and even most writers on Tarot. Historically it is very plausible, but just not esoteric enough for most people with an interest in Tarot.)

Before a further suggestion, a brief aside.

In Chapter Two the importance was noted of the Art of Memory, or Theatre of Memory, to medieval scholars and the Hermetic Philosophers. The Art of Memory is not just filing knowledge away in the right place; it is also the retrieval and linking of different data; today's computerized hypertext is really just a new version of the same principle. Ramón Lull's Art enabled him to link the Attributes of God with the stars and planets and their influences, the elements and humours and much else, all through a classification system based on a letter-notation.

People also used mnemonic devices, often based on word-play and images, to aid memory. One of the best-known is the fish, initially a far more common symbol of Christianity than was the cross; the Greek *ichthus* (fish) stood for *Iesous CHristos, THeou Uios, Soter* (Jesus Christ, Son of God, Saviour), and probably referred also to Jesus's words, 'Follow me, and I will make you fishers of men' (Matthew 4:19); today's esotericists also see a reference to the new Age of Pisces (the fish), now being superseded by the Age of Aquarius.

In the Middle Ages such visual symbols were more familiar to most people than they are today; they were a form of visual shorthand. Instead of a name-sign, shops would display a symbol of their trade, such as a bristly pig outside a brush-makers; probably the last to survive to the twentieth century was the striped barber's pole, though the stylized 'M' of a certain fast-food chain has become a universal symbol.

What applied to trade also applied to more abstract concepts. Medieval morality plays abounded with stock figures who were instantly-recognizable archetypes; in today's more 'sophisticated' society the nearest equivalents are the characters in pantomimes, and the cliché of white and black hats for the goodies and baddies in hack Westerns.

It should be remembered also that the majority of the medieval population was illiterate or, at best, semi-literate. The frequent depiction of Bible stories in stained-glass windows has been called 'sermons in glass'. When church services – and the Bible – were in Latin, which only the educated spoke and understood, a visual reminder was useful for the common people. (In passing, one of the 'crimes' of the Cathars was their translation of parts of the Bible into the vernacular.)

Returning, then, to Tarot, could its original purpose have been much the same as that of a series of stained-glass windows? The Fool is the unnumbered card; in some packs he is at the beginning; in others at the end. In his journey through life he has to take account of both civil and religious authority; he needs to have certain inner capabilities, or virtues; he will be tempted, and have to withstand temptation; he will have to make difficult choices; he will have to keep all the various tensions of his life in balance; he will have to cope with sudden, unexpected, apparently calamitous setbacks; he will have to seek wisdom if he is to dispense wisdom. But if he keeps his heart pure and his eye set firmly on the Heavenly City, he will reach there in the end. All of this, and much more, can be found in the pictures on Tarot cards.

The idea is not unique to Tarot. Around 1470 the *Ars Memorandi*, a block print, showed the four gospels in pictorial form, with each image containing small emblems which were mnemonic devices for incidents or stories in the gospels.

Tarot is a pictorial allegory. The images would have been familiar to a late-medieval, early-Renaissance audience, steeped not only in Christian symbolism but also in the Greek and Roman mythology of the classics. Whether they originated with Petrarch's *Triumphs* or not, it is quite possible that the pictures could have been used to tell more than one story; if each card was indeed an *aide-mémoire*, it would contain within it many resonances which would connect up in different ways with those of other cards. More than one play can be performed by the Theatre of Memory.

Another look taken at Tarot later on in the book will suggest a further possible concept behind it.

THE PUBLISHING
OF ESOTERIC KNOWLEDGE

Before examining the growth of modern Rosicrucian Orders it may be useful to take a quick glance at some of the significant texts in the Rosicrucian and related esoteric fields.

In Chapter Two a number of works were mentioned. The *Corpus Hermeticum* was translated into Latin in 1471; Francesco Giorgi and Henry Cornelius Agrippa were just two of many Renaissance writers who pursued Hermetic Philosophy. As mentioned above on p. 144, Antoine Court de Gébelin published his *Le Monde Primitif* in 1781, Éliphas Lévi published *Dogme et Rituel de la Haute Magie* in 1855 and 1856, and Papus published his *Tarot of the Bohemians* in 1896.

Before Lévi and Papus, however, came two British books, the second one with quite a curious history. In 1801 Francis Barrett published *The Magus, or Celestial Intelligencier; being a complete system of Occult Philosophy*. It gathered together for the first time in the English language many extracts from

THE
MAGUS,
OR
CELESTIAL INTELLIGENCER;
BEING
A COMPLETE SYSTEM OF
OCCULT PHILOSOPHY.

━━◦€◦꘎◦ᴐ◦━━

IN THREE BOOKS:

Containing the Antient and Modern Practice of the Cabaliftic Art, Natural and Celeftial Magic, &c.; fhewing the wonderful Effects that may be performed by a Knowledge of the

Celestial Influences, the occult Properties of Metals, Herbs, and Stones,

AND THE

APPLICATION OF ACTIVE TO PASSIVE PRINCIPLES.

EXHIBITING

THE SCIENCES OF NATURAL MAGIC;
Alchymy, or Hermetic Philosophy;

ALSO

THE NATURE, CREATION, AND FALL OF MAN;

His natural and fupernatural Gifts; the magical Power inherent in the Soul, &c.; with a great Variety of rare Experiments in Natural Magic:

THE CONSTELLATORY PRACTICE, or TALISMANIC MAGIC;

The Nature of the Elements, Stars, Planets, Signs, &c.; the Conftruction and Compofition of all Sorts of Magic Seals, Images, Rings, Glaffes, &c.;

The Virtue and Efficacy of Numbers, Characters, and Figures, of good and evil Spirits.

MAGNETISM,
AND CABALISTICAL OR CEREMONIAL MAGIC;

In which the fecret Myfteries of the Cabala are explained; the Operations of good and evil Spirits; all Kinds of Cabaliftic Figures, Tables, Seals, and Names, with their Ufe, &c.

THE TIMES, BONDS, OFFICES, AND CONJURATION OF SPIRITS.

TO WHICH IS ADDED

Biographia Antiqua, or the Lives of the most eminent Philosophers, Magi, &c.

The Whole illustrated with a great Variety of

CURIOUS ENGRAVINGS, MAGICAL AND CABALISTICAL FIGURES, &c.

━━◦€◦꘎◦ᴐ◦━━

BY FRANCIS BARRETT, F.R.C.
Professor of Chemistry, natural and occult Philosophy, the Cabala, &c. &c.

LONDON:
PRINTED FOR LACKINGTON, ALLEN, AND CO., TEMPLE OF THE MUSES, FINSBURY SQUARE.
1801.

Title page of The Magus, *Francis Barrett, 1801*

magical grimoires and the teachings of the Hermetic Philosophers on astrology, alchemy and other esoteric subjects. Its detailed title page began:

> Containing the Ancient and Modern Practice of the Cabaliftic Art,
> Natural and Celeftial Magic, &c; fhewing the wonderful Effects that
> may be performed by a knowledge of the Celeftial Influences, the
> Occult Properties of Metals, Herbs and Stones . . . [14]

The second book was *A Suggestive Enquiry into the Hermetic Mystery* by Mary Anne Atwood (née South). This was the result of many years' study into the whole wide-ranging subject area by her father Thomas South and herself, and is said to be an extremely impressive compilation of esoteric thought from ancient times up to their own day. [15] Atwood published her book in 1850, then changed her mind, apparently persuaded by her father that such knowledge should not after all be in the public domain. She recovered and destroyed as many copies as possible, and the book effectively vanished for over half a century, not appearing again until 1918. (Lindsay Clarke makes use of this story as the basis of his award-winning novel *The Chymical Wedding* (Jonathan Cape 1989).)

The twentieth century saw a number of books published whose contents would have horrified those who guarded the secrets in previous years. A.E. Waite's *Book of Ceremonial Magic* came out in 1911; Aleister Crowley's *Magick in Theory and Practice* was published in 1929; and Israel Regardie revealed the entire Golden Dawn ritual in a series of books between 1937 and 1940. In 1957 the Sufi esotericist Idries Shah published *The Secret Lore of Magic*, containing many of the most famous (or infamous) magical grimoires including 'The Key of Solomon', which had been prohibited by the Inquisition.

But in the late nineteenth century the main influence on nascent esoteric groups, for better or for worse, was still Éliphas Lévi.

MODERN ROSICRUCIAN ORDERS

The best-known Rosicrucian Orders today are based in the USA; indeed, reading their literature, one could almost be forgiven for thinking that Rosicrucianism is an invention peculiar to the United States; it is so tied in (at least from their claims) with US history – which is so dear to Americans – and with the Great Ideals of the Constitution and Independence and Freedom and the American Dream. Half the great heroes of American history seem to have been either Rosicrucians or Freemasons, which might or might not have come to much the same thing at the time. Middle-class, educated, movers and shakers of society: for Americans more than anyone

THE RESURGENCE OF ESOTERIC SOCIETIES

else, it seems, there is an urge to belong to societies. Furthermore, it has to be known that they belong, and that they are high in the hierarchy (social status); but not what they believe and do (secrecy).

Perhaps it is because their history is so short, and because they have no royalty, nobles and knights, and no idealized and romanticized medieval past, that so many Americans delight in pageantry, costumes, ranks, and insignia of office. This is a sweeping generalization, of course, but there is surely an element of truth in it.

Because the main language of North America today is English, it is easy to forget that white Americans came from all over Europe: there were Scots and Irish, Dutch and Germans, French, Italians, Scandinavians, and others, including Jews from several central European countries. Many were free-thinkers of one sort or another; their religious, political or other ideological beliefs did not fit in within their own lands. They took their independent beliefs with them to the New World.

This is an idealized image, but again it must contain some truth.

Most esoteric societies claim a continuity with the past, a heredity or ancestry, rather than just a continuity of ideas. The oldest Rosicrucian Order in the USA is the *Fraternitas Rosae Crucis*, based in Quakertown, Pennsylvania under the corporate name of the Beverly Hall Corporation. By using the names *Fraternitas Rosae Crucis*, Fraternity of the Rosicrucians, or Rosicrucian Fraternity of itself, the FRC is making the claim to be *the* legitimate Rosicrucian Order in the USA.

'All authority is invested in the Supreme Grand Master and his Council of Three and but one such Council can legitimately exist in a country. Such are the Ancient Landmarks of the Fraternity. The Order retains its original name: *The Fraternitas Rosae Crucis*.' In the same paragraph on 'Authority and Legitimacy' is found, 'It is required that the Neophyte be regularly enrolled in an Organisation having received its authority from a source which is a *direct continuation* of the original exoteric body.' Earlier in the same leaflet the FRC say, 'The Fraternity has continued in America without interruption since prior to 1773.'[16]

According to the FRC the Council of Three in 1774 consisted of Benjamin Franklin, George Clymer and Thomas Paine; during the American Civil War its members were Paschal Beverly Randolph, General Ethan Allen Hitchcock and President Abraham Lincoln. Hitchcock was apparently a member of the Grand Lodge of France and, through his intercession, 'In 1856, Paschal Beverly Randolph received authority from the Grand Dome of France to establish a Grand Lodge ... In 1874, Freeman B. Dowd became the Supreme Grand Master of the Supreme Grand Lodge of the Rosicrucians

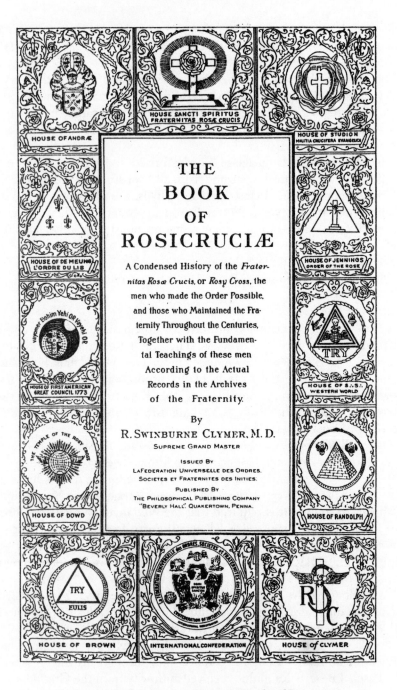

Title page of R. Swinburne Clymer's Book of Rosicruciae
(Fraternitas Rosae Crucis)

in America.' He was succeeded in 1905 by Reuben Swinburne Clymer, who later became 'Supreme Grand Master for both North and South America as well as for all of Europe'. These were not all of Clymer's titles.

> In 1907 he was chosen Supreme Grand Master of the Æth Priesthood by authority of the *Council of Three*. Later he became Exalted Grand Master of the *Illuminatae Americanae*; Supreme Grand Master of the Order, Temple, Brotherhood and Fraternity of Rosicrucians (of the Western World), and Hierarch of Imperial Eulis; Member of *L'Ordre du Lis* and Order of the Rose; Supreme Grand Master *La Fédération Universelle des Ordres, Sociétés et Fraternités des Initiés*, i.e. Confederation or Fraternity of Initiates of the World.

Clymer's importance came from the fact that 'Originally there were a number of authentic Occult Fraternities in America. As the Grand Masters of these Fraternities passed on, they delegated their authority to Dr R. Swinburne Clymer; thus, over a period of years, all Occult Fraternities were merged into a single organisation and under a single Supreme Grand Master'[17] – emphasizing again the FRC's claim to be the only legitimate Rosicrucian Order in the USA.

For the FRC, as for all Rosicrucian and indeed nearly all esoteric organisations, their authority stems from their pedigree. Stripping the above down to its basics, and putting to one side the supposed eighteenth-century history, Randolph founded the FRC in 1858, and it was small and slow-growing until Clymer took it over in 1905, eight years after joining it. But where did Randolph's own authority come from? He had apparently been initiated into several different Orders in Europe. The Supreme Grand Master of the Conclave which made him Supreme Master for the Western World in 1858 was Éliphas Lévi, the French occultist, former trainee priest and somewhat uncertain scholar who wrote some extremely influential books on magic, and contributed to the esoteric interpretation of Tarot.

It was a link to European esoteric organizations; but a certain amount of doubt can be cast on those organizations themselves. The same can be said of the origins of the other major US Rosicrucian Orders.

The Rosicrucian Fellowship was founded in 1907 by Max Heindel (1865–1919), born Carl Louis von Grasshoff to a German father and Danish mother, who in his teens went to Glasgow to study engineering in the shipyards. Moving to the USA, he joined the Theosophical Society in Los Angeles. In 1907 he travelled to Germany, where he had a mystical experience, was tested by an etheric Elder Brother of the Rosicrucian Order, was found fit to be the recipient of esoteric teachings, and was 'given instructions as to how to reach the Temple of the Rose Cross, which was near the border between Bohemia and Germany.' There he was given the teachings which formed his book, *The Rosicrucian Cosmo-Conception*, published in 1909. Heindel met Rudolf Steiner, founder of Anthroposophy, in Germany; it is generally thought that his teachings incorporate many of Steiner's, though Marie-José Clerc, President of the Rosicrucian Fellowship, disagrees.

> We are not at all a blend of any other movements . . . Yes, Max Heindel was originally involved in Theosophy; yes, he met Rudolf Steiner, but was not at all influenced by him as the Teaching given in the *Rosicrucian Cosmo-Conception* was given to Max Heindel by the Brothers of the Rosicrucian Order, in Germany.

Heindel's widow explains in more detail:

> The Rosicrucian Fellowship, founded by Max Heindel under the direct guidance of the Elder Brothers of the Order, is the authorised representative for the present period of the ancient Rosicrucian Order, of which Christian Rose Cross, or Christian Rosenkreuz is the Head. This Order is not a mundane organisation, but has its Temple and Headquarters on the etheric plane. It authorised the formation of the Fellowship by Max Heindel for the purpose of carrying the Western Wisdom Teachings to the Western people. In earlier ages the Order carried on its work through various secret societies in Europe and elsewhere; but the growth and advancement of the people of the United States have in recent years reached such a point that the Order deemed it advisable to establish an exoteric center here for the extension of its work. The Rosicrucian Fellowship is its latest manifestation in physical form, putting out the most up-to-date version of the Rosicrucian Teachings, in twentieth-century scientific terms, which are at the same time simple and devoid of technical abstractions.
>
> The particular work of the Fellowship . . . is to disseminate the esoteric doctrines of the Christian religion, since the Rosicrucian Philosophy is an esoteric Christian philosophy. It is destined to become the universal religion of the world, because the Christ is to have charge of human evolution during the present Great Sidereal Year of approximately 25,000 years.[18]

Like the original Rosicrucians, but unlike some of the other present-day Rosicrucian Orders which specify the amount of the monthly 'freewill' offering, the Rosicrucian Fellowship makes no charge for its work. It has correspondence courses in Philosophy, Bible and Astrology; 'we consider Astrology as a part of Christianity . . . because we consider the 12 Constellations as the 12 Divine Hierarchies of the Bible,' says Clerc. Its healing work 'is an important part of our work and carried on through the Invisible Helpers'. These are members of the Fellowship working while they sleep at night, under the guidance of the Elder Brothers.

Esoteric symbols of the Fraternitas Rosae Crucis

The Rosicrucian Fellowship currently has 7,000–8,000 members; 'our requirements are rather high', says Clerc.[19]

The *Societas Rosicruciana in America* (SRIA) was founded in 1909 by some members of the *Societas Rosicruciana in Civitatibus Foederatis*, founded in 1880 as an American branch of the Scottish branch of the *Societas Rosicruciana in Anglia* – which is commonly known as the Soc Ros, and is an Order open only to Master Masons (see p. 159). The SRIA wanted to open up its esoteric teachings to non-Masons. The main influence on the SRIA was one of its founder members, George Wilmslow Plummer (1876–1944), who led it further in the direction of esoteric Christianity. Both he, and later his widow 'Mother Serena' (1894–1989), were consecrated bishops by heterodox archbishops, founding their own Holy Orthodox Church in America.

The SRIA, also known as the Society of Rosicrucians, Inc, and the Rosicrucian Society of America, 'is a lineal descendant and, in America, the branch of the Society first formulated by Christian Rosenkreutz, the esoteric pseudonym of a spiritual Leader and Adept who was born AD 1378 and died in 1484.'[20] It claims to be 'in most complete harmony with all *legitimate* mystical schools and orders', but it is fairly unusual in its attitude to 'competing' American Rosicrucian and other esoteric bodies.

> While there are many organizations in our land which in varying degrees are similar to ours, there are some others with which we have nothing in common. In stating what this Society strives to avoid we are being quite definite that we do not condemn, attack, nor countenance the attacking of any other organization, for we know that insofar as it is dedicated to some Ideal, every organization serves some useful purpose, even though not the best one.[21]

Most outsiders encountering Rosicrucianism today first come across AMORC, the Ancient and Mystical Order Rosae Crucis, sometimes known simply as the Rosicrucian Order. Unlike most of the other Rosicrucian Orders, which require one to search them out, AMORC advertises openly and widely in magazines and newspapers.

In its promotional literature AMORC skates over its immediate history:

> Since the 17th century there has been a consistent existence and perpetuation of the Rosicrucian Order. However its structure has often been elusive because in past centuries various conditions and persecutions necessitated that limited public awareness of the Order be

maintained . . . Today the Rosicrucian Order, AMORC, is a thriving non-profit, educational, cultural, and fraternal organisation consisting of thousands of men and women in over 100 countries throughout the world.[22]

AMORC is thought to have around a quarter of a million members today.

AMORC was founded by Harvey Spencer Lewis in 1915 in New York. The reason for it keeping quiet about its pedigree is probably that it received its authority not from a Rosicrucian order as such, but from the German branch of the Ordo Templi Orientis; the British branch of OTO was headed by Aleister Crowley, whose personal reputation is hardly pure and spiritual. It is fair to mention, though, that the German branch split away from Crowley's organization in 1916, which was when it authorized Lewis to head a lodge.

H. Spencer Lewis and AMORC were roundly attacked by R. Swinburne Clymer of *Fraternitas Rosae Crucis*, who took Lewis to court in 1928. The bitterness between the two groups is still very much alive. According to Dr Gerald E. Poesnecker, Supreme Grand Master of FRC,

> To make a short synopsis of the Rosicrucian Fraternity in America, one could simply say that the AMORC group for their own purposes attempted to usurp the name Rosicrucian, and Dr Clymer for the FRC sued in a civil lawsuit. After an appeal, the final Court decision was that the name Rosicrucian was public domain and could be used by anyone.[23]

Lewis accused Clymer of being a fraud, while Clymer, having in mind AMORC's origins with the OTO, attacked 'the boastful pilfering Imperator with his black-magic, sex-magic connections'.[24] The row apparently also involved the Rosicrucian Fellowship.

Poesnecker continues:

> As far as the difference between the FRC and the AMORC is concerned, one cannot understand its difference unless one is able to understand the nature of the true Initiate Schools. The concept of Soul Growth and Soul Illumination is absolutely vital to all true Arcane Societies and something completely foreign to groups such as AMORC, The Golden Dawn, etc.

AMORC, meanwhile, say on the back of their introductory leaflet, 'The ancient names and symbols of the Rosicrucian Order are registered and pro-tected by the United States Patent Office exclusively in the name of AMORC.' AMORC today appears to have distanced itself completely from

157

any tinge of dubious magical practices; its courses offer a mixture of historical teachings on esoteric religion, and self-improvement.

These are just four of the Rosicrucian Orders based in the USA, with greater or lesser influence around the world. Each claims to be the true successor to the original Rosicrucians, and the only valid holder of the name in the USA. According to A.E. Waite, the claims of all the American Rosicrucian organisations to any sort of legitimacy whatsoever are fallacious; to adapt Henry Ford's dictum, their history is bunk.

Speaking of Paschal Beverly Randolph, Waite says,

> I have worked through such of his volumes as are available here in England, from so-called Rosicrucian dream-books to declamatory sex-reveries, and have concluded that, mountebank as he was, he believed in all his rant and was not lying consciously when this stuff of sorry dreams was put forward unfailingly as the wisdom of the Rosy Cross. This is how it loomed in his mind and this is what it was in dream, for it was a thing of his own making.

As for Heindel and the much-titled Clymer, Waite dismisses them in a single paragraph:

> It would serve no useful purpose to enlarge upon later foundations, like that of Dr R. Swinburne Clymer, who seems to have assumed the mantle laid down by Randolph, or Max Heindel's Rosicrucian Fellowship of California. They represent individual enterprises which have no roots in the past.

Of *Societas Rosicruciana in America* Waite is a little less damning:

> So far as I am acquainted with its activities, the work undertaken is done in an earnest spirit; it has gradually rectified its Latin – at least to a certain point – and is an exponent of esoteric Christianity, as this is understood by its leading spirit. But it has obviously no tradition, no claim on the past and no knowledge thereof. The Transactions... are amazing reading from the standpoint of things put forward under the denomination of the Rosy Cross.[25]

AMORC had presumably not come to Waite's attention by the time he wrote of the others.

Must we then dismiss all the current Rosicrucian organizations as fraudulent or flawed? From a British viewpoint, the American obsession with building corporations, with setting up publishing companies and mail-order correspondence schools, with registering names and symbols as trademarks, and with litigation, are a far cry from the spiritual ideals of the early Rosicrucians. But the point surely is that, brash and businesslike as they may appear to Europeans, these Orders are distinctively American, and are, in one way or another, passing on some version of the Rosicrucian teachings to the American people. A more legitimate complaint might be that they are then re-exporting this highly-Americanized version of Rosicrucianism back to its place of origin, Europe.

Europe has its own Rosicrucian Orders, of which the best known are the *Societas Rosicruciana in Anglia* and the *Lectorium Rosicrucianum*.

As mentioned a few paragraphs ago, the *Societas Rosicruciana in America* (SRIA) started as an American equivalent of the *Societas Rosicruciana in Anglia* (Soc Ros), but with the expressed aim of opening up the teachings to non-Masons. It is likely that each has drifted away from its origins, and in different directions.

The Soc Ros is often seen as a 'side degree' of Freemasonry in England and Scotland, though the Masonic scholar John Hamill, himself a member, says they would argue very strongly that they weren't.[26] However, the Soc Ros is listed among all the other side degrees in Keith B. Jackson's handbook of Masonic Orders, *Beyond the Craft*. Like many of the side degrees it is a specifically Christian Order not open to members of other faiths, which is against the ethos of the basic Craft. It is an arguable point whether it should be seen as a specialist branch of Freemasonry, or as a quite separate body which happens only to be open to Master Masons.

The SRIA openly calls itself a Rosicrucian Order. So, for that matter, does its parent body, the *Societas Rosicruciana in Civitatibus Foederatis* (SRICF), which is basically the American branch of Soc Ros, and which is also only open to Masons; the SRICF used to have a magazine entitled *Rosicrucian Fama*. The English title of the *Societas Rosicruciana in Anglia* is given in Jackson's *Beyond the Craft* as The Rosicrucian Society of Freemasons.

It seems fair to assume that Soc Ros is a Rosicrucian Order.

Soc Ros was founded in 1866 by two Freemasons, one of whom claimed to have learned ancient secrets from some German Rosicrucians, and the other to have discovered some ancient rituals in the Grand Lodge archives in the vaults of Freemasons' Hall. 'It's a good story', laughs Hamill, accepting it as yet another foundation myth.

Its Ordinances say of its members that 'it is expected that they will be of sufficient ability to appreciate the studies of the Society, which consider the revelation of philosophy, science and theosophy', which definitely sounds more Rosicrucian than Masonic. Unless, as is quite possible, these two Masons were simply creating out of whole cloth another group of invented grades and rituals with yet another impressive name, it could be that they were going full circle: attempting to restore to Freemasonry certain esoteric religious elements which had become lost, corrupted or downplayed over the years.

In this they would have been following the example of the Brotherhood of the Golden and Rosy Cross, a German Order which in 1777 published a form of revised constitution, part of which read,

> Masonry has deteriorated on its own part and has passed almost beyond recognition, being profaned and adulterated by so many idle and useless *additamenta* . . . That all this notwithstanding it remains the preparatory school of the Rosy Cross and from this source only can the Order itself be recruited.[27]

If they existed at all, the 'German Rosicrucians' of Soc Ros's founders were quite possibly descendants of this Brotherhood.

Craft Freemasonry has Lodges; the Holy Royal Arch has Chapters; Soc Ros has Colleges, of which there are currently 58 around the world, around three-quarters of these in Britain. It is very much a scholarly Order; its members are encouraged 'to produce papers and deliver lectures as a vital part of College work'.[28]

'They would argue very strongly that they are not there just to provide another set of rituals and another set of regalia for the gong-collectors,' says Hamill. 'They have a very definite purpose which is the investigation of intellectual and esoteric and religious ideas. People who are of a mystical bent would gravitate to the Soc Ros.'

More than solely mystical, perhaps. The original objects of the Soc Ros were 'to afford mutual aid and encouragement in working out the great problems of Life, and in discovering the secrets of nature; to facilitate the study of the systems of philosophy founded upon the Kaballah and the doctrines of Hermes Trismegistus'.[29]

The *Lectorium Rosicrucianum* is based in the Netherlands but has branches throughout Europe, and also in New York and California. *Lectorium Rosicrucianum*, also known as the International School of the Golden Rosycross, was founded as the *Rozekruisers Genootschap* (Rosicrucian Fellowship) in 1924 by two brothers, Z.W. Leene (1892–1936) and J. Leene (1896–1968); the latter wrote numerous books on Rosicrucianism under the name J. van

Cleopatra's Needle, London, was erected by Freemasons in 1878. Has the esoteric knowledge of the ancient Egyptians been preserved by later secret societies?
(Photograph: David V. Barrett)

Above: *The Templar Church, London. At their height, the Knights Templar were the most powerful organization of their time: an Order of soldier-monks who became bankers.*
(Photograph: David V. Barrett)

Right: *Tour du Coudray, in the chateau at Chinon in France, where Jacques de Molay and other Templars were imprisoned when the Order fell in 1307.*
(Photograph: David V. Barrett)

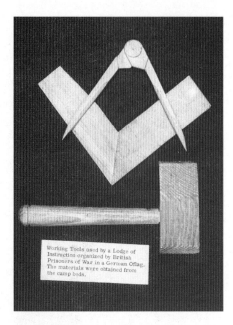

Working Tools used by a Lodge of Instruction organized by British Prisoners of War in a German Oflag. The materials were obtained from the camp beds.

Above and right: *The jewels of speculative Freemasonry are based on the tools of operative masonry.*
(Courtesy of Board of General Purposes, United Grand Lodge of England. Photograph: Matthew Scanlon)

Below: *The ceiling cornice of the Great Temple at Freemasons' Hall, London, showing clear heterodox religious imagery.*
(Courtesy of Board of General Purposes, United Grand Lodge of England. Photograph: David V. Barrett)

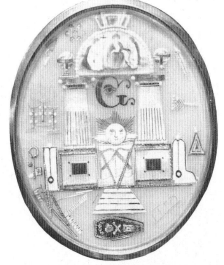

Right: *Tracing boards are pictorial representations of the symbolic truths taught at the different levels of Freemasonry.*
(Courtesy of Board of General Purposes, United Grand Lodge of England. Photograph: Matthew Scanlon)

Below: *The Master Mason's apron of King George VI.*
(Courtesy of Board of General Purposes, United Grand Lodge of England. Photograph: David V. Barrett)

Right: *Hermetic Order of the Golden Dawn: Samuel Liddell 'MacGregor' Mathers.* (Photograph copyright, R.A. Gilbert)

Below left: *Dr William Wynn Westcott, founder of the Hermetic Order of the Golden Dawn.* (Photograph copyright, R.A. Gilbert)

Below right: *Hermetic Order of the Golden Dawn: Westcott's lamen.* (Photograph copyright, R.A. Gilbert)

Above: *Hermetic Order of the Golden Dawn: the Seal of the Second Order, RR et AC.*
(Photograph copyright, R.A. Gilbert)

Right: *Rosicrucian Fellowship: representation of an Invisible Helper.*
(Courtesy of the Rosicrucian Fellowship, Oceanside, California)

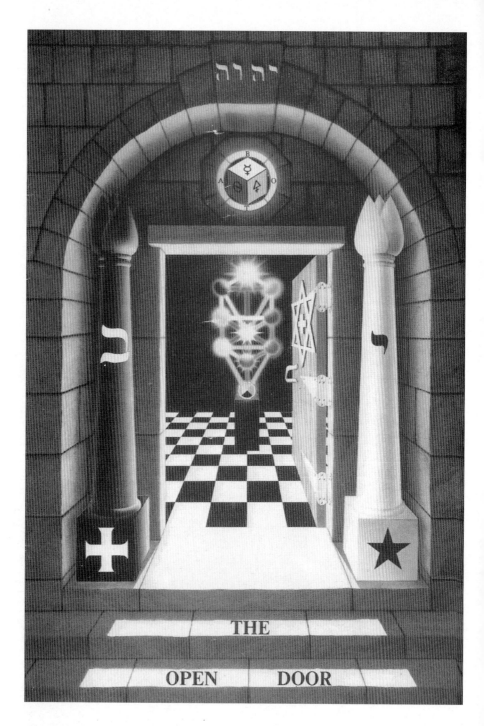

The symbols of the American occult school Builders of the Adytum include the Cabalistic Tree of Life and the pillars of Solomon's Temple.
(Courtesy of B.O.T.A., Los Angeles, California)

Rijckenborgh. For some years it was linked with Max Heindel's Rosicrucian Fellowship, but split away in 1935, giving less emphasis to the cosmic teachings of Heindel, and moving to a strongly Gnostic interpretation of Christianity. As with many of the movements examined in Chapter One, *Lectorium Rosicrucianum* teaches the immanence of God, or the Kingdom of Heaven or, in its words, 'the divine nature–order'.

> The human heart contains a last remnant of this divine nature–order. This remnant, this *spirit–spark–atom*, also called *Divine Spark* or *Rose of the Heart*, calls up in many people a vague memory, called pre-memory, from which emanated a continuous inner drive to seek out the original state of being "with the Father", the state of being immortally at one with God.[30]

Unlike most of the other Rosicrucian Orders, *Lectorium Rosicrucianum* does not appear to claim a pedigree going back to the early seventeenth century; it says it was formed 'in order to promote the world-wide dissemination of the Gnostic universal teachings: the living spiritual core in the original revelations of all the great world religions and mystery schools'.[31]

Among these is the belief, common to many of the early Gnostics, the Manichæans and the Cathars, that the material world is one of 'imperfection, darkness and evil'. But this belief is not gloomy and pessimistic. 'It is exactly the other way round. The Gnosis taught and demonstrated the path of liberation. It reminded man of his origin and showed him the way back. And the Gnostic teachers exemplified this path for their pupils by their own lives . . .'[32]

This emphasis on purity of living, on morality, on setting an example, of being a light burning in this world of darkness, is found in all the Rosicrucian Orders, in the mystery schools, and also, in slightly different words, in Freemasonry. Part of the purpose of such movements, as will be shown in the final chapter, is that the individual spiritual reawakening will lead to a better life, which will lead to a general improvement of society.

Such was the aim of the first Rosicrucians; it is likely that it was also the aim of the Cathars.

There is one further European Rosicrucian Order which should be mentioned, for its influence on other Orders. This is the Kabbalistic Order of the Rosy Cross, which was founded in 1888 by two followers of Éliphas Lévi's teachings, the Marquis Stanislas de Guaita and Joséphin Péladan; its aim was to restore the esoteric spiritual element which had been at the heart of Freemasonry, but which had become almost completely buried beneath manufactured rituals. Unsurprisingly it concentrated on study of Lévi's interpretation of Cabala and Tarot, and of other ancient wisdom systems. Certainly at one stage, in contrast to that of the earliest Rosicrucian Orders, its membership was exclusively Roman Catholic; Lévi himself had trained for the Catholic priesthood at Saint-Sulpice, and had in fact been ordained a deacon, but was expelled from the seminary before becoming a full priest, for speaking too openly about his heterodox beliefs.

One of the Order's members was Gérard Encausse, who later achieved fame as Papus, a writer on Tarot and the occult. Papus's *The Tarot of the Bohemians* used cards designed by Oswald Wirth, a close friend and student of the Marquis de Guaita. Papus later joined the Golden Dawn temple in Paris.

Internal disputes soon split the Order; one offshoot, the Order of the Catholic Rose-Croix of the Temple and the Grail, was founded by Péladan in 1890. H. Spencer Lewis, the founder of AMORC, was at one time a member of Péladan's Order, and undoubtedly borrowed much of its teachings. The Hermetic Order of the Golden Dawn, as will now be seen, also leaned heavily (usually without attribution) on Lévi's teachings. It should be remembered that Paschal Beverly Randolph, founder of the American *Fraternitas Rosae Crucis*, also allegedly received his authority from Lévi.

Péladan was also the 'custodian' of the moribund Order of the Temple, founded in 1805 by Bernard-Raymond Fabré-Palaprat. This was to re-emerge nearly two centuries after its founding, via several other Orders, as the Order of the Solar Temple (see p. 81).

THE HERMETIC ORDER OF THE
GOLDEN DAWN

The best-known occult society of the last century or so, and one of the most influential despite its short life, was the Hermetic Order of the Golden Dawn (HOGD). For those who require an actual organizational lineage rather than just one of ideas and ideals, the HOGD offers plenty of direct offspring, though the legitimacy of its own parentage is more than questionable.

Among non-esotericists the HOGD tends to have a bad reputation, mainly because one of its best known members was Aleister Crowley, who from all accounts was an extremely unpleasant, power-hungry individual who delighted in shocking people with not just his acceptance of, but his pride in his own wickedness.

It is not the function of this book to attempt to rehabilitate Crowley's name. He was almost certainly all the things said against him, and more, and hardly a shining example of esoteric beliefs or morality. It should be mentioned, however, that a number of experienced and respected esotericists say that, whatever his character, Crowley's understanding of the occult should not be dismissed.

It should also be pointed out that much of Crowley's reputation arose after he had left the HOGD, and that in fact he was only a member of it for a year before being expelled, along with its one remaining founder.

The Hermetic Order of the Golden Dawn was founded by Dr William Wynn Westcott, a London coroner, Dr William Robert Woodman, a retired physician, and Samuel Liddell 'MacGregor' Mathers, of no fixed occupation. All three were Freemasons, and all three were leading members of the *Societas Rosicruciana in Anglia*, the Soc Ros; Woodman and Westcott were successive Supreme Magi.

Soc Ros had claimed to be based on some old Rosicrucian manuscripts supposedly found in the archives of Freemasons' Hall, and on some secret teachings from a German Rosicrucian. Westcott claimed to have come across some further papers, this time sent to him by an elderly clergyman in 1887; they were enciphered, but when rendered into plain text revealed the bare details of five rituals of an occult society called Golden Dawn. In a move reminiscent of the birth of the immediate-post-Manifesto Rosicrucians some 270 years earlier, Westcott decided to form such a society in Britain. It was necessary to have a triumvirate at the top (as with the Council of Three of the American *Fraternitas Rosae Crucis*, described on p. 151); he recruited Woodman, then Supreme Magus of Soc Ros, and Mathers, asking the latter to write some detailed rituals based on the fragments in the manuscript.

It has been seen, and will be seen again, how important it was for Rosicrucian and other esoteric Orders to have a lineage, to give them authority. Westcott invented a German Order called the *Goldene Dämmerung* (Golden Dawn) and its leader, a certain Fräulein Sprengel, and had letters forged from her granting authority to form a British Order. Mathers, meanwhile, was formulating detailed rituals. The degrees of the Order of the Golden Dawn bore a marked similarity to those of Soc Ros.

COMPARED SYSTEMS OF DEGREES

Soc Ros	*Golden Dawn*
First Order	**Outer Order**
	0°=0° Neophyte
I Zelator	1°=10° Zelator
II Theoricus	2°=9° Theoricus
III Practicus	3°=8° Practicus
IV Philosophus	4°=7° Philosophus

Second Order	**Second Order**
V Adeptus Minor	5°=6° Adeptus Minor
VI Adeptus Major	6°=5° Adeptus Major
VII Adeptus Exemptus	7°=4° Adeptus Exemptus
Third Order	**Third Order**
VIII Magister Templi	8°=3° Magister
IX Magus	9°=2° Magus
	10°=1° Ipsissimus

In fact, the Soc Ros, like several other Rosicrucian Orders, had themselves borrowed this system of degrees from the Brotherhood of the Golden and Rosy Cross, the late eighteenth-century German Order mentioned on p. 103. (There is today some disagreement about whether the grade 10°=1° Ipsissimus was part of the original HOGD structure or not, though Israel Regardie mentions it in his book of Golden Dawn teachings.)

Most of the early members of the HOGD were recruited from Soc Ros; all of these, therefore, were Master Masons. Initially all members of the HOGD were only in the Outer Order, except the three Chiefs, who were Adeptus Minor, and who were supposedly subject to three Secret Chiefs who were Adeptus Exemptus; in fact these latter were Woodman, Mathers (who had, of course, devised the rituals and the examinations), and Fräulein Sprengel (i.e. Westcott). The Third Order were not of this world; they were from the Astral Plane, possibly equivalent to the Great White Brotherhood of the Theosophists,[33] or the Elder Brothers of the Rosicrucian Fellowship – or even, perhaps, the concept of Baron von Hund's Unknown Superiors.

From one viewpoint, the creation of the HOGD was entirely spurious. The lineage was a fake, and Mathers's rituals were largely blue-sky creations. (Whether the Soc Ros was similarly created out of whole cloth is less certain; there apparently could be an element of truth in its foundation myth.)

From another point of view, though, certainly as the HOGD developed, it was as sound and as valid as any esoteric organization, and more so than many. Whether it was in any way a true successor to the 'genuine' Rosicrucian Orders must be debatable, but it certainly claimed to be in direct descent from the traditions of Christian Rosenkreutz. Its members included Freemasons, Rosicrucians, Theosophists, and people well-versed in occult history, rituals and philosophy, in Egyptology, in mythology, in alchemy and astrology, in Cabala and Tarot and numerology and much else. All of these were drawn together in the HOGD. It was not simply a club for esoteric dilettantes who liked dressing up and going through odd rituals; it took its subject matter seriously. The HOGD teachings have now been published,[34] and reveal, among many other things, that members had to work hard to pass from grade to grade.

One of the main initiatory rituals of the HOGD's Second Order took place in a seven-sided vault based on that in which Christian Rosenkreutz's uncorrupted body is supposed to have been found; the resurrection symbolism is also closely linked to that of the 'raising' of a Master Mason, whose initiation also involves the representation of a grave. The initiatory rituals were not simply theatre, as many describe those of Freemasonry; 'properly performed, [they] could act as a powerful stimulus to the active imagination and spiritual aspiration of the candidate'.[35]

The HOGD based much of its teachings about Cabala, Tarot and the theory of ritual magic on the writings of Éliphas Lévi (1810–75). Unlike Lévi, who appears to have been more of a theorist rather than a practitioner of magic, the HOGD developed a complex working system of ritual magic. This was based on Lévi's three laws of magic – the force of the will, the astral medium, and the theory of correspondences – with the addition of a fourth factor, directed imagination. Most ritual magic practised in the West today stems directly from HOGD theory and practice.

Both Mathers, within the HOGD, and Crowley, after leaving it, developed correspondences way beyond Lévi's ideas. Each Hebrew letter (and hence number, as letters were also used for numerals) had its own meaning, just as the Norse runes do; the 22 letters were each associated with a path between the Sephiroth of the Cabalistic Tree of Life; there were further correspondences with the astrological planets, the twelve signs of the zodiac, and the four elements; with the Major Arcana of Tarot; with notes of the musical scale; with colours; with Hindu gods; with Roman gods; with animals, real and imaginary; with plants, real and imaginary; with precious stones; with magical weapons; with perfumes; with the Greek alphabet; with geometrical shapes; with metals; with parts of the body; and with much else besides. The tables of 'a few of the principal correspondences' take up 21 pages in Appendix V of Crowley's *Magick in Theory and Practice*. If an adept wished to invoke a particular spirit or its essence for a particular magical working, he or she would go through the tables of correspondences and select the relevant plants, precious stones, colours for cloths or candles, scents for incense, and so on, to use in the ritual.

Correspondences are a complex extension of the idea of sympathetic magic: if two things are similar, or connected in some way, then one can be used to influence the other – or, in a more psychological explanation, to help the practitioner to focus his or her mind more clearly.

The Order of the Golden Dawn flourished for a few years, setting up Temples in Weston-super-Mare, Bradford and Edinburgh, in addition to the original Isis–Urania Temple in London. Famous members over the next decade included the poet W.B. Yeats, the supernatural writers Arthur Machen and Algernon Blackwood, the esoteric historian A.E. Waite, the tea heiress Annie Horniman, and the West End actress (and mistress of, among others, George Bernard Shaw) Florence Farr; unlike the Soc Ros which gave birth to it, the HOGD was open to both men and women. At its height it had over 300 members, more than a third of them women.

The real activity now was in the Second Order, which around 1891 was renamed the *Ordo Rosae Rubreae et Aureae Crucis* (*RR et AC*) – in English, the Order of the Rose of Ruby and Cross of Gold. Mathers wrote rituals for it, and suitable members of the Outer Order were invited to take examinations and be initiated into it; the remainder were kept ignorant even of its existence.

The name of the Second Order is clearly taken from the Brotherhood of the Golden and Rosy Cross; Westcott, Woodman and Mathers, as senior members of Soc Ros, would have been well acquainted with the history of Rosicrucian societies. It is thought unlikely that there was any *actual* connection between the HOGD and the eighteenth-century German Order.

Then everything began to fall apart. There were several reasons, one of which was the personalities – and personality clashes – of its leaders. Woodman died in 1891, and Mathers assumed more and more control. Mathers had moved to France, but almost his sole source of income was the generosity of Annie Horniman, one of the leading lights of the HOGD; eventually she grew tired of Mathers's imperious nature, and cut off her funding in 1896. In response, Mathers expelled her from the HOGD. Although still exercising autocratic control over it, Mathers devoted less and less time to the HOGD; instead he devoted much of his attention to, of all things, a revived Jacobite cause: a small group planning to restore the House of Stuart to the Scottish throne (compare the Chevalier Ramsay as discussed on p. 94).

It was generally believed that in 1897 the civil authorities in London (possibly tipped off by Mathers) discovered that Westcott was involved in an occult society, and told him that this was not suitable behaviour for a senior coroner; Westcott resigned his position in the HOGD. It is possible, however, that Mathers had simply threatened Westcott with exposure of the truth about Fräulein Sprengel. Westcott's place as leader of the HOGD in England was taken by Florence Farr, who was an incompetent administrator; the detailed examination system fell into disarray, and individual members of the HOGD began to perform unauthorized and unsupervised magical experiments.

Worse was to come. A young man, Aleister Crowley (1875–1947), joined the HOGD in November 1898. A year later he had passed through all the stages of the Outer Order, and demanded initiation in the Second Order. Florence Farr and other senior members did not believe he was a suitable person, and refused him admittance to the Order. Crowley went to Mathers in Paris; Mathers initiated him and sent him back to London, apparently to wrest control of the whole HOGD from Farr and her colleagues. At about the same time Mathers revealed to the HOGD that the Fräulein Sprengel letters were fakes.

In the ensuing uproar, the London Temple expelled not just Crowley but Mathers – the last of the original founders – himself. Annie Horniman returned, and discovered the mess that Florence Farr had let everything drift into. W.B. Yeats took over the leadership of the Outer Order for a year.

Having stuck his neck out for Crowley – and lost his Order at least in part because of him – Mathers later fell out with him, and the two fought a vicious magical war for some time.

The HOGD split into several factions. Retaining the old Isis–Urania Temple and the old name (but changing Hermetic to Holy), A.E. Waite changed the emphasis of the HOGD from ritual magic to mystical Christianity. Those interested in continuing the HOGD's work in ritual magic formed a new Order, *Stella Matutina* (the Order of the Morning Star). A few who stuck with Mathers formed the *Alpha et Omega* Temple; Mathers, however, stayed in Paris until his death in 1918.

ALEISTER CROWLEY

Crowley (born Edward Alexander Crowley) went off to form the Order of the Silver Star, or *Argenteum Astrum* (A∴A∴), based on the hidden Third Order of the HOGD, in 1907. (The standard convention of Masonic and occult societies of the time was to use three dots between initials; for convenience this convention is not being followed in this book.) Over the next few years he published many of the secrets of the HOGD in his Order's magazine *The Equinox*. Crowley was obsessed with power and with sex; he must have been delighted in 1912 to be invited to head the British branch of the *Ordo Templi Orientis* (OTO), the Order of the Temple in the East. This gave him the title 'Supreme and Holy King of Ireland, Iona and All the Britains in the Sanctuary of the Gnosis'.

The OTO had been founded in 1906 by two German Freemasons who had connections with both the Rite of Memphis and Misraim (founded by a very influential but somewhat eccentric Freemason, John Yarker) and the German branch of the Theosophical Society. Probably picking up on ideas

167

of Paschal Beverly Randolph, who had in turn picked up teachings from Lévi and others, they believed that the hidden secret at the heart of Rosicrucianism and Freemasonry was sex-magic. (By the time R. Swinburne Clymer took over the *Fraternitas Rosae Crucis* the emphasis on Tantrism, or sex-magic, had been dropped.) As has already been noted on p. 157, H. Spencer Lewis's AMORC owes its origins to the OTO; this later gave ammunition to Clymer when the two men and their organizations fell out in court. Like the FRC, Lewis dropped sex-magic from his movement's teachings; AMORC today prefers to forget its early connection with the OTO.

It is commonly assumed that Crowley later became head of the entire OTO; this is not in fact the case, though at a conference in Germany in 1925 he claimed authority over the whole German Rosicrucian movement – a claim that was rejected by the leaders of the various German Orders. Some of them did, however, accept his authority as a high adept, and published translations of some of his works. Even this was too much for others, and German Rosicrucianism split into pro- and anti-Crowley factions.

In 1920 Crowley founded the Abbey of Thelema at Cefalu in Sicily. He took the name and the idea from Chapter 57 of the first book of François Rabelais' wonderfully scurrilous satire *The Histories of Gargantua and Pantagruel*, first published in 1532. This also provided his famous dictum, 'Do what thou wilt shall be the whole of the Law', which (probably largely because of Crowley's own licentious behaviour) is taken by most critics to be a recipe for licence. In fact, Rabelais had intended it to mean that those whose will was in line with God's will would naturally perform only virtuous actions, so no other Law was necessary. St Augustine had said much the same. Crowley believed that the Thelemic Age would take over from the Christian Age. Partly because of his strict upbringing by Plymouth Brethren parents, he was vehemently opposed to Christianity; in this, as well as in much else, he was at variance with the great majority of the esotericists covered in this book.

After various scandals, in 1923 Crowley was thrown out of Sicily. Although he wrote pro-German propaganda during the First World War, when he was living in the USA, Crowley was somehow later involved in the seedier side of espionage for MI6, the British Secret Intelligence Service. Through his membership and leadership of various esoteric societies, and through his intelligence work, Crowley had many influential connections, including his brother-in-law Gerald Kelly, who was later President of the Royal Academy, the MP Tom Driberg, and writers Denis Wheatley and Ian Fleming, in addition to those he knew through his brief membership of the HOGD.

In a curious aside, Crowley was a significant influence on L. Ron Hubbard, creator of the psychoanalytic system of Dianetics and founder of the controversial Church of Scientology. In 1945 Hubbard stayed for some time at the home of Jack Parsons, a rocket scientist and a senior member of the Los Angeles OTO. In a letter to Crowley, Parsons said that Hubbard was 'the most Thelemic person I have ever met and is in complete accord with our own principles'.[36] Parsons and Hubbard are said to have worked major sex-magic rituals with a 'scarlet woman' in an attempt to conceive a 'moonchild' – the antithesis of Christ – as first proposed by Crowley in his Book of the Law (1904) and fictionalized in his novel *Moonchild* (1929).

This account is challenged by the Church of Scientology, which claims that Hubbard was working as an undercover detective investigating black magic. However, several years after Crowley's death, in a lecture in Philadelphia in 1952, Hubbard described Crowley's writings as 'a trifle wild in spots but is a fascinating work in itself', and referred to Crowley himself as 'my very good friend'.[37]

Born in 1875, the year of Éliphas Lévi's death, Crowley believed he was a reincarnation of Lévi – and also of Cagliostro, John Dee's sidekick Edward Kelley, and the Borgia Pope Alexander VI. In his occult career he went as high as it is possible to go: in 1916 he was self-initiated to the grade of Magus, and in 1921 to the supreme level of Ipsissimus. Crowley celebrated excess, in sex, drink and drugs, and delighted in the media appellation 'the wickedest man in the world'. It did him little good; he died, in poverty and with few real friends, in 1947, leaving his unpleasant reputation as 'the Great Beast 666' behind him.

MODERN MYSTERY SCHOOLS

Sometimes known as Schools of Occult Science, most modern Mystery Schools can trace their origins, by one route or another, to the Hermetic Order of the Golden Dawn which, as has been seen, saw itself as the Rosicrucian Order of its day.

It could be said, with some justification, that A.E. Waite hijacked the HOGD, and that the HOGD's true successor was actually *Stella Matutina*, which continued until the mid-1930s. W.B. Yeats stayed with *Stella Matutina* until the early 1920s; other well-known names involved in the group included Dion Fortune, Israel Regardie and Constance Wilde, wife of Oscar Wilde. The teachings, rites and ceremonies of the Golden Dawn, as revealed by Israel Regardie between 1937 and 1940, were actually the teachings, rites and ceremonies of *Stella Matutina*, and it is from *Stella Matutina*, rather than from Waite's version of the HOGD, that most of today's esoteric societies have grown.[38] Waite's HOGD faded out in 1914; in 1916 he founded the

Fellowship of the Rosy Cross which, although it never had a large membership, included the mystical writer Evelyn Underhill and, for ten years, the esoteric novelist Charles Williams.

In 1922 Dion Fortune (born Violet Mary Firth, 1891–1946), inspired by *Stella Matutina*, founded the Christian Mystic Lodge of the Theosophical Society. After a disagreement with Mathers's widow, she renamed this the Fraternity of the Inner Light, and set it up as a separate order in 1928; it later became the Society of the Inner Light.

The Society of the Inner Light today bases its teachings mainly on Dion Fortune's books *The Mystical Qabalah* and *Cosmic Doctrine*, and also recommends her *Esoteric Orders and their Work, The Training and Work of an Initiate, Practical Occultism in Daily Life*, and *Sane Occultism*. It lays most emphasis on the Cabala, the Bible, and the mythology of the British Isles. From its publicly-available literature, it seems to have three main differences from most other esoteric schools: it doesn't appear to study Tarot; it specifically will not allow gay, lesbian or bisexual members; and it lays an exceptional emphasis on members being

> Raised with experience in the British tradition; i.e. fairy tales, nursery rhymes, and folk stories; full knowledge of the legends and myths of our history i.e. heroes; Alfred, Arthur, Drake, Nelson, saints and sages; George, David, Patrick, Shakespeare, at al.; Power centres; Iona, Glastonbury, St. Albans, Canterbury and Walsingham.[39]

This emphasis on 'Britishness' might have some connection with the claims of the then Fraternity of the Inner Light to have worked on the spiritual/psychic plane in 1940 to protect Britain against German invasion.

At least two other esoteric societies have sprung from the Society of the Inner Light. The Servants of the Light was established in 1972 in Jersey by former Society of the Inner Light member W.E. Butler (1898–1978), as a 'school of occult science'. Although its deepest teachings are still secret, both Butler and its present director Dolores Ashcroft-Nowicki have published several books about ritual magic, and the latter has designed an esoteric Tarot pack, based on Servants of the Light teachings and highlighting many of the Golden Dawn traditions which have been muddied in various other packs.

The more recent London Group was also founded by a former member of the Society of the Inner Light. Yet another former member has written several very sound books on both the history of magic, and the spiritual quest, under the name of Gareth Knight; he has also designed a Tarot pack.

Those are all British-based societies. In the USA, Builders of the Adytum (BOTA) is an esoteric society founded in the early 1920s by a former member of the Chicago branch of the Hermetic Order of the Golden Dawn, Paul Foster Case (1884–1954), who is widely accepted as one of the most thoughtful authorities on both Tarot and Cabala. Like most modern esoteric schools, BOTA stresses that, although it is openly offering teaching which was formerly restricted to a few, it is not a quick and easy path: 'your sincerity, your desire, and your willingness to work will be the sole measure of your accomplishment ... For you to be successful in our Work, your personal goals must correspond to those of the Order: personal enlightenment, self-transmutation, and service to Life.'[40]

BOTA aims to help seekers gain 'a higher state of conscious awareness' through study of Cabala, Tarot, spiritual Alchemy and esoteric Astrology; it stresses that it doesn't mean their common trivialized expressions: 'these Hermetic arts and sciences are by no means deluded imaginings or ignorant superstitions that some persons suppose them to be.' For associate members, this is by correspondence course; there is a more advanced ritual group called a Pronaos into which members might qualify to be initiated 'after completing certain lessons and demonstrating harmonious fraternal qualities'.

BOTA's introductory booklet ends with a statement which shows the heredity of Gnosticism, Rosicrucianism and the HOGD: 'The way to illumination now stands open before you. Look well within yourself and may the Light of Divine Understanding guide you. L.V.X.' The Order of the Golden Dawn, following the early seventeenth-century Rosicrucians, used 'L.V.X.' to represent *Lux*, the divine light; it was believed significant that the three letters can all be found within the shape of the Cross.

Most of these groups emphasize the value of study – of Cabala, of Tarot, of the Grail romances, of the teachings of esoteric authorities through the ages – and, like the *Lectorium Rosicrucianum*, emphasize in one way or another the recognition (*gnosis*) of God within, and the mystical union of man and God.

Rudolf Steiner's Anthroposophical Society, an offshoot of the Theosophical movement founded in 1913, is another approach to the same idea, but with a greater emphasis than most present-day esoteric societies on linking science and religion; in this, Steiner was probably closer to the original Rosicrucians. Steiner was a member for a while of the Rite of Memphis and Misraim, and might also briefly have been a member of the German OTO.

It is thought that Steiner took the name Anthroposophy from the title of a book by the Rosicrucian Thomas Vaughan, *Anthroposophia Teomagica*, published in 1650. Vaughan, twin brother of the metaphysical poet Henry Vaughan, had been a priest and a scholar of medicine and alchemy.

While Theosophy is largely Eastern-orientated, Anthroposophy is closer to esoteric Christianity; its study-groups were popular for many years among intellectual, free-thinking clergy, and its spiritual ideas still have an influence in esoteric Christian circles. To most people, however, through its Waldorf Schools it is known more for its reforming ideas in education, particularly of mentally and physically handicapped children. In this, too, it holds to the original Rosicrucian ideal of benefiting humanity at large; it is perhaps achieving this more than most of the other Esoteric movements put together.

Steiner also, as has been seen, influenced Max Heindel's Rosicrucian Fellowship. It is an occult principle that everything is connected to everything else; this is certainly the case with esoteric societies.

Aleister Crowley's development of the HOGD and *Ordo Templi Orientis* teachings has also spawned a number of successors, including the deliberately misspelled Thee Temple Ov Psychick Youth, or TOPY, which has branches in England, Germany, Sweden and the USA. Such groups often teach and practise Thelemic Magic – basically sex-magic – and for obvious reasons keep themselves fairly well hidden. According to esoteric authority Richard Cavendish, the 'k' in Crowley's spelling of Magick stands for *kteis*, Greek for the female genitals.[41]

Other groups with links to the Crowleyan side of the esoteric include the Nu–Isis Lodge, the Order of Maat, the Knights of the Solar Cross and the International Order of Chivalry, Solar Tradition; the last of which, under the name Order of the Solar Temple, came into prominence in 1994 and 1995 when large numbers of its members committed mass suicide and/or were murdered by its leaders.

This book throughout has shown the close connection between secret societies and esoteric religion. There is also a lot of overlap between small secretive societies and small alternative religious movements, often known as sects or cults, especially some of those with a New Age emphasis. To outsiders their beliefs sometimes seem literally incredible, but it has long been observed that people will believe anything if it's marketed in the right way. Some of the stranger movements involve magic, some sex, some drugs. The more outlandish the beliefs, and the more demanding the guru-figure, the more strongly, it seems, the members commit themselves to the movement. Cynics see them all simply as a means of exerting power and making a lot of money.

As a deliberate exercise to test people's gullibility, in 1969 an Indian journalist placed an advertisement in the *Village Voice* in Greenwich Village, setting himself up as a guru; he was astonished, and a little frightened, at how quickly he gathered disciples.[42] A little more mischievously, the authors of a 1965 book on the supernatural, intrigued and amused at the weird beliefs of some of the movements they had examined, mentioned in passing

> the Free Union for Creative Karma, of Los Angeles, which holds as a
> basic tenet the 'enabling' quality of sensuality freed from outer restraint
> but disciplined from within – a quality that can apparently release man
> from the karmic wheel of action/reaction.

They were more than a little bemused to discover some years later, when one of them visited Los Angeles, that the cult they had invented as a joke in their book now actually existed.[43]

The 'dawning of the Age of Aquarius' was under way long before the musical *Hair!* brought it to a wider attention. Whether in a 'secret society' or in some form of guru, seekers will always find their seers; today the difficulty is that of choosing among them. America especially proliferates in mail-order enlightenment. Some, including most of the Rosicrucian societies and Golden Dawn offshoots, have an esoteric pedigree; others are individual people wanting to share their personal vision.

The secret knowledge, the hidden teachings, the revelation now published for the benefit of the world, is not identical in every case. The teachings themselves might be different, or the way of approaching them, or the language used to describe them. Some emphasize ritual, others quiet contemplation, others a more intellectual approach. But all, in one way or another, teach a path to *gnosis*: not just knowledge, but recognition, realization, acceptance, understanding, the apprehension of the divine.

A brief mention of two quite different examples of organizations founded on 'one man's teachings' will suffice to illustrate this. The first is British, the second American.

The Realization System describes itself as 'practical psychology', and is very much in the mould of personal development or self-help courses – what Norman Vincent Peale called the power of positive thinking. Indeed, its publisher says, 'We are a mail-order company specialising in the sale of semi-educational, self-improvement books and courses on a range of subjects';[44] these include effective speaking, rapid reading, and so on. As an organization it is only very peripherally connected to the subject of this book, but the connection is valid.

The author of the Realization System was Daniel A. Simmons, a member of the Society for Psychical Research at the same time as was Sir Arthur Conan Doyle. The introduction to the course speaks of 'a new conception of the human mind and of the relation of its deeper phases to the Creative Intelligence and a new and better conception of its marvellous hidden powers'; it describes its teachings as 'the liberating truth'; 'the teachings of the System come like a blaze of all-illuminating light, revealing the open gate to the Realm of Realization'.[45]

Although the course as a whole is couched largely in psychological rather than spiritual terms, the similarity to the spiritual enlightenment of *gnosis* is unmistakable.

The Fellowship Press in Indiana, USA, exists to publish 'the books of one person only, William Dudley Pelley. There is no church, nor do we sponsor organised study groups, although we are pleased to supply books for those that do. While the books we publish are metaphysical and philosophical, which Mr Pelley called collectively "Soulcraft", we are not concerned with any kind of ritual or occult practices.'[46]

But the booklets and fliers from the Fellowship Press show the similarity to other esoteric teachings:

'Religion' and 'Science', in short, are beginning to be recognized as parts of the same Truth, of the same Reality, as indeed they must be. The books . . . are not attempting to supplant Christian teachings. They are instead trying to separate out of them the superstitious dogma accumulated over the centuries, and make clear many of the allegories and enigmas of ancient scripture. Over all, they present a working philosophy of what Life is all about, why you are in it, what the purposes are behind adversity, what goals you are achieving, and can achieve, or which you have not yet dared to dream . . .

As Christ Jesus was divine, so are all men divine in Original Essence, gaining to Holy Stature by illuminations of Wisdom acquired of material experience.

Again, the comparisons are unmistakable.

The *Soulcraft Scripts* fill twelve large volumes at $20 each. The flier for *Excerpts from the Soulcraft Scripts*, four smaller volumes at $28 for the set, reads, 'If your time is limited, you need this shorter road to the Ancient Wisdom!'

The older adepts might have disapproved, but they weren't living in late twentieth-century America.

ESOTERIC TAROT

In recent years a large number of Tarot packs have come out of some of these esoteric movements.

How close to Golden Dawn teachings are the various packs which have appeared from former members? For example, Case and Waite both show the Lovers card as a naked woman and man standing beneath an angel with outstretched arms. The traditional Marseille design shows a man standing between two women; it symbolizes the hard choice between sensuality and spirituality, rather than the romantic love now usually associated with this card.

The original Golden Dawn Lovers card, as described in the HOGD teachings published by Regardie, is quite different again: it shows a scene from Greek mythology. 'Andromeda is shown manacled to a rock, the dragon rising from the waters at her feet. Perseus is depicted flying through the air to her assistance, with unsheathed sword.'[47] Not only the picture, but the meaning is quite different. The dragon represents fear, and the waters stagnation; Perseus's sword is 'striking off the fetters of habit and materialism'. The descriptions of several of the other cards – in particular, the Fool and the Wheel of Fortune – are also substantially different from those of Waite and Case. These designs, as described, can be seen in the Golden Dawn Tarot, created by Robert Wang, and based on Regardie's own hand-drawn pack.

The usual theory for the discrepancy is that Waite and Case were both continuing to conceal some of the deeper Golden Dawn secrets; a more prosaic explanation could be that Regardie's book describes the *Stella Matutina* designs, and that these might actually have been different from Moina Mathers's original Golden Dawn designs, remembering that Waite was a member of the original HOGD, not, as Regardie was, of *Stella Matutina*. An alternative explanation is that Waite's later, more mystical version of the HOGD might have changed some of the designs from Mathers's more magic-orientated original.

Everybody borrowed from everybody else; everybody disagreed with everybody else; thus were the present-day symbolic interpretations of Tarot cards formulated.

Aleister Crowley was also, if only briefly, a member of the original HOGD; his dismissal from it was one of the causes of its fragmentation. His Thoth Tarot (painted to his direction by Lady Frieda Harris), quite apart from renaming many of the cards, is radically different from any of the other HOGD-inspired packs; his esoteric ideas had moved on considerably from those of the HOGD.

The designs of *Le Tarot Symbolique Maçonnique*, the Masonic Symbolic Tarot, are also very different in many ways, though more readily recognizable than Crowley's. Unusually the designer and the artist are the same person, Jean Beauchard; he has incorporated many aspects not just of Freemasonry but of Cabala into his designs, which have a strongly geometric basis. According to Beauchard, in a rather awkward translation,

> Tarot and Freemasonry carry similar traditional thought and participate as well in the evolution of the spirit of humanity of which they are amongst the driving motors. Their end thought actually is identical: Freemasonry, a philosophical school in its intrinsic nature, has as its goal the research and the comprehension of the individual himself and of his relationship with the Universe . . . The Tarot, as far as it is concerned, is primarily a revealer and a means of investigation. The reflection which the Tarot proposes by the aid of the signs and their possible associations, brings the keys to the individual for the understanding of his proper self.[48]

The Masonic Tarot Lover card (not Lovers, as in most packs) strongly emphasizes the idea of choice between the sensual and the spiritual, the mundane and the esoteric.

The Servants of the Light (SOL) Tarot, although in some cards showing boldly-drawn reinterpretations of the designs, is generally much closer to Waite and Case than it is to the Regardie/Golden Dawn version; where there are differences between Waite and Case, it follows Case.

(Interestingly, although the Lovers card in this pack, as in Crowley's pack, is closer to Waite and Case than it is to either Regardie or the Marseille, the interpretation of the card in both SOL and Crowley stresses another concept, openness to inspiration.)

The SOL pack was painted by two different artists to designs by Dolores Ashcroft-Nowicki, director of Servants of the Light, which was founded by W.E. Butler, a former member of the Society of the Inner Light, which had been founded by Dion Fortune, a former member of *Stella Matutina*, which was a continuation of the Hermetic Order of the Golden Dawn. Recent paths of esoteric succession are at least well-documented.

The topic of Tarot will be taken up once more at the end of this book (see chapter six), to suggest that its development might be even more closely linked to the continuance of esoteric thought than is normally realized.

CHAPTER FIVE

SECRET SOCIETY –
THE DARK SIDE

NOT ALL secret societies have esoteric roots, and not all secrecy is within secret societies. In this chapter secrecy will be treated in three quite different areas: crime, politics and government. Secret societies have been deeply involved in nationalist movements and their opponents; the IRA and the Orange Orders in Northern Ireland are obvious examples, as were the Boers, from whom apartheid eventually arose in South Africa. The chapter also has a discussion of the nationalist roots of two of the most visible present-day criminal organizations. First, however, a brief look at the involvement of secret societies in European politics.

FREEMASONRY AND REVOLUTIONS

In a previous chapter a link was noted – however slight, and however romantically idealized – between some Scottish and French Freemasons and the Jacobites. That revolution failed; but two others succeeded, with the active involvement of individual Freemasons: in America and in France. Ironically, in view of their oaths of secrecy about their own affairs, Freemasons tended to be in favour of freedom of speech, along with the associated freedoms of religion and assembly. Like the Rosicrucians they were, at least initially, anti-Catholic; many were also anti-monarchy.

Freemasons, in fact, were in the forefront of secular republicanism in the eighteenth century.

It should be emphasized that there is no real evidence (despite the efforts of conspiracy theorists) of any organized plotting by Freemasonry or Rosicrucianism as organizations, nor even by individual Lodges of Freemasons or Rosicrucians, to turn the world upside down. It was far more the case that freethinking intellectuals in different countries did not exist in a vacuum; they were aware of the development of ideas by other freethinkers, even on the other side of the world. And some, though by no means all, of these individuals were Freemasons or Rosicrucians of one sort or another, or belonged to other societies.

The possible involvement of Freemasons and other esotericists in the birth of the United States has already been considered in chapter two of this book; in a quite different way, they were also influential in France.

Denis Diderot, leader of the French Encyclopædists, was a Freemason; so were several of his colleagues including, towards the end of his life, Voltaire (François-Marie Arouet). The *Encyclopædia*, which published its first volume in 1751, could justifiably be called the intellectual stimulus for the French Revolution; it emphasized independent thought, and the brotherhood of men; it was soon banned by the authorities, towards the end of what is now called the *ancien régime*.

It is undoubtedly true that several men who were either Freemasons or who were strongly sympathetic to Freemasonry were involved in the early days of the French Revolution. By the time of the Terrors, however, they were as likely to meet Madame la Guillotine as was anyone else.

When things settled down after the Revolution, Freemasonry became socially respectable and officially acceptable again. With Reason the new religion, French Freemasonry made one change to its statutes which still divides it from English-based Freemasonry: it scrapped the membership requirement of belief in God. The Grand Orient Freemasonry of France – which, like English and Scottish Masonry, soon spread its influence abroad – was thus seen as openly atheistic and antagonistic to the Roman Catholic Church. The Carbonari, a nineteenth-century Italian secret society with

A Belgian Grand Orient Masonic medal from 1832
(Robert Macoy, *General History, Cyclopedia and Dictionary
of Freemasonry*, 1850)

strong links to Freemasonry, and dedicated to a united (and secular) Italy, was also opposed to the power of the Church.

Between them, the Grand Orient and the Carbonari were directly responsible for the attitude of the Vatican to Freemasonry, which to this day it regards as an ungodly and politically subversive organization. The United Grand Lodge of England has long protested that its original version of Freemasonry is something quite different, but to no avail; the Vatican looks out of the window and sees Grand Orient Masonry, and declares that if a Catholic becomes a Mason, he has automatically excommunicated himself. (Apparently, by the 1990s, many individual Catholics treat this prohibition in much the same way as they do the Church's stance on birth control; they come to their own decision in the light of their own conscience.)

According to Masonic scholar John Hamill, a number of senior Grand Orient members recently 'broke away and re-established Italian Freemasonry on British lines as the Regular Grand Lodge of Italy, which is now recognized by the British Grand Lodges'.[1] It remains to be seen whether this move will affect the Vatican's opinion of Freemasonry.

The Roman Catholic Church is not fond of neo-Templar Orders either. Bernard-Raymond Fabré-Palaprat, founder of the Order of the Temple (see p. 181), also founded the Johannite Church in the early nineteenth century. Like the various Liberal Catholic and Liberal Orthodox Churches linked to Theosophical, Rosicrucian and some neo-Templar movements, this had clergy who had received irregular but valid ordination by successors to renegade Catholic or Orthodox bishops, the *soi-disant* Wandering Bishops. Apostolic succession continues even if the consecrating bishop has been excommunicated. Though they might wish it otherwise, in the eyes of Rome the priests and bishops of these unorthodox Christian Churches have technically been validly (though illegally) ordained and consecrated. Luc Jouret, leader of the Order of the Solar Temple (see p. 181), was an ordained priest in one such French independent Church.

It can be said with some justification that Freemasonry in Britain has always been more of an Establishment organization, and that on the Continent it has always been more revolutionary, both socially and politically; this is probably a result of the differing social and political environments in Britain and on the Continent, rather than stemming from Freemasonry itself. Freemasonry has been banned by Fascist governments in Germany, Italy and Spain, and by Communist governments in Central and Eastern Europe. Britain got its own Revolution out of the way in the mid-seventeenth century, and has been a relatively stable democracy ever since; there has been no need for British Freemasonry to be politically subversive.

OCCULT SOCIETIES AND NAZISM

Much has been written on Germany's National Socialist (Nazi) Party's involvement with the occult; a lot of this is misconceived pseudo-scholarship with the aim of painting an intellectual magical background to Nazism or, alternatively, of blackening the occult in general through guilt by association. The actual relationship was both complex and confused; it is only possible to give the bare bones of it here.

Nazism, like many parties and rulers before and since, used whatever it could to grant itself both intellectual and social credibility, and popular support. Thus it drew on the genetic theories of Mendel, the philosophy of Nietzsche and the music of Wagner; thus it also latched onto the various Templar and Teutonic Orders of knights. Through them it realized the importance of symbolism for speaking straight to the heart; it took the existing symbols of the swastika and the *sig* rune and adapted them for its own use.

According to modern Odinist John Yeowell, 'The Nazi party itself appropriated many of the outward symbols and trappings of heathenism [i.e. the old Norse/Germanic religion] in order to emphasise their claims to be the true inheritors of ancient German traditions and virtues and to harness the spiritual yearnings of the German people.'[2]

The Germanic/Nordic mythological emphasis came largely from Guido von List (1848–1918; the 'von' was a spurious affectation); he created a new version of the Runic *Futhark* or alphabet known as the Armanen system, about which Rune expert Bernard King says 'it forms the basis of most Nazi rune-lore and is as suspect in its origins as it is in its applications'.[3]

The *Ordo Novi Templi*, or Order of New Templars was founded in 1907 by Jorg Lanz von Liebenfels (1874–1954), who had much the same idea as the Chevalier Ramsay and Baron von Hund in the eighteenth century, but specifically applied to Germany and extreme right-wing German nationalism. Similar ideas surfaced in the Germanen Order from 1912 and the Thule Society from 1918, with even more extreme versions of the same thing. They believed in the purity of the German blood, and were rabidly anti-Semitic. Although they were opposed to Freemasonry, which they saw as a Jewish conspiracy, they adopted many Masonic elements in their organization and ritual.

It seems to have been these Orders which first made use of the swastika in German nationalism; until then it had been an ancient and powerful religious symbol of the sun and of the continuing cycle of life.

The Thule Society was closely connected with – and, indeed, funded – a very minor right-wing political party, the German Workers Party; Adolf Hitler joined this in 1919, took control, changed its name to the National Socialist German Workers Party – and the rest is history.

Although it is indisputable that Hitler based much of the mythos, mystique and method of the Nazi Party on such societies, he later banned all secret societies, including Freemasonry; he had taken what he needed from them, and did not want any competition. The Party itself was to be the religion of the German people. The tremendous importance given to the swastika flag, the greeting with the Nazi salute, the undisguised ritualism of the great rallies, all were religious in their appeal to the people.

The structure of Nazism was itself built on the structure of secret societies. Membership of the Party was open to all who were worthy to join, but it was at the same time a great honour to be allowed to join. Only the elect could join the inner Party, the SS, which was consciously modelled on (an interpretation of) the Knights Templar and other élite Orders, which used occult symbolism in its regalia, and which built its headquarters in the form of a Grail castle.

Nazism created a new symbolism of right-wing politics by appropriating and redefining existing symbols, and in doing so changed, perhaps for ever, our perception of those symbols. The swastika now 'means' anti-Semitism, hatred, persecution and genocide. The *sig* rune now 'means' fear. Modern followers of the old Northern religion, whether they call themselves heathens, Odinists or Asatru, constantly have to fight off the outside perception that they are right-wing; their situation is not helped by the fact that neo-Nazi groups still make use of this symbolism.

***

There are also still secret societies with links back to the *Ordo Novi Templi*, and also to an earlier non-Masonic Order of the Temple founded by Bernard-Raymond Fabré-Palaprat in 1805. Through a complex line of succession which included the Sovereign and Military Order of the Temple of Jerusalem (founded in Belgium in 1932), the Sovereign Order of the Solar Temple (1950s) and an AMORC-offshoot, the Renewed Order of the Temple (*c.* 1970; these last two were both French), Fabré-Palaprat's Order eventually gave birth to the ill-fated Order of the Solar Temple in the late 1980s.

According to one academic researcher the leader of the Order of the Solar Temple, Luc Jouret, was involved with various other dubious neo-Templar Orders 'long enough to enter in the orbit of influence of groups whose ties with the French SAC, with the Italian P2 Lodge (see p. 188) and with several countries' secret services seem probable in view of court and parliamentary findings'. (SAC, *Service d'Action Civique*, is 'a private French right-wing organisation with ties to the Gaullist party, halfway between a private secret service and a parallel police'.)[4]

Although both Freemasonry *per se* and the more legitimate and open neo-Templar societies are social and/or esoteric religious organizations which are no more right-wing, no more criminal and no more dangerous than any of the other secret societies in this book, there is well-documented evidence that many of the smaller and more secretive organizations are – politically, economically, socially and racially – extremely right-wing. There are identifiable links between the Mafia and P2, and certain small neo-Templar, pseudo-Rosicrucian, Theosophy-offshoot and Masonic-related organizations. According to the editors of *Open Eye* magazine, ultra-right-wing, anti-Semitic neo-Templar groups are also now infiltrating the New Age movement.⁵

Those who wish to construct conspiracy theories have plenty of raw material to draw on.

THE KU KLUX KLAN

The Ku Klux Klan, known for its lynchings of black people in the southern American states, began as a specifically Christian alternative movement to Freemasonry. Its name came from *kuklos*, Greek for 'circle', with the Scottish word 'clan' to emphasize the ideal of brotherhood. Its rituals, initiation ceremonies and oaths were borrowed and adapted from Masonry, but its aims, from the start, were quite different.

True, it pledged mutual aid to its members, and stressed the concept of brotherhood, but its initial impetus was largely political. In the last third of the nineteenth century, the later right–left differentiation between the Republican and Democratic parties was effectively the other way around; southern Democrats still supported slavery, while the northern Republicans held more democratic beliefs. The agricultural southern states were poor, and felt oppressed by the industrial north. The outcome of the Civil War (1861–65) emphasized the differences; the abolition of slavery in 1863 aggravated Southern feelings. Not only were they defeated in battle; not only were they poor; not only were they dominated and oppressed by the north; not only were corrupt northern businessmen – carpetbaggers – taking advantage of their depressed condition; but the blacks were free and uncontrolled, running wild, threatening the honour and purity of white Christian women and girls.

The fact that there were few if any actual cases of black men raping white women was irrelevant.

The KKK was founded by Nathan Bedford Forrest, a Confederate Army general. It was opposed not just to the freedom of blacks, but to northerners and Republicans. Effectively, it was still fighting the Civil War.

In 1865 the first southern whites donned robes and Hallowe'en-type masks, and rode around pretending to be ghosts, terrorizing blacks. The idea spread through the southern states like wildfire; within three years Forrest claimed half a million followers, members of the KKK and of several other organizations. It was very quickly out of the control of Forrest or anyone else. Anyone who wanted to commit a robbery, rape or murder donned a hooded cloak first. Blacks were frankly terrified, and with good reason; but any acts of defence or retaliation on their part simply served to intensify (and worse, to 'justify') the attacks on them.

In 1869 Forrest realized just how little control he had over the KKK when he ordered the Klansmen to disband, and was ignored. The 'Invisible Empire' he had established across the southern states had taken hold.

After Forrest's departure, any semblance of military discipline vanished. Klan leaders in different states adapted the rituals and oaths, emphasizing the idea of ghosts and ghoulies. For those taking part, largely the downtrodden poor, it was welcome fun, an escape from the depression which ruled their daily lives. Murders, shootings, lynchings and rapes continued. American Masonry, disgusted by the Klan and all its workings, and perhaps fearing the possibility of guilt through association because of the original borrowings from Freemasonry, condemned the KKK absolutely.

The Federal government, now under the presidency of General Ulysses S. Grant, the northern commander at the end of the Civil War, cracked down. In 1870 the 15th Amendment was ratified; this granted the vote to citizens, regardless of race. This was followed in 1875 by the Civil Rights Act, which gave blacks the right to serve on juries. KKK members suddenly found themselves being jailed for their offences. Order, albeit racist order from a 1990s perspective, was restored, and the Klan died down for a few years.

It was revived in 1915 in Alabama by William Joseph Simmons. Where the earlier Klan had in practice basically been an excuse for louts to commit crimes, Simmons's organization was intended to be more of a fraternal secret society along the lines of the Freemasons, of which (as well as of several other Orders) Simmons was a member. He developed the rituals, initiating new members by dubbing them Knights with a naked sword. The Bible was present and, of course, the American flag; this was both a Christian and an intensely patriotic society.

Five years later Simmons was sidelined by two public relations experts, Edward Young Clarke and his mistress Elizabeth Tyler. They let Simmons remain as Grand Wizard, but took over the organization of the Klan. Two years after that, having used their expertise in publicity and organization to kick-start the KKK as a powerful force, they in turn were ousted by Hiram Wesley Evans.

The main target was still blacks, but Jews, Catholics and other un-desirables had replaced the Republicans and northerners as additional objects of hate. The Klan was White Anglo-Saxon Protestant, and proud of it. The membership was still largely poor working-class men, blue-collar red-necks who wanted targets on which to turn their hatred, but now it had influence.

By the mid-1920s the Klan was sufficiently well organized and powerful to have some four million members, and to have US senators and state governors under its control. Small-town America was flexing its muscles. The burning cross and the Bible were a terrifyingly potent combination. Immorality was rooted out wherever it could be found, or invented. KKK members might be just as immoral themselves, but the hood protected them. They maintained fear by lynchings and torture; they maintained control of small towns by openly boycotting businesses which dared to oppose them.

Quite suddenly it all fell apart again. The main cause was the trial of David C. Stephenson, Grand Dragon of Indiana, for raping, mutilating and murdering a black girl. Jailed for life, Stephenson released a testimony detailing corruption and naming names including, among others, a sheriff, a mayor, a congressman, and a governor. Ordinary Southerners had had enough, and left the Klan in droves; by 1927 membership had plummetted to 350,000. The KKK broke up completely during the Second World War, only to be reborn immediately after the war with the aim, once again, of keeping blacks in their place.

This time the authorities were more prepared for it. There were still murders, bombings and tortures, but from the White House to individual state government to local communities, opposition to the Klan became apparent. The KKK was a spent force. It still fought vehemently against the growing power of blacks, but the Civil Rights movement of the 1960s, after some bloody battles, caught the popular imagination, and had the stronger moral voice.

The Ku Klux Klan still exists, but it is now very small, and it no longer has any real power. Its views, however, have lingered on. 'Liberal' is a dirty word in the southern states; the 1960s are viewed with horror and disgust. Janice Ian's song 'Society's Child' in 1966 and Jeannie C. Riley's 'Harper Valley PTA' in 1968 were banned by radio stations in the south; 'Society's Child', about a white girl going out with a black boy, 'engendered a steady stream of racist correspondence and outright death threats . . . we got so much virulent hate mail from the South'.[6] Both songs portrayed small-town America just a little too accurately for comfort. Racism and intolerance were alive and well in the late 1960s, and still are today in the 1990s.

The small-town red-neck mentality found two new avenues, each with God on its side: one, the 'Moral Majority', in the 1990s calling itself the Christian Right, which has schoolteachers sacked for teaching evolution, and which is powerful enough to back a candidate for the Republican presidential nomination, just as the Klan did at its height in 1924; and the other: assorted militia or survivalist groups – the extreme end of the American gun lobby – who claim to be more patriotic than Capitol Hill, and will blow up government buildings to prove it. For the more extreme Bible-Belt Americans, God, the gun and the flag seem to be almost equal in sacredness.

Today's red-necks often wear white collars, and don't wear pointed hoods, but they still have 'an autocratic impulse to impose one's values on others ... an élite conviction of one's own superiority ... a sense of self-righteousness, sanctimoniousness and complacency'.[7]

This is Baigent, Leigh and Lincoln speaking of American Fundamentalism. The similarity to the Ku Klux Klan becomes even stronger as they continue:

> Fundamentalism rests not on the acknowledged Christian virtues of charity, forgiveness and understanding, but on war – on imaginary epic conflict between the self-styled 'forces of God' and those of His adversary. Reality is reduced to a simple matter of 'us' and 'them'. The creed defines itself by virtue of its opposite, defines its adherents by everything and everyone that they are not. Whatever seems opposed to certain basic tenets – not of Jesus usually, but of the congregation and its own idiosyncratic interpretations of scripture – is, ipso facto, damned.

These are today's descendants of 'those old sectarians who substituted intolerance for charity, persecution for friendship, and did not love God because they hated their neighbours'.[8]

The survivalist militia groups are secret societies; it's difficult to tell how many there are, or how many members they have, or what their true agenda is. The 'Christian Right' are out in the open, but again, their numbers, and their true agenda, are difficult to assess. But from their speech and actions, it is clear that they wish to restrict the actions, speech and beliefs of others.

Many observers have described such Fundamentalism, of whatever faith, as religious fascism. It is *not* being suggested here that all Fundamentalists are fascists. Many, probably the overwhelming majority of Fundamentalists within Christianity, Islam and other religions, are sincere, honest, good people with a deep and devout belief in God. They, like everyone else, are entitled to their beliefs. But when their beliefs become an 'ism' which attempts to deprive others of their own right to freedom of belief and freedom of expression, *then* one needs to worry. The spirit of the KKK lives on.

A tiny minority can have a disproportionate effect on the wider majority of society. This is precisely the same fear that is often expressed about secret societies.

THE MAFIA

The word 'mafia' is often used today to mean a powerful self-perpetuating clique, which needn't be Italian, or even criminal – in other words, loosely, a cabal or secret society. The infamous criminal organization of the Mafia is little more than a century old, though its roots can be traced back over 500 years, perhaps even 700 years.

In its birthplace, Sicily, the Mafia is known as *onorata società*, the Honoured Society. Sicily has had its fair share of foreign rulers over the centuries, including the Arabs, the Normans and the Spaniards. Although some sources say that the word *mafia* is of nineteenth-century origin, and is Sicilian dialect for 'swank, swagger or bluster', others suggest that it is derived from the Arabic for 'place of refuge'; certainly, the native Sicilians were often in need of such. Their stronger members fought against the invaders; they protected the defenceless against foreign domination. They were bandits and terrorists, but generally they were on the side of their own people. They were opposed to the imposition of the rule of law, and were a thorn in the side of anyone trying to enforce the law, avenging what they saw (probably quite rightly) as wrongs against the oppressed people.

This changed in the mid- to late nineteenth century. The Mafia had become strong enough that no ruler of Sicily could enforce the law without their active cooperation; under Garibaldi's ostensible rule, it was the Mafia who actually ran the country. They were employed by absentee landlords to manage their landed estates, the *latifundia*. Having power at last, even though only semi-official power, they behaved just like any other rulers of Sicily, imposing their rule often brutally on the people they had formerly protected. It's easier to collect taxes and rents when you have a gun in your hand.

Much of the immigration to North America in the late nineteenth and early twentieth centuries was of European peasants who, for a variety of social and political reasons, were starving in their home countries, or who were forced off their own lands. The stories of the Irish potato famine and the forcible displacement of Scottish crofters are well known. Much the same happened in Sicily and the Italian mainland: social changes forced the peasants out. When hundreds of thousands of Sicilians – some say as many as a million – emigrated to the USA, the Mafia moved with them.

The basis of Mafia organization is the family. Countless films, and almost as many news stories of court cases, both showing judges and witnesses gunned down in the streets, have made us aware of the godfathers, the heads of these families, whose word is absolute law. A Mafia family is not a normal nuclear family, and hardly even a sociologically-standard extended family; it is far more like a Scottish clan, with the godfather, the *capo* or head, as the clan chief. Whether family members would willingly die for him (as for the leaders of the Assassins) is doubtful; but they would certainly kill for him, for the honour of the family.

For decades the Mafia families, governed from Sicily, ran organized crime in American cities, particularly Chicago and New York: extortion, protection rackets, bootlegging, drugs, gambling and prostitution. They were powerful enough to buy off many police chiefs and local politicians. From their point of view, they kept crime under control; independent petty criminals were not tolerated. The Mafia policed their own territory; their own name for themselves, *Cosa Nostra*, means 'Our Affair'. Mafia bosses seemed genuinely offended when anyone had the temerity to arrest them.

This is the popular image of the twentieth-century Mafia; many commentators paint it as largely fictional. According to Professor Maldwyn A. Jones, 'most of the Mafia stereotype is based on misconception or hearsay. There is no proof that the highly organised international conspiracy in which many people believed has ever existed.'[9] The Mafia and the equally infamous Black Hand Gang, he suggests, were either labels adopted by gangsters of Sicilian or wider Italian descent to reinforce their regime of terror, or labels applied to them by the sensation-hungry media; each reinforced the other. The myth of the Mafia was largely a product of red-neck American dislike, distrust and persecution of Italian immigrants (compare the Ku Klux Klan on p. 183).

When a number of elderly 'godfathers' were arrested in March 1996, their defence attorney said that they weren't godfathers but grandfathers; what is more, he would prove not only that they were not *mafiosi*, but that the Mafia did not exist in America.

This may, technically, be more or less accurate. In the early 1930s a group of American-born gangsters calling themselves *Unione Siciliana* killed off many of the old family leaders and took control of much of the organized crime. Certainly the idea of looking after the downtrodden, part of the ethos of the original Sicilian Mafia, no longer seemed to be a part of American 'Mafia' activities. On the other hand the inviolable code of silence, the *Omertà*, is still strong; the few who have broken it have generally not lasted long.

Such an oath of silence about the membership, the activities and the secrets of the organization is common to most secret societies including, of course, Freemasonry. There is an interesting and more specific parallel in that both members of the Mafia and Master Masons swear to respect the chastity of the wives, sisters and daughters of other members. However different they are in other ways, both movements have a strong sense of internal honour and, within their own terms, of moral rightness; both look after their own; and both, more pragmatically, would wish to avoid the internal dissension that such behaviour would inevitably bring. It is going too far, though, to follow the anti-Masonic writer Martin Short's suggestion that 'the similarity in their oaths makes one wonder if both organisations have a common ancestry.'[10] There is no evidence for such an idea, and much evidence against it, in both the nature and the history of the two organizations. P2, which is treated next, is a special case.

In Sicily itself, and in Italy in general, the Mafia is alive and well and still powerful, despite periodic attempts to destroy it. In 1926 Mussolini's Fascists began a campaign, which was very nearly successful, to wipe out the Mafia; the previous year they had banned Freemasonry and other secret societies. Whether in secret organizations or in the rule of terror, a totalitarian state doesn't want competition from freelancers.

In more recent decades, from time to time there have been purges by the authorities, and in retaliation the police chiefs and judges most troublesome to the Mafia have found themselves gunned down or blown up. There are persistent allegations that Italian political campaigns are financed by Mafia money, and persistent calls for politics to be cleaned up. Politicians come to power on anti-corruption platforms, only to find themselves implicated in allegations of corruption. Governments tend to be rather short-lived. Italy, in short, continues to be Italy.

P 2

The Italian-based organization *Propaganda Due*, usually known as P2, could be called part of Freemasonry, part of the Mafia, or simply part of corrupt politics, business and high finance. Indeed, it exemplifies what has already been said in this book about Masonic corruption: a corrupt individual will join whichever organizations he thinks will best further his interests. In the case of P2, however, this was the *raison d'être* of the organization.

The actuality of P2 makes most conspiracy theories look rather unimaginative.

P2 was founded in the mid-1960s by Licio Gelli, who had fought for Franco in the Spanish Civil War, had worked as a liaison officer between the Nazis and the Italian Fascists during the Second World War, and had helped organize the Nazi escape route to South America. In 1954 he moved to Argentina himself; there he became closely associated with General Perón and other right-wing political leaders. He also, according to some sources, simultaneously spied for the Soviet Union. In 1972 he became Argentina's economic advisor to Italy.

Some years before this, in 1963, he had joined a Lodge of Grand Orient Freemasonry in Italy. Italian Lodges had to provide lists of their members to the government; Gelli conceived the idea of a sort of 'super-Lodge' which reported to no one except himself, and which would consist only of the most influential people; he named it after a nineteenth-century Lodge, *Propaganda*. From the start it was illegal, if only because it was not formally registered, and did not hand over its membership list to anyone; the Grand Orient suspended P2 partly for this reason, but not until after the scandal broke. Apparently it was so well hidden that the Grand Orient leadership were not aware of it until then.

The membership of P2 at its height was a conspirator's wildest dream; it included senior military personnel, senior civil servants, senior politicians, newspaper editors, and top bankers, businessmen and industrialists. It also included a number of highly-placed officials – some of them priests – within the Vatican; this despite the papal edict forbidding Masonic membership to Roman Catholics on pain of excommunication.

There were somewhere between 1,000 and 2,400 members in Italy alone, and all of them were top people: generals, admirals, cabinet ministers, judges, presidents of international companies, and the head of the Italian Secret Service, while at least one bishop and a cardinal were either members of P2 or closely linked with it.

As the leader, or *Il Venerabile*, Gelli was the only person who knew the identity of all the members of P2; even the leaders of the various cells and branches only knew their own members. When necessary, Gelli used black-mail and corruption to induce people to join, and to maintain his hold over all the members. Through P2 and its branches, members and contacts, Gelli's influence extended through large parts of Europe, the USA, and much of South America. P2 was in a position where it could 'persuade' key members of governments to swing particular decisions which were to the financial advantage of Gelli and other members. Just as Freemasonry is often accused of being, P2 really was a mutual aid society on the grand scale.

Being based in Italy, and involved in dubious financial transactions, money-laundering and so on, P2 was from the start linked with senior members of the Mafia; deals which benefited one could also benefit the other. In addition, the Mafia connections could also arrange for the permanent removal of anyone who was being a particularly troublesome opponent.

P2 was bust open in 1981. Files found in Gelli's Tuscany villa revealed some of the membership itself, and the areas of business, politics and other professions in which they worked. Gelli himself had vanished. During the Falklands War the following year he surfaced for long enough to negotiate the sale of Exocet missiles from France to Argentina. Later in 1982, Roberto

Calvi, head of the Banco Ambrosiano, was discovered hanging beneath Blackfriars Bridge in London. Archbishop Paul Marcinkus of the Vatican Bank, a close associate of Gelli, Calvi and other major P2 figures, was eventually found guilty of fraud in 1984. The Sicilian banker Michele Sindona, who had close Mafia connections and was a P2 member – and a financial advisor to the Vatican – had already been imprisoned in 1980 for 25 years.

It is interesting to observe the various conspiracy theories about P2.

Martin Short states that '"Men of goodwill" in Britain, France and Italy would bluster that P2 had nothing to do with "regular" Freemasonry, but this was a lie and those who uttered it were either fools or knaves.'[11]

Stephen Knight claims that P2 was, from the start, a front for the KGB, to enable it to infiltrate Western politics and banking. His argument appears to be that as P2 had Masonic connections, and (he believes, but probably incorrectly) KGB connections, and as the KGB quite naturally infiltrates wherever it can, including not just the security services but also British Freemasonry, then 'Britain stands in danger of a social calamity at least as great as that which struck Italy... Evidence published here for the first time indicates that British Freemasonry, without realizing it, has become a time-bomb which could explode at any moment.'[12]

In contrast, Baigent, Leigh and Lincoln argue that P2 channeled CIA funds for various undercover anti-Communist purposes. Unsurprisingly, they also reveal possible links between P2 and the Prieuré de Sion, though they are reluctant to accept these, preferring to see links between P2, the right-wing Catholic organisation Opus Dei, the CIA and the Knights of Malta.[13]

No-one yet seems to have 'proved' that P2 is the executive arm of the Illuminati, though for ardent conspiracy theorists, this probably goes without saying.

One of the very few well-argued conspiracy theories is David Yallop's *In God's Name*, which puts a strong case for Pope John Paul I having been murdered; among the conspirators were the Vatican 'civil service', the Vatican Bank, 'the tyrannical despot'[14] Cardinal John Cody of Chicago – and P2, which had its fingers in every possible corrupt pie. John Paul I, as well as planning to relax the Church's conservative position on contraception, had been about to overthrow the tables of the money-changers in the Vatican; they got to him first.

Yallop's book is closely argued; he doesn't make logical leaps from 'could be' to 'is'; he also doesn't resort to sensationalist journalese – his central thesis is sensational enough to speak for itself without the necessity for purple prose. Perhaps this is why his theory has attracted a large amount of support from people who dismiss most other conspiracy theories as crackpot. So far as P2 is concerned, almost anything is believable.

And it's anyone's guess whether branches of P2 are still in existence.

THE TRIADS

The Triads are known for their involvement in crime among the expatriate Chinese population. Because of the 'protection' they offer to Chinese businesses, in exchange for a financial contribution, they have been dubbed the Chinese Mafia. It is only really in the last half-century that they have become primarily a criminal organization; before that they were political groups with religious symbolism, freedom-fighters for deliverance from foreign rulers of their country: again, like the original Mafia.

Chinese secret societies, sometimes called Tongs, go back to the time of Christ, and many of them – the Red (or Carnation-Painted) Eyebrows Society, the Copper Horses, the Iron Shins, the Yellow Turbans, the White Lotus Society – are the stuff of legend, and of genuine history. The last-named fought to liberate China from the Kublai Khan's Mongols in the fourteenth century. The White Lotus, the Illustrious Worthies and the White Cloud fought against the Manchu rulers in the eighteenth century. In the nineteenth century there were, among others, the Three Incense Sticks, the White Feather, and the White Lotus again. Many of these societies had as their ostensible goal the restoration of the Ming Dynasty, though outside observers say that most of them simply wanted to throw out whoever was currently in power and take control themselves. The famous Boxer Rebellion in Peking (Beijing), in 1900, was sparked off by secret societies, notably the Fist for Righteous Harmony Society, whose famed ferocity was a result of their belief in their magical invulnerability.

The entire history of secret societies in China exemplifies the saying, 'One man's terrorist (or brigand, or bandit) is another man's freedom fighter'.

Many of these societies raised and maintained the devotion of their members through esoteric rituals; some were associated with monasteries, and learned powerful meditation techniques which made them disciplined, dedicated and almost invincible warriors. Their initiation rites and rituals drew heavily on Taoist and Buddhist beliefs; both religions were often driven underground by Confucian rulers, giving them a popular appeal, power and mystery which the societies drew on. It is also thought that the Gnostic religion of Manichæism influenced some of the societies.[15] Some Masonic scholars have found correspondences between the initiation rites of Chinese secret societies, particularly the Triads, and the rituals in Freemasonry, particularly the 3rd Degree (Master Mason's) initiation and some of the 'Higher' Degrees, with their emphasis on resurrection symbolism.

The societies also often had the advantage of being led by failed candidates for the Civil Service, educated men with a grudge against the government. In outlying districts and in small villages (and as in medieval Europe, much of China was small villages), where government power didn't really reach, the effective local government was often the societies, ruling from behind the scenes through a combination of benevolence, fear and superstition.

The Triads are almost certainly descended from the White Lotus, and were founded, according to a richly symbolic legend, in 1674; thus they have a body of political, patriotic and religious background to give them some legitimacy – more so than many of the esoteric societies of the West. The English name Triad refers to the three elements of their original name, the Brotherhood of Heaven and Earth; their symbol is usually a triangle, with the sides representing Heaven, Earth and Man. The alternative name of Tongs, more common in the USA, simply refers to their meeting halls.

The Triads were closely associated with the initial rise to power of Dr Sun Yat Sen in 1912. He was a Triad member, and his Kuomintang Party which finally overthrew the Manchu dynasty in 1911 was linked to the Triads. In the war for supremacy in China in the 1940s, both sides – Mao Tse-Tung's successful Communists, and Chiang Kai-shek's defeated Nationalists – made extensive use of secret societies. Mao Tse-Tung ended up with mainland China, while the Nationalists retreated to Formosa (now Taiwan) in 1949.

In the aftermath of that war, many Chinese fled abroad. There were already large populations in Hong Kong, Singapore and the Philippines; now those few who were able to leave China also moved to the West. So did the influence of the secret societies.

With the background they have, it is easy to see how the Triads maintain their power wherever the Chinese go. Like the original Mafia, they look after their members like brothers, as a benevolent association; but like Fundamentalists, if you are not for them, you are against them, and are treated as opponents. Away from China, the Triads' political motivations have turned to criminal ones, using the same skills they have honed for centuries. Wherever they have influence, they control gambling, prostitution and drugs, the seamier side of the entertainments industry – once again, like the Mafia.

In the USA, the Mafia have traditionally been strongest on the Eastern seaboard and in the industrial cities of middle America; the home of the KKK is the South; the Triads seem to be strongest on the West Coast, particularly in California.

In Britain there are currently four major Triad societies: the Wo Shing Wo, the Wo On Lok, the 14K, and the San Yee On. Most members are ex-Hong Kong Chinese, though increasingly they are recruiting Malaysians, Vietnamese and others, including second-generation (British-born) members.

The Chinese population in Britain in 1994 was between 130,000 and 200,000; this is expected to increase, perhaps even double, with the reversion of Hong Kong to China. Whether this will mean a concomitant increase in Triad activity remains to be seen.

The well-publicized violence of the UK Triads tends mainly to be inter-group fighting over their 'turfs', rather than directed at outsiders, but it can easily catch up anyone in the Chinese business community, especially if they are under pressure from two competing groups. 'It is this potential for violence which promulgates the fear these thugs feed from. It is this fear within the Chinese community that I find the most worrying,' says a Metropolitan police officer with experience of the Triads in both Hong Kong and London.[16]

GOVERNMENT SECRECY

It was said at the beginning of the book that the priest vies with the prostitute and the spy among the world's oldest professions. The prostitute (even the temple prostitute) lies outside the scope of this book, but there is space for the spy.

Ever since there have been rulers and governments, there have been spies. They might be freelance informers – information mercenaries working for the highest pay – or they might be part of a government department. Spies have always spanned all social classes, from grubby street ruffians to the élite of society. (Going back to the sixteenth century it is almost certain that, in different ways, John Dee, Giordano Bruno and Christopher Marlowe were all spies.)

As with secret societies, recruitment of spies has often been on personal recommendation, and all recruits are carefully 'vetted'. In Britain all intelligence officers have to sign the Official Secrets Act – a close equivalent to taking initiation vows: the commitment to secrecy lasts for life. Astonishingly few former Freemasons, or former members of other initiatory societies, ever break their vows. The same applies to former spies.

The three main branches of British intelligence are the internal Security Service (MI5), the foreign Secret Intelligence Service (MI6), and Government Communications Headquarters (GCHQ), which specialises in signals intelligence (sigint).

Like many governments, the British government is paranoid about its secrets, as the following examples illustrate.

I worked for GCHQ from 1979 to 1985 before returning to journalism. In 1987 I wrote two feature articles for *Computer Weekly*[17] about the work at GCHQ, based on an authorised visit and interviews with senior staff. Whilst giving as much 'public domain' information as possible about signals intelligence and cryptanalysis in order to make the articles worthwhile, I was determined not to reveal any secrets about this establishment. Not only had I signed the Official Secrets Act, but I genuinely had no desire to compromise the work of GCHQ.

GCHQ insisted on vetting the articles, which is against normal journalistic practice, but under the circumstances was understandable. They also insisted that no mention be made in the articles of my former employment at GCHQ, and that one of the articles must appear under a joint byline with the deputy editor. The reason for both impositions is interesting in that it reveals a very useful ploy used not only by GCHQ but also by others, including the Freemasons, to maintain their secrecy.

Many other journalists had written about GCHQ from an outsider's viewpoint. For example, Duncan Campbell of *New Statesman* was very accurate in most of his articles, which were based on a lot of meticulous research and a little inspired guesswork; inevitably, though, there would usually be one or two minor inaccuracies. This allowed GCHQ to respond, quite truthfully, that Campbell's pieces were based on surmise and contained a number of errors – which sounds like a blanket refutation, but is not necessarily anything of the sort.

In *World Freemasonry*, United Grand Lodge librarian John Hamill and R.A. Gilbert mention 'what purported to be exposures of Masonic ritual' in the early days of Freemasonry, and also a 1965 television programme which 'enacted, inaccurately, some of the more dramatic parts of the ritual.'[18] Both statements give the impression that the exposés were substantially incorrect; neither in fact actually says or necessarily means this. 'Purported to be exposures' doesn't mean that they weren't, while 'inaccurately' could simply mean that a single foot movement or hand gesture was incorrect, or that the wrong person was given a phrase to say. Hamill has confirmed in conversation that this is substantially the case.

Official denials should always be examined carefully.

GCHQ's fear was that, if the byline mentioned that I had formerly worked for them, readers would rightly assume that the articles were entirely accurate, and so GCHQ would not be able to hide behind the usual dismissal. Having a joint byline served the same purpose; even if it were known that I had worked for GCHQ, readers could not be sure which parts had been written by me, and so were accurate, and which had been written by my 'co-writer', and so possibly contained inaccuracies.

In the event, the subterfuge was rendered ineffective by stories in both the *Guardian* and *New Scientist* naming me as the writer who, 'as an ex-employee, could not be denounced as a journalist with no real knowledge of what is going on.'[19] The *Guardian* drew an apposite comparison: GCHQ's management 'argued – as the government does in the case of Mr Peter Wright's MI5 memoirs – that it was one thing for an outsider to write about the organisation but quite another for a former "insider" to do so.'[20]

After publication of the first article, GCHQ warned that permission might be withdrawn for publication of the second – which, like the first, had already been vetted. Meetings were held at Directorate level at GCHQ to consider the text of the second article and decide whether they dare allow publication. I rewrote it, making absolutely certain that there was nothing in it that was even Restricted, the lowest level of official secrecy, let alone Confidential, Secret, Top Secret or VRK (Very Restricted Knowledge).

The problem turned out to be that, although not one single piece of information in either article was classified, GCHQ feared that the way that all the individual Unclassified details *were put together* made the articles as a whole Top Secret.

This is not as crazy as it sounds. W.E. Butler, founder of the esoteric school Servants of the Light, said something very similar about the fact that a lot of the ritual used in magic is now in the public domain:

> The question arises, why should the various magical orders have sworn their initiates to secrecy concerning these things which are of common knowledge? The answer is, that in those orders and fraternities which were genuine the information given in these various sources *was combined in a particular pattern*, and it was this *pattern* which was the real object of secrecy.[21]

But really, GCHQ had simply panicked.

A similar situation a few years earlier shows again just how paranoid governments can get, and just how silly it can all become.

In 1970, journalist Peter Laurie wrote *Beneath the City Streets*, an examination, drawn largely from information already in the public domain, of Britain's secret plans for keeping the machinery of government going in the event of a major war. If Westminster and Whitehall disappear under a mushroom cloud, Britain will continue to be run from Regional Seats of

Government (RSGs) scattered all over the country, often buried deep beneath town halls or police stations. There is also a communications network, linking the RSGs via the microwave towers which dot the landscape.

Laurie was severely reprimanded for publishing that book. Although the location of any individual RSG or microwave tower is Unclassified (for example, the Telecom Tower near Oxford Street in London is hardly hidden away), it seems that a map of the UK showing several of them is Top Secret. The *pattern*, again.

In 1979 Laurie wrote a new, updated edition of his book. Not wanting to get into further trouble, he sent a draft of it to the Home Office, the Foreign Office, MI5, MI6 and so on, explaining that he had no wish to break the Official Secrets Act by publishing any official secrets. Could he publish this new edition?

The answer was 'No', because the book contained official secrets.

Laurie offered to take out whatever material was causing the problem. He was told that this was not possible, because this would mean telling him official secrets. When he protested that he obviously already knew these secrets, because he had written the book, he was told that this wasn't the point; if they told him which parts of his book to take out, they would be telling him which parts were official secrets, and he wasn't authorised to know that.

Realising he was getting nowhere, Laurie removed most of the references to sigint and GCHQ, which he thought was probably the most sensitive information, and published the book. He probably guessed right; he wasn't prosecuted.

Such paranoia is not unusual in the world of government secrecy; books by Chapman Pincher and Nigel West (the pseudonym of the former Conservative MP Rupert Allason) reveal plenty of similar cases. These include agents of MI5 and MI6 tailing each other around London for months, each thinking the others were subversives or agents of a foreign power, simply because the two organizations were so jealous of their own secrets they weren't communicating with each other.

Although the policies of 'need-to-know' and 'compartmentalized knowledge' can sometimes cause more trouble than they're worth, there are very sensible reasons for them; there are many things which do require the highest levels of secrecy. If a careless word at an embassy cocktail party were to reveal how successful Britain was at intercepting and decrypting another country's communications, a simple change of cypher equipment or cypher key generator could throw away years of painstaking work at GCHQ. Another careless word could cause the life of a long-term, well-established British agent abroad to be threatened, or at the very least, cause him to be sent home, and his ring of contacts and informers to be bust open.

Lord George-Brown, a former Foreign Secretary (1966-68), raises a disturbing point about security, and the trustworthiness or otherwise of members of the security services and the Diplomatic Service – and, by extension, MPs and Ministers of State. If someone is under suspicion, he writes,

> Inevitably, much of the evidence in such cases is hearsay or almost unprovable deduction, and one must reckon with the natural wish of colleagues to protect, as it were, a fellow-member of the club, especially when they don't know, and can't really be told, the full extent of the matter. This clearly happened in the case of Burgess and Maclean.[22]

MPs themselves are a club; very senior civil servants – 'the Whitehall mandarins' – are a club; members of MI5 and MI6 are a club; the British establishment, whether in public office or not, is a club. Most of these people also belong to various gentlemen's clubs; some belong to that huge but secretive club, the Freemasons. Without casting any aspersions against any of these organzations, or their rules, regulations, restrictions, customs or obligations regarding 'mutual support' and 'members in need', it is not in the slightest surprising if individual members look out for the interests of each other, especially if they are friends and dinner and drinking companions. Over the years favours, large and small, are traded; when someone is potentially in trouble, fellow 'club' members are likely – rightly or wrongly – to help them out.

The sort of 'corruption' of which critics accuse Freemasonry is not the fault of Freemasonry any more than two members of any other club helping each other is the fault of that club. In most cases it's questionable whether it's even corruption. Really, it's simply human nature, for good and for bad.

But those who spend their lives looking for evil, will find it everywhere.

CHAPTER SIX

THE ETERNAL QUEST

THIS BOOK has covered a lot of ground. With the exception of some of the previous chapter, the emphasis has been mainly on the esoteric background and nature of movements which, rightly or wrongly, are seen by outsiders as secret societies. Various threads have become apparent during the course of the book; now it is time to draw some of them together. This final chapter should not be seen as a Conclusion *per se*, if only because any conclusions are bound to be tentative; it might better be seen as a Summary plus Suggestions.

WHY PEOPLE JOIN
SECRET SOCIETIES

In the case of most Freemasons, probably the main reason for their membership is social: a men-only form of companionship and mutual support which has changed little since the days of Mithraism, and serving much the same function as the pub darts club, or the little league baseball team, though a considerable cut above either. In some cases Freemasonry is a family tradition: a son (or 'lewis') following in his father's footsteps. For some, membership is undoubtedly seen as a means of advancing their own careers, of getting on good social terms with future business contacts. For others with a social conscience, it provides a means for charitable giving, of their money and their time. For some, it's the secrecy which appeals: belonging to something and knowing things which the majority of people don't.

For most, it seems, the rituals of the first three degrees are little more than play-acting, a bit of mumbo-jumbo they're prepared to go through as their initiation into the club. A few take it more seriously; they look at the surface symbolism and see something deeper. These are the ones, along with some seeking social advancement or a rise up the 'club' career ladder, who take the higher degrees, up to 33rd degree, and who join related Orders.

A few others, who have studied the esoteric background of Freemasonry before joining it, already have a good idea of what they're looking for. They're prepared to put up with the social side of fairly low-level Freemasonry in order to study the deeper mysteries.

Rosicrucians, too, have a number of motivations. Some are initially attracted by the promise of power: increasing their memory, becoming more successful in everything they do. Their motivations are only a little different from those of people who respond to the 'Increase your sexual attractiveness' ads in the men's magazines. Once they realize they have to study comparative religion, mythology and history, astronomy and astrology, chemistry and alchemy, and the complexities of Cabala, few of these will last for much more than the first few months of lessons.

Others, right from the start, genuinely want to get closer to God; they feel a lack in traditional Christianity, and are looking for the Christ-spark within themselves. Their motivations are spiritual rather than particularly esoteric. Others, again, know something of the background of Rosicrucianism before they join. They know about the power, they know about the spiritual search, and they're already fascinated by the studies. They use what they learn from Rosicrucianism as a springboard for their further personal researches into the esoteric.

The Schools of Occult Science attract those who already know something about Cabala, the deeper symbolism of Tarot, comparative religion, esoteric Christianity, mysticism, those who have encountered the Western Mystery Tradition, and who want to study it in more depth under the guidance of experienced teachers. Some may have tried the more open Rosicrucian Orders, and have found them both too broad and too shallow. They've worked their way through the side-salad and the bun; now they want the meat.

COMPETING TRUTHS

To the outsider, there often seem to be contradictions in what they know of the teachings of secret societies, not only between different societies, but within individual ones.

One of the most important aspects of any esoteric teaching is that the same statement may have two or more quite different meanings – factual and allegorical, exoteric and esoteric – and may reveal different layers of meaning at different levels of learning. This explains the outsider's impression of the apparent wilful contrariness of, for example, the eleventh-century esoteric Ismaili school in Cairo, or its adaptation in the Assassins, where at each level of initiation the student discovered that what he had learned at the previous levels was false.

It was not that the previous teachings were actually false as in untrue; rather that in the light of the new revelations they could be seen to demonstrate only a very limited understanding.

The converse is also the case: it is often said of the Hermetic Philosophers that they were able to accept two mutually contradictory statements as equally true. This is not as perverse as it seems. In everyday usage we speak of the Sun rising in the morning and setting in the evening, and moving across the sky in between, while in fact knowing that the Earth is actually rotating on its axis while orbiting around the Sun. But both statements are true. The astronomical version is a scientific statement; the other is a perceptual truth.

Max Heindel examines this point while discussing two different translations of Genesis 1:1.

> Much has been said and written as to which of these two interpretations
> is correct. The difficulty is, that people want something settled and
> definite. They take the stand that, if a certain explanation is true,
> all others must be wrong. But, emphatically, this is not the way to
> get at truth, which is many sided and multiplex. Each occult truth
> requires examination from many different points of view; each
> viewpoint presents a certain phase of the truth, and all of them are
> necessary to get a complete, definite conception of whatever is under
> consideration.[1]

From the viewpoint of the esotericist, this is the problem with exoteric religion, particularly orthodox Christianity, and even more particularly Evangelical Christianity. As was seen earlier in discussion of Freemasonry, Fundamentalist Evangelicals especially see Christianity as an exclusive religion; if it is true, as they believe it is, then all other religions must of necessity be false: made up by man, but inspired by the Devil. Within Christianity (and the same applies to a lesser extent within several other religions) there is even further exclusivity; each of a thousand different sects believes that it alone has the truth.

Such tunnel vision, of course, leads to argument, dissension, antagonism, and even to war. The smaller the differences between two groups, the more bitter, it seems, are the disagreements.

This doesn't apply to just Christianity, nor indeed to only exoteric religions. Esoteric movements can also have tunnel vision and stubborn pride. The history of occult societies, as for example with the *Fraternitas Rosae Crucis* and AMORC, is littered with disputes; it is also littered with schisms. Considering their emphasis on spirituality this may or may not be 'right', but it is quite understandable. If you receive messages from Hidden Masters on the etheric plane, whether they are from the Great White Brotherhood of Theosophy and its many offspring, or from spirits or *dæmons*, your messages are unlikely to agree in every respect with someone else's messages. This becomes most apparent when the leader of an esoteric religious movement dies, and his or her putative successors vie with each other for supremacy, each claiming to have had a personal revelation that they were to be the new leader. It often ends with the religion splitting into two or three, with members dividing to follow the several different leaders, each of whom claims to be the one true successor. In the US in particular it sometimes leads to lawsuits, each group staking its claim to the original name and organization (and to its property and funds).

One of the classic American examples, perhaps surprisingly, is not either a Christian or a Theosophical movement; it is the large number of competing groups each claiming to be the true successor to Radhasoami Satsang, a religious movement founded in 1861 in the Sant Mat tradition of esoteric Hindu/Sikh-inspired movements, originally from Northern India. Although they all appear, to the outsider, to be teaching much the same thing, each apparently claims to have the only true, full and perfect distillation of the Truth. Some, like ECKANKAR, present themselves as the first time the Truth has ever been taught in its entirety, and seem to ignore the fact that their teachings are borrowed from earlier movements.

So far as such esoteric organizations are concerned, it doesn't seem to occur to most of them that it is permissible for them to have different emphases within their overall teachings. At least two of the major Rosicrucian organizations concentrate on physical healing in addition to spiritual truths; others concentrate on personal development. This doesn't have to mean that any one of them is 'right' and all the others 'wrong'. But still, some claim to be the only true and legitimate bearers of the Rosicrucian mantle.

An Evangelical minister, explaining the bad behaviour of some of his congregation, once said, 'Christians are human too'. The same applies to esotericists; they can be just as selfish and bitchy as anyone else. They can also have the added temptation, especially if they have risen up through several levels of initiation, of the sin of spiritual pride.

Members of esoteric organizations are supposed to work for the greater good of mankind, just as Christians are supposed to obey Jesus' command to love one another. Sometimes they fail; sometimes they're human.

ESOTERIC LINEAGE

However laudable their aims, is any of these present-day organizations, or their eighteenth- or nineteenth-century forebears, with all their uncertain lineages – is any of them actually Rosicrucian, as many of them claim? Again quoting A.E. Waite:

> It seems undeniable therefore that the links are broken everywhere. The various associations and sodalities which have claimed the generic title exhibited in the early seventeenth century, rose up in their day, advancing their particular claims, and they died also in their day – again so far at least as any records are concerned. *It is above all things probable that their connection one with another was in the bond of union furnished by an identical name and a certain consanguinity of intention, whatever the intention was.*[2]

If we accept that as a valid premise, then it has removed one of the problems: the 'apostolic succession' of authority through proven lineage which so many Rosicrucian-type movements struggle so hard to claim. Quite simply, it doesn't matter. We know, almost for a fact, that the very first people to take up the Rosicrucian mantle in the early decades of the seventeenth century simply assumed the name that had been handed to them in the three Rosicrucian Manifestos – unless, of course, they themselves were the anonymous writers, in which case they had cobbled the shoes they then stepped into. What is as certain as anything can be in this whole field, is that the Rosicrucian Brotherhood, the Fraternity of the Rosy Cross, did not exist until the *Fama Fraternitatis* appeared in 1614. At least, not under that name, as a distinct, discrete order.

The people who became the first 'Rosicrucians' were pursuing exactly the same studies after 1614 as before. The *Fama* simply gave a new name and a more unified identity to the Hermetic Philosophers who had been studying alchemy and astrology and medicine and Cabala and geometry and architecture – and, note carefully, the spiritual philosophy underlying and encompassing each and all of these – for decades before.

As for today's societies – *Fraternitas Rosae Crucis*, *Societas Rosicruciana in Anglia* and *in America*, the Rosicrucian Fellowship, AMORC, *Lectorium Rosicrucianum* and others, and those which don't actually use the term Rosicrucian in their name, such as BOTA and Servants of the Light – their organizational lineage is unimportant if, in Waite's words, they have 'a certain consanguinity of intention', which they clearly do. True, they also have many differences in emphasis, but so did Pico della Mirandola, Francesco Giorgi, Henry Cornelius Agrippa, Paracelsus, John Dee, Giordano Bruno and the rest.

Each pursues the truth in his or her own way.

There are still some, both inside and outside today's variety of esoteric societies, who claim a direct and actual lineage back from, say, the Freemasons to the Hermetic Philosophers and Renaissance alchemists, to the Knights Templar and/or the Cathars; some make claims right back to the Greek and Egyptian magical philosophers of 2,000 or more years ago.

True, not all the Cathars were wiped out in massacres such as Béziers and Montségur. Some, with their beliefs, survived. And it is more than probable that when the Templars were disbanded and their leaders burned, some Templars went underground, banding together in small numbers, maintaining careful touch with each other, keeping their secrets and their rituals alive.

But however tempting it would be to believe that these hidden few managed to keep up their secret numbers and preserve their beliefs and rituals century after century, to re-emerge as the Rosicrucians or the Freemasons, there is no real evidence that this occurred.

Just as unscrupulous antique dealers sometimes create a convincing but false provenance for items with an uncertain or non-existent history, so, for example, did William Wynn Westcott for the Hermetic Order of the Golden Dawn, with his faked letters from 'Fräulein Sprengel'; Samuel Liddell 'MacGregor' Mathers's 'ancient' rituals were the icing on the cake. With perhaps less deceit and more self-delusion, some of the early historians of the Freemasons did just the same, inventing an impressive but spurious history.

As for all the chivalric Orders and Rites within Freemasonry, it is far more than merely likely that these were all eighteenth- and nineteenth-century inventions, and nothing more. The whole of Masonic ritual is based on what they themselves (at least today) acknowledge to be legends rather than historical accounts. But does this make them untrue, or make Freemasonry a fake?

The importance of myth is not its factual basis; it is the message it contains. Jesus made up stories (dignified by the term 'parables') to make moral points, or to paint a concrete analogy of an abstract idea. Few actually believe that a man called Christian Rozenkreutz actually lived out his story for 106 years, and that his uncorrupted body was found in its tomb 120 years after his death. And it makes no difference to modern-day Freemasonry whether a few Knights Templar kept themselves together for four centuries, or not; the facts are unimportant if the message lives on.

It is unlikely that those who created the Rosicrucian myth, and the perpetuation-of-the-Templars myth, were deliberately creating falsehoods to deceive people, any more than Jesus was lying when he told the story of the Good Samaritan. They were generating a mythos, a story to be remembered for what it teaches. A more fruitful enquiry than whether or not Pierre d'Aumont succeeded Jacques de Molay and sailed to Scotland, is why a Freemason selected the Templars to be the spiritual forebears of his new Masonic Rite.

Here is Waite again:

> If the Templars had a secret knowledge – and this is one hypothesis concerning them – it is certain to have been communicated from without the circle of chivalry, not to have originated in preceptory or chapter-house. To that secret centre the Order would have looked in the day of utter dereliction [i.e. when it was destroyed by Philippe le Bel], and could we turn in the same direction a light on this question of survival might yet reach us. There are many mysteries of chivalry and after more than a century of speculation – though we have ingarnered various materials – we have constructed no certain theory as to anything which lay behind it. In literature, in symbolism and by evasive suggestions of intention which manifest there and here, the student stumbles continually on apparent traces of something *perdue* in the deeps which may have cast up the rough, feudal Knighthood as a veil of its hidden project. I do not know that as such it is more than part and parcel of that strange growth of secret life which characterised the Middle Ages. On this side and on that it opens paths of speculation, and I know not where they may lead.[3]

The remainder of this chapter follows some of these paths of speculation, to see where they might lead – and to see, perhaps, if there could indeed have been 'something *perdue* in the deeps'.

———

The true lineage, as was said earlier, is not in the underground continuance of secret orders, but in the pursuit of similar ideas and ideals: a spiritual lineage. Much of this book has been about esoteric religious beliefs, classed as heresies by the orthodox mainstream; it has shown how the same ideas crop up again and again, and how the people with these ideas, these beliefs, have again and again been condemned and persecuted.

But even when these beliefs have been restricted, whether by persecution or by choice, to a select few, there has always been the urge, common to the Cathar *perfecti*, the original Rosicrucians, and the Freemasons today, to benefit mankind as a whole. This is an easily-missed but vital point, which is at the very heart of the enquiry.

THE QUEST FOR THE HOLY GRAIL

For whatever reasons, twelfth- to thirteenth-century France was buzzing with esoteric spirituality; it was also red with the blood, or dark with the ashes, of heretics. Whether by accident or by design, the principles, the ideals and the ideas of these heretics were preserved in such a way as to have a remarkable and continuing effect on society.

There are already far too many conspiracy theories linking the Freemasons and Rosicrucians back through the Knights Templar to the Holy Grail. We are all familiar with those glorious 'unified theory' books which link whatever the author wants to link. Throughout such books, in every argument, we read 'perhaps . . . it could be that . . . is possibly . . . may be . . . might be . . .'; then by the following chapter these surmises have become facts to be built upon with yet further mights and maybes into yet more 'facts'.

However, as A.E. Waite says so succinctly, 'They prove nothing whose thesis proves too much.'[4] This book has included its fair share of 'perhaps' and 'could be', but has always labelled them as such; no attempt has been made to turn supposition into fact. What follows is not an 'inescapable conclusion', nor even a 'strong conjecture'; although it has been arrived at independently during the course of researching and writing, much of it is not even original to this book. Just call it a series of thoughts which might be worth pursuing.

THE ARTHURIAN ROMANCES

Every year sees yet more Arthurian novels published, usually as fat trilogies; historical fantasy is a popular genre. Most of these blithely set Arthur and co. in a late-medieval or early-Renaissance court, just as most Arthurian films feature glorious pavilions and jousting. A few authors strip away the twelfth- to fourteenth-century accretions, and write about a Dark Age warrior–leader instead of a glorious King of All Britain. If any historical fiction can be said to be accurate, these latter are certainly more so, historically, than the vast majority. If Arthur lived at all, as a historical personage, he and his court were nothing at all like the characters and settings of the Arthurian romances purporting to depict him and his kind.

This is because the medieval Arthurian romances did just what religious paintings of the time did: without any attempt at historical realism, they set their characters (whether Arthur or Jesus) in an idealized setting of their own time.

But why was the Arthurian cycle suddenly so popular? Where did it suddenly spring from? What, if anything, was its purpose, its *raison d'être*?

To answer these questions, instead of stripping away the late medieval trimmings in search of the historical Arthur, the exact opposite is needed: to discard for the moment whatever factual basis there might be behind the tales, and to look instead at what they say of the times in which they were written. *Why* were they written? What was so important to the writers that they had to create these wondrous tales out of (almost) whole cloth?

Remaining after the historical basis has been stripped away are chivalry, courtly love, the Grail, and questing knights. These are what the French romance writers were writing about, not a Dark Age British king at all; Arthur was little more than a convenient peg on which to hang what really concerned them.

Each of these four concepts will be treated in the next few pages, after a brief consideration of the Arthurian romances themselves, their significance and the influences on their writing.

Today, in Britain, the more scholarly Neo-Pagan groups and individuals, who tend towards the esoteric in their studies and interests, are often deeply committed to what has become known as the Matter of Britain, particularly the Arthurian and Grail cycles. This is unsurprising; Neo-Paganism in any country usually explores the mythology of that country.

What is a little more surprising is that at least two of the esoteric societies, or Schools of Occult Science as they sometimes call themselves, also focus strongly on this material, in addition to their studies of Tarot, Cabala, and Greek/Egyptian magico-philosophy. The Servants of the Light recommended book list gives nearly 30 titles of Arthurian books, most of them specifically on the Grail. SOL was founded by W.E. Butler, a former member of the Society of the Inner Light, and this latter organization, for this day and age, is quite extraordinarily British-chauvinist; it insists that candidates must be British-born, and have 'full knowledge of the legends and myths of our history i.e. heroes . . . saints and sages . . .'[5] Its founder, Dion Fortune, was for many years associated with Glastonbury, rightly or wrongly the main centre of Arthurian and Grail attention in Britain.

Why should esoteric organizations which study and teach the complexities of Cabala, surely the ultimate in intellectual spiritual contemplation, be bothered with Arthuriana?

The clue lies in the dating. Geoffrey of Monmouth, who was as likely to have been Breton as Welsh, wrote his largely fictional *History of the Kings of Britain* in Latin around 1136. The Norman-French Wace used this in 1155 as the basis for his *Roman de Brut*, which turns it from an heroic tale into a story of courtly romance, and also introduces the Round Table to the story. Chrétien de Troyes wrote five romances between at the earliest 1159 and at the latest 1190; the last of these, *Perceval* or *Le Conte del Graal*, introduces the Grail for the first time. *Perceval*, though unfinished, is clearly a parable of the journey from ignorance to knowledge; the Grail is described as a mystery. The idea of the Grail being a sacred chalice, either the cup from the Last Supper or the cup which was used to catch the blood of Christ on the Cross, did not appear until Robert de Boron wrote *Joseph d'Arimathie*, probably in the late 1190s. Layamon, an Englishman, put Wace's *Brut* back into English, dropping much of the courtly romance, around the turn of the twelfth and thirteenth centuries. The four Continuations of *Perceval*, by different hands, date from between 1200 and *c.* 1240. Each says more about the Grail than Chrétien de Troyes did.

THE SPIRITUAL CULTURE

This is not the place to provide an in-depth study of the late medieval spirituality of the Grail romances, and in any case, there are others far better qualified to do so – Caitlín and John Matthews, R.J. Stewart and Gareth Knight in particular. Here, then, a simple comparing of some dates.

- The Crusades took place between 1095 and 1272. Jerusalem was won in 1099, lost in 1187, recaptured in 1229 and lost again in 1244.
- The Assassins began in 1090, and were influential until around 1250.
- The Knights Templar were founded in 1119, and came to an end between 1307 and 1314.
- The Cathars existed from *c.* 1150, had largely been crushed by 1209, and were effectively wiped out, in France at least, at Montségur in 1244.
- The idea of courtly love, written and sung about by the Provençal troubadours, migrated to northern France (possibly with returning Crusaders) in the middle of the twelfth century.
- The Cabalist *Sefer ha-Bahir* was written in Provence around 1175. Medieval Cabalism developed in Provence in the twelfth century and remained strong there; it spread from Provence to Spain, where the *Sefer ha-Zohar* was published *c.* 1285.
- The medieval mythologizing of the Arthur story, with the French emphasis on chivalry and courtly love, and the introduction of the Grail, occurred between *c.* 1155 and *c.* 1190.
- Languedoc or Provençal culture was largely wiped out by the middle of the thirteenth century.

It is not being suggested that there were direct causal links between all of these; what *is* being pointed out is that some very interesting events occurred in France, particularly southern France, or involved the French, in the twelfth and early thirteenth centuries.[6] There were a lot of heretical ideas around during that period. There was an emphasis on mysticism, on an individual search for and personal relationship with God, in contrast with an unquestioning acceptance of the Catholic insistence on salvation only via the Church. The Muslim Assassins, the Gnostic Cathars, the Christian Templars, the Jewish Cabalists, all in different but mutually comprehensible ways sought to get closer to God. (It is true that we don't know the Templars' beliefs; but if they had been completely orthodox it is unlikely that the Church would have used the specific charges of blasphemy and heresy to destroy them.)

Gnosticism and its descendant Catharism believed that the material world itself is evil. Not all the heterodox religious movements looked at in this book believed this, but they did have certain things in common. It seems that the main 'heretical' beliefs which have consistently refused to fade away are that:

- there is One Creator God, whatever he is called in different religions
- there is a constant battle between the good principle and the evil principle
- there is a part of God in each one of us
- by recognizing the God within we may become one with the God without.

CHIVALRY

There are two well-known and widespread religious movements today which are, from an orthodox Christian viewpoint, heretical, and yet which are accepted and respected by many Christians. These are the Quakers and the Unitarians. It has been said of both that their Creed consists only of the first four words of the Apostles' Creed – 'I believe in God' – and that any further details are between the individual believer and his or her God. The Quakers are also well known for their dictum 'There is that of God in every man', which should by now be a familiar concept. Both groups are respected partly for the honest simplicity of their belief, and partly for their good works in society.

Present-day Rosicrucians and Freemasons teach their members that by improving the individual person, they can have a beneficial effect on society. In Biblical terms, a few grains of salt can flavour an entire meal. There is perhaps a similarity with the heretical religious movements examined in this book. The Cathar *perfecti* did not impose their chosen way of life on the ordinary *bonshommes*, but there is no doubt that the latter, who had a deep respect for their spiritual leaders, benefited (as also did the orthodox Christians who lived comfortably alongside them) if only in that there was less coercion and more tolerance in their society – at least, until the Albigensian Crusade.

Chivalry, in the Arthurian romances, meant that a knight should be a good force in society, rather than just lining his pockets with booty, as was too often, if not usually, the case in brutal reality.

Chivalry also meant that a knight should fix his thoughts on God, and be a holy man as well as a fighting man. Until the Knights Templar there was rarely any connection between the two; soldiers were often brutish, and got blood on their hands; in contrast, monks (at least in theory) lived Godly lives and kept their hands clean of blood. But the Knights Templar brought the two together: a fighting man who had also made his vows to God. Could this be where the idea of chivalry in the Arthurian romances came from?

COURTLY LOVE

The Cathars, as has been seen, believed that sexual intercourse was to be avoided because it tended to result in babies being born, which meant more sparks of the Divine trapped in human bodies. Non-sexual relationships of mutual respect and love were encouraged.

In Catharism women as well as men could be *perfecti*; the religion had several well-respected and well-loved female leaders, including Esclarmonde of Foix, who helped found a Cathar convent, and who owned Montségur. Women were not, as in Catholicism, second-class citizens with no spiritual authority and no material rights. They were equals of men.

The mystical religions, whether Jewish Cabalism, Christian Gnosticism or Manichæism or Catharism, or Islamic Sufism or the Assassins, sought a knowledge of God and a close personal relationship with God. Often they spoke of the Wisdom of God in Greek terms as Sophia, or described the indwelling presence of God in Cabalistic terms as the Shekhinah; both of these were female. Sufi poetry saw no contradiction in using the language of sensual love to describe the joy of their closeness to God. God might still be thought of mainly in masculine terms, but the mystical religions had re-covered the Pagan concept of the Eternal Female Principle.

As the poems and songs of the Provençal troubadours, extolling the beauty of love, worked their way north, were they mingled en route with Cathar, Templar, Cabalistic and other esoteric beliefs current in southern

France? Taking all these ideas together, was this the origin of the devoted but chaste 'courtly love' which was the ideal of so many of the Arthurian romances?

THE GRAIL

What of the Grail itself? The traditional image is of a cup, a communion chalice, usually richly decorated with jewels and engravings. But the Old French word *graal*, from the medieval Latin *gradale*, simply meant a serving dish or platter, used to bring the meal to the table in stages.[7]

In the first known reference in the romances the Grail was not described as a cup. In Chrétien's *Perceval* or *Le Conte del Graal* can be read, 'A damsel who came with the two youths held in her two hands a dish [*un graal*]; she was beautiful, well-attired and noble. When she came in there with the dish she was holding there appeared such brightness that at once the candles lost their brightness as the stars do when the sun or moon rises.'[8] In another early romance the Grail is a stone with healing powers; in another it is the head of Christ; and in another it is a book written by Christ.

The concept of the Grail can be found in several traditions; it is often traced back, for example, to the Cauldron of Ceridwen in Celtic mythology. But researchers who go searching for a physical Grail – a cup, or anything else – are missing the whole point.[9]

The Grail is, like so much else in the Arthurian cycle – and indeed, in all religious stories – a symbol. In most of the Grail stories the Grail has to do with sustenance and plenty. As a cup it can be full of the Water of Life, or the Blood of the Saviour, or it can be overflowing with God's life and love. As a dish or platter it can be filled with the bounteousness of God's gifts, of life itself. It is a cornucopia.

As a stone – usually a green stone – it is said to represent Lucifer, not as the Christian Devil, but as the Light-bringer: as the Morning Star, or as the Angel of Light, or as Christ's elder brother, or even as the Zoroastrian Ahura Mazda. A name, like any symbol, may represent many things. For those who automatically equate Lucifer with the Devil, for instance, it should be pointed out that this identification wasn't made until the fourth-century St Jerome, who misread the single Bible reference (Isaiah 14:12) as a proper name instead of a probable reference to the Morning Star, Venus. In any case, the verse is actually talking in symbolic terms about the King of Babylon. And in theological terms even the Evangelical *New Bible Dictionary* says that the *title* (rather than *name*) of Lucifer should more properly be applied to the risen Christ in his ascended glory than to the Devil.[10]

The Grail-as-stone, whatever colour it is and whether or not it represents Lucifer, is always seen as an agent of healing – physical, mental, emotional and spiritual – a word which literally means 'making whole' (*heal*, *whole* and *holy* all come from the same root, the Old English *hal*, *halig*). It has obvious links with both the Emerald Tablet of Hermes Trismegistus, and the Philosopher's Stone of alchemy; the first is usually summed up in the phrase 'As above, so below'; the second brings not just health (wholeness) and holiness (wholeness), but immortality and oneness with God (the ultimate wholeness).

What of the head of Christ? It too has obvious links, first with the head of the Celtic God-king Bran the Blessed, from the *Mabinogion*, and secondly with the talking head of either the thirteenth-century alchemist Albertus Magnus, teacher of Thomas Aquinas, or his close contemporary, the monk and scientist Roger Bacon, who was imprisoned for his 'heretical' teachings. The point of the Grail-as-head is that it speaks, and speaks the words of Christ; it is the words that are important, not the head, be it made of wood, brass or flesh.

Clearly the same applies to the Grail-as-book. It is entirely unimportant, save as a curiosity, whether it was physically written by the hand of Jesus; again, it is the words that are important.

Or perhaps the Word: 'In the beginning was the Word' (John 1:1) is talking about Christ, in the recognizable terminology of the Greek philosophers of the day.

But if we are talking about the words of Christ, rather than the Word-as-Christ, this is clearly not just referring to the New Testament accounts of his life and teachings; otherwise, the Grail would simply have been a Bible. The Grail is veiled in mystery; most of the time it is hidden. Could it be symbolic of the hidden words of Christ, the secret teachings of Jesus?

It has already been mentioned that there were a number of Gospels and other writings circulating in the first few centuries of Christianity, before the New Testament canon was eventually fixed in AD 367 by Athanasius. Biblical scholars have long known that the Gospels of Matthew and Luke were based on Mark, with large sections of a now-lost 'Sayings of Jesus' known as Q, from the German *quelle* meaning 'source' – and there are clear resemblances between the reconstructed Q and one such non-canonical work, the Gospel of Thomas, which begins 'These are the secret sayings which the living Jesus spoke', and which has clear Gnostic overtones. Even the New Testament Gospels tell us that there are other writings; Luke begins:

> Forasmuch as many have taken in hand to set forth in order a
> declaration of those things which are most surely believed among us,
> even as they delivered them unto us, which from the beginning were
> eyewitnesses, and ministers of the word; it seemed good to me also,

211

having had perfect understanding of all things from the very first, to write unto thee in order, most excellent Theophilus, that thou mightest know the certainty of those things, wherein thou hast been instructed (Luke 1:1–4);

while John's Gospel, as we have it now, ends with an added verse at the end of an added last chapter:

And there are also many other things which Jesus did, the which, if they should be written every one, I suppose that even the world itself could not contain the books that should be written (John 21:25).

Esoteric Christians say that the words of Jesus himself imply that not all his teachings were for the general public: 'And he said unto them, Unto you it is given to know the mystery of the kingdom of God: but unto them that are without, all these things are done in parables' (Mark 4:11); also, 'But without a parable spake he not unto them: and when they were alone, he expounded all things to his disciples' (Mark 4:34). Thus there were open teachings, often veiled in parables, given to everyone; and secret teachings, including the real meaning of the parables, given only to the inner circle.

If the Grail represents the secret teachings of Christ, known to the early Christian Gnostics, to the Manichæans, and perhaps to the Cathars, then the legend of the four *perfecti* escaping from Montségur with 'the treasure of the Cathars' could refer to their teachings; perhaps they did indeed escape with the 'Grail'.

THE QUESTING KNIGHTS

And so we come to the questing knights of the Grail mythos. Their chivalric code demanded courtesy, good behaviour and good works. Their courtly love meant not just chaste devotion to an individual lady, but deep respect for the very essence of woman. These were very much new concepts so far as medieval knights were concerned. They were sent to search for the Grail, and for many it was a life-long search. Whether the Grail symbolizes the life or love of God, the bounteousness of God, the wholeness of God, or the secret teachings of Jesus, the importance of the knights searching for the Grail is that *individuals* are questing for God. Finding the Grail is usually seen as attaining mystical union with God. 'It is difficult to resist the conclusion that the light of the Grail is the radiance of the Divine Presence, which is also the radiance of immortality,' says the esoteric scholar Richard Cavendish.[11]

Freemasonry has Degrees of the Knights of Constantinople, the Red Cross of Babylon and St Lawrence the Martyr, and Orders of the Knights of St John, the Holy Sepulchre, the Red Cross of Constantine, the Knights of Malta – and, of course, the Knights Templar. The Confederation of Initiates, a sort of umbrella group of certain Rosicrucian Orders which recognize each other as authentic, includes the Knights of Chivalry Order of the Holy Grail.

These are almost certainly all relatively modern creations, rather than in any way descendants of ancient Orders. The point is not whether or not there is a lineage; it is the fact that these more recent secret societies, secretive societies, or even 'societies with secrets', feel the need to link themselves with the concept of chivalric knighthood, as exemplified in the questing Grail knights.

It is not just courtesy and good works, though a member of the Society of the Inner Light 'is expected to remedy defects in his own nature and practice more assiduously a civilised way of life'.[12]

It is not just respect for women, though the equality of men and women is taken as given in all the Rosicrucian and sub-Rosicrucian movements; and even the all-male 'official' Freemasonry emphasizes strong respect for women: in what today seems rather old-fashioned language, Freemasons always refer to women as 'ladies'.

The chivalry of all these organizations is something more than social niceties or proto-feminism. It is the continuing knightly quest for the Holy Grail.

Here is just one example: 'Masonry is designed to produce regeneration in the individual life . . . The characteristics of a true Mason are humility, purity, fidelity and perseverance.'[13]

These are also characteristics of the questing Grail knight.

And so the ideas of chivalry, of courtly love, of the Grail and the personal quest for the Grail were written into the Arthurian romances – and so, at least to some extent, passed into court society. The tales were being told, and people, hearing them, absorbed the power of the ideas within them. Individuals, and society, were changed because of them.

Within a couple of centuries, though, with further additions to the Grail literature, substance had given way to form, content was less important than packaging, surface appearance was more important than the ideals within. This always happens; Chrétien de Troyes warned of its likelihood when he had Perceval mistake the mere possession of armour for the state of being a knight.

The message needed to be restated, in a different form for a different age.

THE DEVIL'S PICTURE-BOOK

The 'psychic historian' Graham Phillips asserts 'The view of most modern historians is that the Tarot probably originated with the Albigenses',[14] though with no supporting evidence whatsoever for such a bold claim. The 'inventor' of Tarot, or his exact era, is not known. If there is any connection at all between the Cathars and Tarot, it is likely to be an indirect one. The Cathars were more or less eradicated in 1244, in France; the earliest surviving Tarot packs are from *c*. 1445, and are from Italy. However . . .

Tarot, as has been shown, connects well – or can be made to connect tolerably well – with several other esoteric systems: Cabala, astrology, Celtic mythology, Runes and Norse mythology, Egyptian and Greek mythologies, among others.[15] It is not to be thought that someone sat down one day, pen or brush in hand ready to draw the cards, with the Tree of Life, maps of the

The Papess, or Female Pope, Oswald Wirth and Marseille designs
(Papus, *The Tarot of the Bohemians*, 1896)

heavens, and the *Mabinogion* spread out on the desk in front of him or her. The complex correspondences which have been drawn between Tarot and other esoteric systems are *ex post facto*. The reasons they can be made are two-fold: first, mankind's innate ability to see patterns in anything, from entrails to clouds to flames to dreams to ink blots, and to match one pattern onto another, which lies at the heart of most soothsaying and fortune-telling; and second, the fact that all these systems and mythologies stem from related peoples and from their esoteric concepts of the relationship between themselves and the Divine.

A lot of ideas have been proposed for the origin of Tarot; some are plausible, others quite ridiculous. Probably in reaction to these latter, some writers eschew all such ideas, saying that the occult symbolism of Tarot was invented in the late eighteenth and the nineteenth centuries, which is largely true, and that Tarot was originally simply an attractive card game.

This last is just as ludicrous as Antoine Court de Gébelin's assertion that Tarot is the ancient Egyptian Book of Thoth. Even in the very earliest packs, many of the cards are clearly religious. The Cary–Yale Visconti pack, dated 1440–45, has Fortitude, Faith, Hope, Charity, Death and Judgement; the Visconti-Sforza pack, *c.* 1450, has the Pope, the Papess, and Judgement, among others; the Charles VI pack (1470–80) has the Pope, Temperance, Fortitude, Justice and Judgement; the Ercole d'Este pack (1475–80) has the Pope, and the cards for the Star, the Moon and the Sun clearly show astrological study. These packs also have Death, the Hanged Man, the Lightning-struck Tower, the Wheel of Fortune and the World, all of which have religious connotations.

There cannot be any doubt that the Tarot images, from the very beginning, had religious significance. The imagery is not just religious, but largely Christian; and not just Christian, but in some cases esoteric Christian.

To take just one example, the Papess or Popess – sometimes turned into Juno in later Classical-inspired packs, and more often into the High Priestess in modern packs – was, in the Visconti-Sforza pack, very clearly a female pope, wearing the papal triple tiara. She may well, as most authorities think, have represented the popular medieval myth of the ninth- or eleventh-century Pope Joan; or she may have been Sister Manfreda or Maifreda di Pirovano, a relative of the Visconti family and a member of the small Milanese sect of the Guglielmites, who was burned by the Inquisition in 1300, the year in which the sect believed she would become pope; or she may have been a reference to the sexual equality in Catharism, such a contrast to the position of the Catholic Church. Whichever, in one way or another she represents the esoteric, heterodox concept of female spirituality.

The six essential interrogatives taught to trainee journalists – Who, What, When, Where, How and Why? – are all fascinating when applied to the origins of Tarot; but the one to concern us here is the last. Why were these particular religious images used on sets of cards designed and made – hand-painted, and richly embossed with gold leaf – for the Italian nobility?

What follows in this section is a hypothesis, offered in the hope that others will follow it up, whether it be to provide further supporting evidence or to shoot it down in flames.

While Tarot quite possibly had as a primary pictorial basis the *Triumphs* of Petrarch – itself exemplifying the virtues of Classical Greece – it also embodied from the start some aspects of Cabalistic thought (strong in southern France and northern Spain); and some Gnostic ideas most recently seen in Catharism (southern France and northern Italy); and – as Arthurian literature strayed from its original ideals – the essence of the quest for the Grail (all of France, but at least in part inspired by the Provençal troubadours and taking in the ethos of that area's heterodox beliefs and culture); and all that within a Theatre of Memory *aide-mémoire*. If stained-glass windows were orthodox sermons in glass, then Tarot was heterodox beliefs on card.

Any supposedly Egyptian elements were Greek/Egyptian magical–mystical–philosophical concepts as passed on through the Neo-Platonism which became such a powerful spiritual and intellectual influence in the Renaissance. The whole was presented in a pictorial format which would be understandable by the people of the day – familiar social and religious images – just as paintings of Christ were put in a late medieval or early Renaissance setting.

With some regret, but with firmness, those 'standard' Tarot images, which nineteenth- and twentieth-century esotericists have spent so much time analyzing, must be put out of mind – the Hanged Man with his legs crossed in a figure 4, the exact creatures climbing up and down the Wheel of Fortune, the figure of Temperance with one foot on land and one in water, the crayfish and the dogs in the Moon card, and so on – and all the detailed symbolism from these familiar images. They were later design features, no doubt added for very good reasons, but not in the original Tarot images.

How can one even guess at the original symbolism? The Hanged Man might perhaps originally have represented a heretic about to be executed; they were sometimes burned upside down. The Tower – in early packs often called Lightning, and sometimes called the House of God – could perhaps have represented the divine reproval of those who build a tower to God, whether the mythical Babel or the vast and corrupt edifice of the established Christian Church. From the images on the very earliest packs the card now called The World probably represented originally the Christian's hope and destination, the City of God, the Heavenly Jerusalem; in medieval maps

Jerusalem, the Holy City, was always shown at the centre of the world.

Whatever the original symbolism, it is now difficult if not impossible to find it under the layers of accretions of symbolism of the following centuries. The symbolism was relevant to its day, to the mind-set of the people for whom the first Tarot packs were designed.

Paradoxically, this frees us, if we wish, to redesign and redefine Tarot within whatever new symbolic parameters we wish. Those Tarot purists who complain that modern packs have strayed from the original designs (by which they tend to mean Rider–Waite, or at the earliest, Marseille) forget that the pictures always *have* changed. The Visconti-Sforza Fool (*c.* 1450) is quite different from the Charles VI Fool (*c.* 1470–80) and the Ercole d'Este Fool (*c.* 1475–80). The same applies to other cards. The world-views change; the images change; the precise symbolism changes.

Then, with the advent of printing, Tarot suddenly became widely and cheaply available. The images were more crudely executed, and inevitably copying errors crept in. (For example, the well-known image of the Hermit holding a lamp was originally an old man holding an hourglass, representing time.) Tarot changed from being a rich symbolic library for the educated nobility to no more than a popular card game with interesting pictures.

Tarot, like the Grail stories, lost its initial sense, the ideals represented within the pictures; substance gave way to form again. There is no evidence that the Hermetic Philosophers of the fifteenth and sixteenth centuries, with their emphasis (theoretical or practical) on Cabala, astrology, alchemy and magic, saw anything significant in Tarot. Did Cornelius Agrippa or John Dee own a Tarot pack? This, quite simply, is not known.

The eighteenth- and nineteenth-century occultists, with all their bad scholarship, at least realized that there was more to Tarot than a pretty card game. Whatever their ideas, misconceived or otherwise, they brought Tarot back to the attention of those interested in esoteric religion. The Hermetic Order of the Golden Dawn, for good or for bad (or both), leaped on Tarot and added their own interpretations.

Today, esoteric schools such as Builders of the Adytum and Servants of the Light use Tarot for study, for teaching, for meditation, for spiritual illumination, for religious ritual – and not, generally, for divination. Their teachings include Cabala, Gnosticism, the Grail, mysticism; they honour the Divine Feminine. Tarot's own Wheel of Fortune has thus gone full circle: after centuries first as a card game and then a fortune-telling device, Tarot has come home.

As has been seen with the Church's treatment throughout history of those with divergent beliefs, whether they be labelled heretics, magicians, witches or whatever, it has always been standard practice to calumnize and demonize heterodox beliefs and practices. From the narrow viewpoint of orthodoxy (or today, of Fundamentalism), anything which is not sanctioned by themselves is evil; anything heterodox is, by definition, of the Devil.

If Tarot is indeed a pictorial memory-theatre of Classical Pagan, Neo-Platonist, Gnostic, Cabalist, Grail and mystical beliefs – and alchemy and astrology also fit into it well enough – then, *from the Church's point of view*, the Devil's Picture-Book is not a bad description.

In a nutshell, the established Church has to be vehemently opposed to all these belief-systems, which have surfaced again and again in different forms throughout history; if they caught on widely, as they did in southern France in the twelfth century, they would make the Church completely irrelevant.

One of the most sound Tarot authorities today, Rachel Pollack, expresses it clearly and simply: 'the goal remains the same despite the system – a reunion of the self and the divine.'[16]

And that would put hierarchical religion out of business.

THE CONTINUING
REVELATION

Just before the previous section, it was said of the Grail romances, which were becoming little more than pretty stories, that 'The message needed to be restated, in a different form for a different age.'

Tarot originated some time in the late fourteenth or early fifteenth century as, it is suggested, an esoteric *aide-mémoire*, heterodoxy on card. A century or so later, with the invention of cheap printing methods, it had become a popular card game, and any message it contained had become forgotten. The message needed to be restated, in a different form for a different age.

In 1614 the *Fama Fraternitatis* appeared; it called on those adepts, generally known as the Hermetic Philosophers, who desired to benefit the world, to make themselves known.

It is quite categorically *not* being stated that throughout history there has been a continuing secret band of initiates who have guarded a secret Truth, and from time to time have launched a wider dissemination of esoteric, heterodox ideas. What is being suggested is that these ideas just won't go away, however much they may be pushed out of public view. Every now and then, probably quite independently, someone who had discovered for himself the value of esoteric teachings seems to have decided to share what he had found

– not necessarily in the wide-open marketplace, but with others who would recognise the clues. So, for example, the Hermetic Philosophers studied alchemy and Cabala, usually alone; one or more of them decided to write and publish the Rosicrucian Manifestos.

In the late nineteenth century a handful of British members of the *Societas Rosicruciana in Anglia* started a new society; its membership should be wider, including non-Masons and women; its esoteric enquiry should be deeper. The Hermetic Order of the Golden Dawn was born.

In the early twentieth century a group of Americans decided that the teachings of the *Societas Rosicruciana in Civitatibus Foederatis* should not be restricted to Freemasons. *The Societas Rosicruciana in America* was born.

In the late 1930s the *Stella Matutina* had lost impetus and members; rather than risk its (originally Golden Dawn) teachings vanishing altogether, Israel Regardie broke ranks, and his vow of secrecy, and published all its teachings and rituals. The secret teachings were made public.

Time and again over the centuries, someone brings the hidden teachings out into the light. But time and again they are pushed back into the dark again, either by the established Church, or by such as the eighteenth-century Age of Reason or the nineteenth-century Age of Scientific Rationalism; or in the late twentieth century by science on the one hand and Fundamentalism on the other. Orthodoxy appears determined to wipe out heterodoxy.

———

There are many, very different, versions of orthodox, exoteric Christianity. They share the same God, the same sacred text, similar creeds, and probably some of the same hymns; but the supremacy of the pope, the veneration of Mary, the doctrine of transubstantiation and so on are anathema to Evangelicals, while the lack of a priesthood and sacraments of some Evangelical Churches are anathema to the Catholic Church. Yet both are seen as legitimate varieties of the multi-faceted organism which is the Christian religion.

In contrast, the more mystical, more Gnostic, more esoteric varieties of Christianity are regarded as heresy, or even as anti-Christian, by most denominations within mainstream Christianity. Perhaps it is because ortho-dox, exoteric denominations say of themselves, in effect, 'There is one way to salvation, and this is it,' while esoteric Christians generally say, 'There may be many ways to salvation; here is the road-map, here are the signposts; now you follow your own route.'

Esoteric spiritual beliefs stick in the craw of orthodox believers, of what-ever religion. Christian critics of secret societies often, at some point, come up with the argument, 'If these people really do have some wonderful spiritual truth, it's not right that they should keep it to themselves; they should share it with everyone, just as we proclaim the good news of Christ crucified.'

But that is the very difference between exoteric and esoteric religion.

The great world-religions have been ordained to teach in their respective manners the same truths as the Mystery systems have taught. Their teaching has always been twofold. There has always existed an external, elementary, popular doctrine which has served for the instruction of the masses who are insufficiently prepared for deeper teaching; and concurrently therewith there has been an interior, advanced doctrine, a more secret knowledge, which has been reserved for riper minds and into which only proficient and properly prepared candidates, who voluntarily sought to participate in it, were initiated. Whether in ancient India, Egypt, Greece, Italy or Mexico, or among the Druids of Europe, temples of initiation have ever existed for those who felt the inward call to come apart from the multitude and to dedicate themselves to a long discipline of body and mind with a view to acquiring the secret knowledge and developing the spiritual faculties by means of experimental processes of initiation of which our present ceremonies are the faint echo.[17]

W.L. Wilmshurst is speaking here of Freemasonry; he could as easily have been speaking of Rosicrucianism or one of the modern Schools of Occult Science.

Anyone finding this quotation élitist should consider three points. First, esoteric teachings are always available for those who wish to pursue them; 'Seek and ye shall find.' Second, recall what happened when esoteric Christianity did come out into the open in southern France in the twelfth and thirteenth centuries. And third, if Freemasonry is, as Wilmshurst claims, in the same line of esoteric spirituality, then it is making such teachings openly available to anyone (if male); the only restriction is the awareness of the initiate to what is being placed before him – and that was always the case.

Throughout this book certain ideas have cropped up over and over again. Throughout history these same (or similar) ideas have surfaced, and flourished, and in most cases died. Either they have been stamped on and stamped out, or they have faded away, or they have ossified. The Cathars are the obvious example of the first, the Freemasons of the last.

But the ideas have never gone away altogether. The Manichæan version of Gnosticism resurfaced in Catharism. Neo-Platonism resurfaced in the philosophers of the Renaissance. The alchemists became the Hermetic Philosophers, who spawned the Rosicrucians. The Hermetic Order of the Golden Dawn gave birth to (among others) the Society of Inner Light, which itself sparked off the Servants of the Light.

Today, more than at any time in history, individual spirituality is out in the open. One can find books on Cabala, on Rosicrucianism, on spiritual growth, not only in specialist shops but in high street bookshops; one can even buy the secret teachings of the Golden Dawn in their entirety. There are not only specialist publishers, but specialist imprints of the major publishing companies. 'Mind, Body, Spirit', 'New Age', 'Esoteric': the labels proliferate.

The ideas are on open display. In many ways this is good, but there are three possible dangers. The first is commercialization: thousands of books, dozens of Tarot packs, crystals, pendulums, self-help kits of many varieties. The second, related to this, is the difficulty of finding the pearl in a sea full of oysters. The third is the rise of Fundamentalism, which is implacably opposed to what it sees as the Devil's work.

A NEED FOR SECRECY?

Is there still any need for secrecy, whether in the Freemasons, the various Rosicrucian or occult schools, or any other secret societies? Only they can answer for themselves, but a general outsider's view might be: 'If they have nothing to hide, why not dispense with the secrecy, come out into the open, and so lose all the suspicion attached to them. If they do have something to hide, what?'

One reason for secrecy was given right at the beginning of this book, by the Lemurian Fellowship. It is worth quoting again: 'the Lemurian lesson material is available only to qualified students. Not because it is "secret" but because each lesson's information provides a basis for the next; along with this the Fellowship teachers' guidance to each student according to his individual needs makes the deeper benefits possible and adds to the uniqueness of Lemurian Training.'[18]

In other words, it is progressive, cumulative teaching.

It is not generally considered a good idea to try teaching post-Einsteinian physics to someone who hasn't mastered basic Newtonian physics – even though the more complex teachings often overturn what we learned in our schooldays. A skilful novelist can break rules of grammar to good effect; but a sensible English teacher hammers those rules into pupils without exception. It may be a tautology, but at every level of understanding we can understand what we are taught at that level. The next level might show that the previous one was a gross over-simplification – or even that it was incorrect, but needed to be learned in order that the contradiction of the next level would have a basis.

Even those esoteric societies which are comparatively open rarely reveal the details of their initiation ceremonies. The widow of the founder of the Rosicrucian Fellowship gives another reason why this should be so:

> . . . his consciousness is lifted to the level required for the Initiation which he is being given. This is the reason why the secrets of true Initiation cannot be revealed. *It is not an outward ceremonial but an inward experience.* This description is the nearest to what Initiation really is that can possibly be given to one who has not experienced it himself. There is no secret about the pictures in the sense that one would not tell it, but they are secret because no earthly words are coined which could adequately describe such a spiritual experience.[19]

A.E. Waite says much the same in his brief discussion of the subject of Masonic secrecy in his *Encyclopædia*. The true secrets of Freemasonry, he says, are not the handshakes, the closely-guarded Words, the jewels or insignia or the internal layout and decorations of a lodge. All of these, in any case, have been public knowledge almost since Freemasonry began. Even the workings of the different degrees can be found in full detail in books in most public libraries. According to Waite,

> The true secret is the peculiar life of Masonry which is incommunicable to the uninitiated by the irrepealable nature of things. There is a sense in which Masonic symbolism is a part of this life . . . the Mysteries are not taught openly even in the Orders themselves, being acquired in the course of the life. What happens actually is that certain Keys are put into the hands of the Brethren, as each initiate in his turn passes through the successive Grades; and it is for him – if he is able – to open the Temple into which they do or may give entrance. It comes about in this manner that there are always Mysteries behind the Mysteries and a more withdrawn adytum behind the Holy of Holies, because growth in the knowledge of Masonry is growth in its life and consciousness.'[20]

Interestingly, the Builders of the Adytum (which means 'inner temple') call their Tarot cards 'Keys'.

There is also the very vital point that many of the esoteric societies claim that their initiates are able to improve their mental powers – not in the sense of telepathy, invisibility or walking through walls, but in the sense of vastly improved memory, self-confidence and personal authority. According to W.L. Wilmshurst, Freemasonry offers much the same:

> In fact, part of the purpose of all initiation was, and still is, to educate the mind in penetrating the outward shell of all phenomena, and the value of initiation depends upon the way in which the inward truths are allowed to influence our thought and lives and to awaken in us still deeper powers of consciousness . . .

> . . . the neophyte Mason who aspires to Mastership. He will become conscious of an increase of perceptive faculty and understanding; he will become aware of having tapped a previously unsuspected source of power, giving him enhanced mental strength and self-confidence; there will become observable in him developing graces of character, speech and conduct that were previously foreign to him.[21]

This, of course, is dependent on the Mason understanding and applying the inner depths of the teachings, rather than just going through the motions by rote, as many undoubtedly do; it does, however, help explain why Freemasons tend to be very capable and successful people.

Such increases in personal powers are quite real. They are very clearly open to abuse. When coupled with ritual, whatever one's views on magic, they become even more powerful. A self-seeking individual could do major harm to others through abusing such powers. The Builders of the Adytum insist on associate members 'demonstrating harmonious fraternal qualities' before they allow them to be initiated into the higher levels.

It should also be remembered that ritual has power of its own, whether this be explained in spiritual or psychological terms. Even someone with no religious beliefs can be moved by the spectacle of a Roman Catholic high mass, or the serenity of an Anglican Prayer Book Evensong. This is what has been lost in modern 'plain speech' services: the grandeur, the peacefulness, the sense of mystery, the *otherness* – or perhaps simply the beauty of poetic language – evoked by the old rituals. Initiates taking part in a Masonic ritual, or any other esoteric ritual, will be changed by it to some extent, even if they have no perception of its inner meaning.

As discussed above, esoteric societies from the Rosicrucian Manifestos to the present day all speak of society benefiting through the personal development of their members. Most stipulate that candidates at the lowest level should be of good character, but unless initial entrance is by invitation only, they often have to depend on the candidate's own word for that. Interestingly Freemasonry, if it sticks to its own rules, not only bans women from membership (they are, after all, in a patriarchal society, traditionally weaker of intellect and will) but also bastards and men with physical disabilities – both, historically, sure signs of unfitness of character.

A carefully-graded course of instruction over several years, with initiation to the next level never being assumed as automatic, but always being by invitation, means that the more senior (and presumably wiser) adepts can keep a careful check over the rise of members through the grades. Those judged unsuitable in their character for the next level of knowledge find their way blocked. This unsuitability might only become apparent after a certain level has been reached.

This was the problem with Aleister Crowley. After only a year he had progressed through the Outer Order of the Golden Dawn, and demanded initiation into the Second Order. The leaders of the Order refused on the grounds that he was morally unsuitable. The ensuing events rapidly led to the break-up of the Hermetic Order of the Golden Dawn. With the example of Crowley still sharp in their memories nearly a century later, it is little wonder that today organizations descended from the HOGD are wary about who they allow to join them. All such groups are protective of their secrets; for some, even their existence is a closely-guarded secret. Secrecy not only protects those within, it also keeps out undesirables.

The recognition signs and the wording of the rituals in Freemasonry are supposed to be kept secret. Speaking more generally of the Mysteries lying behind Freemasonry, one writer mentions

> . . . the secrecy and the intense watchfulness and carefulness of the
> stewards of the Mysteries lest the secret doctrines find expression on
> the lips or through the action of unfit persons to possess the secrets.
> For the secret power of the Mysteries is within the signs. Any person
> attaining to natural or supernatural states by the process of
> development, if his heart be untuned and his mind withdrawn from the
> Divine to the human within him, that power becomes a power of evil
> instead of a power of good. An unfaithful initiate, in the degree of the
> Mysteries he has attained, is capable, by virtue of his antecedent
> preparations and processes, of diverting the power to unholy,
> demoniacal, astral and dangerous uses . . . [22]

Hence, at each stage of initiation, only certain information is revealed; it is also why, in Freemasonry as in other societies, entry to the higher levels is by invitation only.

It is common for Fundamentalist opponents to lump together secret societies, esoteric religion, high ritual magic, Neo-Paganism and Satanism as equally 'occult', and their rituals as equally evil. In fact, the power made available through esoteric ritual is neutral, like electricity, or a motorcar, or the contents of a pharmacy. It can be used for good or for evil, to heal or to harm; but usually, like these more mundane powers, it is used only for good.

Secrecy, then, is also to ensure that only those fit to receive powerful knowledge may be allowed to do so.

One further reason for the secrecy of societies should be considered: it might be necessary for their own safety. The growing influence of Fundamentalism has already been noted. Rightly or wrongly (from other people's point of view), Fundamentalists sincerely believe that it is their sacred duty to combat Satan and all his works in any way they can. It is their firm belief that anything which is not of Christ is of the Devil, and their definition of what is 'of Christ' is somewhat narrower than most. The activities of secret societies, especially those (the majority) with some spiritual element, are clearly in danger from increasingly strenuous opposition to their existence because of the attitude of such groups; the equation is simple: heterodoxy is esoteric, esoteric is occult, and occult is Satanic.

Fundamentalists, like everyone else, have every right to their freedom of belief and freedom of speech. It has become more and more apparent in recent years, however, that they believe this gives them the right to constrain the beliefs and the speech of others; they see this as permissible in their fight against Satan. More effective than breaking the law in their prosecution of that fight, though, would be changing the law.

Freedom of speech *can* legitimately be curtailed: for example, for reasons of national security – the Official Secrets Act; or in the greater cause of equal rights for all people, regardless of their skin colour – it is illegal to incite racial hatred in speech or writing. The first is a Government imposition, generally accepted (with some reservations) by most of the population; the second is very widely accepted as right.

Over the last few decades, as Western countries have moved further into a liberal democracy and a multi-cultural environment, there has been a general understanding that one should accept the diversity of different religious beliefs, and accept the right of others to practice their religion as they wish. Occasionally Hindu or Muslim worship is shown on British television; most people would agree that this is a positive development – but not all. There have been complaints when non-Christian religions, both orthodox and heterodox, have been given air-time, even in documentaries about unusual beliefs.

In the last few years there have been calls for a tightening up of the Blasphemy laws. According to the existing Blasphemy Act, one can be prosecuted if a publication contains 'contemptuous, reviling, scurrilous or ludicrous matter relating to God, Jesus Christ or the Bible, or formularies of the Church of England.' Insulting the 'formularies' of Hindus, Muslims, Jews, and even Roman Catholics and Baptists, is quite permissible under the law as it currently stands.

The British Blasphemy law is based on thirteenth-century Church Law, which originally stipulated the death penalty. Over the years public opinion changed, so that blasphemy became not so much a sin against God as an offence against one's fellow man; penalties were reduced accordingly. The law is no longer for the protection of the reputation of God, so to speak, but for the protection of the feelings of believers.

Most people would agree that inciting religious hatred should be as illegal as inciting racial hatred; but at what point should the line be drawn? The phrase 'causing offence' is not a reliable guideline. Most Christians of whatever persuasion would find the assertions that Jesus either didn't die on the cross or didn't rise from the dead, for example, both offensive and blasphemous, and yet many who call themselves Christians believe this – not to mention countless millions of Jews and Muslims. Despite that, anyone suggesting such a belief as a thesis to be considered objectively would be condemned by Fundamentalists; they would be called a blasphemer or a heretic.

Other unorthodox beliefs are also under fire; there have been serious calls by British Fundamentalists for the Witchcraft Act, which was only repealed as late as 1951, to be reinstated.

Fundamentalists are opposed to other people's freedom of belief and worship.

As we pass into the new millennium, it seems that the divide between religious conservatives and liberals, between the orthodox and the heterodox, between Fundamentalists and Freethinkers, is becoming wider and more entrenched. There is a possibility that mainstream Christian MPs could be pressurised by increasingly vocal Fundamentalists into passing legislation which would, ultimately, restrict freedom of speech on religion, and thus restrict the freedom of belief. The Christian Right in America are already almost in a position where they could do this. There is at least one Islamic Republic where it is illegal 'to injure the feelings of a Muslim'; the equivalent could soon occur in America, and not long after, in Britain. One British MP, joint secretary of the parliamentary all-party cult group and also on the Council of Reference of the most outspoken anti-cult organization, has already called for alternative religious movements – 'sects' and 'cults' – to be registered and regulated. It is a small step from that to imposing restrictions on their beliefs and practices. The same would undoubtedly apply to secret societies, most of which have heterodox religious beliefs and rituals.

If this happened, Western liberal democracies would effectively be instituting a new witch hunt. The organisations mentioned in Chapter Four, and their members, could find themselves in serious trouble. As was said near the beginning of Chapter Two, in the Middle Ages the burning of uneducated country women and the burning of highly educated heretical priests were two sides of the same coin. Whatever the spiritual beliefs of individual secret societies might be, including those of mystics within Freemasonry, they tend to be heterodox. For a vocal and increasingly influential few, heterodox equals heretical equals blasphemous equals Satanic.

The need for secrecy might, sadly, be greater than ever.

CODA

EXOTERIC CHRISTIANITY does not usually teach what is one of the central tenets of the Gnostics, the Sufis, the Cabalists, the Cathars, the Rosicrucians, and even the spiritual heart of the Freemasons. It seems appropriate to end this book with a quotation from a book by a leading Freemason of earlier this century, who in turn is quoting a myth from 'the East'. This, in allegorical form, is the starting point of the revelation at the heart of all secret societies with esoteric religious origins:

> From the wise lore of the East, Max Müller translated a parable which tells how the gods, having stolen from man his divinity, met in council to discuss where they should hide it. One suggested that it should be carried to the other side of the earth and buried; but it was pointed out that man is a great wanderer, and that he might find the lost treasure on the other side of the earth. Another proposed that it be dropped into the depths of the sea; but the same fear was expressed – that man, in his insatiable curiosity, might dive deep enough to find it even there. Finally, after a space of silence, the oldest and wisest of the gods said: 'Hide it in man himself, as that is the last place he will ever think to look for it!' And it was so agreed, all seeing at once the subtle and wise strategy. Man did wander over the earth, for ages, seeking in all places high and low, far and near, before he thought to look within himself for the divinity he sought. At last, slowly, dimly, he began to realise that what he thought was far off, hidden in 'the pathos of distance,' is nearer than the breath he breathes, even in his own heart.[1]

CHRONOLOGY

THIS CHRONOLOGY lists some of the significant events covered in this book. Some of the dates, particularly of a process rather than a specific event, are approximate.

660–583 BC	Possible dating of Zoroaster (Zarathustra)
581–497 BC	Pythagoras
c. 90	Vitruvius writes *De Architectura*
c. 100 BC to c. AD 100	Probable origins of Gnosticism
First–fourth century	Works of 'Hermes Trismegistus' written
First–sixth century	Neo-Platonist Schools flourish
Second–fifth century	Mithraism flourishes
216–76	Mani, founder of Manichæism
325	Council of Nicea
367	Content of New Testament officially finalized
Fourth–fifth century	Pelagius, propounder of Pelagianism
Seventh century	Probable origin of Sufism
c. 721–815	Jabir ibn Hayyan (Geber), influential Arab alchemist
Ninth century	John Scotus Erigena
Tenth century	Possible founding of the Bogomils
1090	Founding of the Assassins
1095	Beginning of the First Crusade. Jerusalem is won in 1099, lost in 1187, recaptured in 1229 and lost again in 1244
1119	Founding of the Knights Templar
c. 1143	Emergence of the Cathars
c. 1150	The idea of courtly love, written and sung about by the Provençal troubadours, migrates to

	northern France (possibly with returning Crusaders) in the middle of the twelfth century
c. 1155–90	Medieval mythologizing of the Arthur story, with French emphasis on chivalry and courtly love, and introduction of the Grail
c. 1175	The Cabalist *Sefer ha-Bahir* is written in Provence. Medieval Cabalism develops in Provence in the twelfth century and remains strong there; it spreads from Provence to Spain
1184	Pope Lucius III founds the Inquisition
1193–1280	Albertus Magnus
c. 1200	Origin of the Beguines
1200–50	Languedocian or Provençal culture is largely wiped out
1209	Albigensian Crusade begins against the Cathars
1214–92	Roger Bacon
1215	Founding of the Dominicans
1229	The Northern French annex the Languedoc
1232–1315	Ramón Lull
1233	Dominicans put in charge of the Inquisition
1244	Cathars' last stronghold, Montségur, falls
c. 1250	End of the influence of the Assassins
1272	End of the last Crusade
c. 1285	The Cabalist *Sefer ha-Zohar* is published in northern Spain
1307–14	Dissolution of the Knights Templar; Jacques de Molay burned in 1314
1337–1453	Hundred Years War
1340–74	Petrarch's *Triumphs* written
1347–50	Black Death kills a third of Europe's population
1367	First known mention of playing cards
1378	Supposed birth of Christian Rosenkreuz
c. 1445	Earliest known Tarot pack
1453	Constantinople sacked by the Turks
1471	*Corpus Hermeticum* translated into Latin
1484	Supposed death of Christian Rosenkreuz
c. 1486	Publication of *Malleus Maleficarum*
1492	Jews expelled from Spain and Portugal
1492	Columbus sails to America

Fifteenth–seventeenth century	The Hermetic Philosophers
1614–16	Publication of *Fama Fraternitatis, Confessio Fraternitatis* and *The Chymical Wedding of Christian Rosenkreuz*
1646	Elias Ashmole initiated into Masonic Lodge
1659	Three people executed in Massachusetts for being Quakers
c. 1700	Marseille Tarot pack becomes popular
1701	Act of Settlement ensures Protestant monarchy in England
1707	Act of Union between England and Scotland
1710	Laws of the Brotherhood of the Golden and Rosy Cross published
1717	Formation of first Grand Lodge of Free-masons
1736	Chevalier Michael Ramsay's Oration sparks chivalric interest in Freemasonry
c. 1754	Baron von Hund founds the Rite of the Strict Observance
1776	American Declaration of Independence
1776	Founding of the Illuminati
1777	Reformation of the Brotherhood of the Golden and Rosy Cross
1781	Antoine Court de Gébelin publishes *Le Monde Primitif*
1781	Last person burned at the stake for heresy, in Seville
1789	French Revolution begins
1801	Francis Barrett's *The Magus* published
c. 1834	Freemasons concoct the word Jahbulon
1850	Mary Anne Atwood's *A Suggestive Enquiry into the Hermetic Mystery* published
1855–56	Éliphas Lévi's *Dogme et Rituel de la Haute Magie* published
1858	Founding of *Fraternitas Rosae Crucis* (Beverly Hall Corporation)
c. 1865	Founding of the Ku Klux Klan
1866	Founding of *Societas Rosicruciana in Anglia*
1875	Founding of the Theosophical Society
1888	Founding of the Kabbalistic Order of the Rosy Cross

1888	Founding of the Hermetic Order of the Golden Dawn
1890	Founding of the Order of the Catholic Rosy Cross, the Temple and the Grail
1891–95	Leo Taxil's fabrications against Freemasonry
1896	Papus publishes *The Tarot of the Bohemians*
c. 1900	HOGD splits into several factions, including *Stella Matutina*
1906	Founding of the *Ordo Templi Orientis*
1907	Founding of Crowley's *Argentium Astrum*
1907	Founding of the Rosicrucian Fellowship
1907	Founding of the *Ordo Novi Templi*
1909	Founding of the *Societas Rosicruciana in America*
1910	Rider–Waite Tarot published
1913	Rudolf Steiner founds the Anthroposophical Society
1915	Founding of the Ancient and Mystical Order Rosae Crucis (AMORC)
1920	Aleister Crowley founds the Abbey of Thelema
1920s	Paul Foster Case founds the Builders of the Adytum
1924	Founding of *Lectorium Rosicrucianum*
1928	Dion Fortune founds the Fraternity (later Society) of the Inner Light
1937–40	Teachings and rituals of HOGD revealed by Israel Regardie
1960s, mid-	Founding of P2
1972	W.E. Butler founds the Servants of the Light
1989	Freemasons drop the word 'Jahbulon'
1994–95, 1997	Suicide/murder of members of the Order of the Solar Temple

NOTES

INTRODUCTION

1   Mrs M.W. Menger of the Lemurian Fellowship, personal correspondence, 8 December 1995.

CHAPTER ONE
THE ROOTS

1   L.C. Pascoe, A.J. Lee and E.S. Jenkins, *Encyclopædia of Dates and Events*, English Universities Press 1968, p. 23.
2   Stephen Knight, *The Brotherhood*, Granada 1983, p. 236; and see pp. 117–20.
3   Jack Lindsay, *Byzantium Into Europe*, Bodley Head 1952, p. 324.
4   André Nataf, *The Occult*, W. & R. Chambers 1991, p. 35.
5   See Norman Golb, *Who Wrote the Dead Sea Scrolls?*, Michael O'Mara 1995, *passim*.
6   For more detail on this, see my *Sects, 'Cults' and Alternative Religions*, Blandford 1996, pp. 46–50.
7   Many fourth-century lists omit the book of Revelation; several omit the Epistle to the Hebrews; Eusebius Pamphilus, *c.* 315, says that the Epistles of James, Jude, II Peter, II John and III John were generally received, but doubted by some.
8   Quoted from *The Other Bible*, ed. Willis Barnstone, Harper and Row 1984, p. 302.
9   Leonard George, *The Encyclopedia of Heresies and Heretics*, Robson 1995, pp. 62, 173–5, 263–4.
10 Modern-day numerology, finding Personality numbers and Heart numbers from one's date of birth and the numerical equivalent of one's name, is a very much debased version of *gematria*, the Cabalistic study of the spiritual significance of numbers; as practised by most people, it is no more than a trivialized form of fortune-telling, of as much value as tabloid newspaper horoscopes.
11 Servants of the Light introductory booklet, p. 3.
12 Robert Graves in his Introduction to Idries Shah, *The Sufis*, W.H. Allen, 1964, p. xix; Shah sees it more as an influence than a direct descent.
13 For a more detailed examination of Christian 'heresies' see my *Sects, 'Cults' and Alternative Religions* Blandford 1996.

14 'The spurious charge of sodomy is one of the traditional libels applied by the
Roman Catholic Church to those who question its dogmas.' James McDonald, *A
Dictionary of Obscenity, Taboo and Euphemism*, Sphere Books 1988, p. 17.

15 Rufus M. Jones, *Studies in Mystical Religion*, 1909, quoted in Michael Cox, *A
Handbook of Christian Mysticism*, Aquarian Press edn 1986, p. 96.

16 Emmanuel Le Roy Ladurie, *Montaillou: Cathars and Catholics in a French Village
1294–1324*, Peregrine edn 1984, p. viii.

17 Some authorities say as many as 200,000.

18 M.L. Cozens, *A Handbook of Heresies*, Sheed and Ward 1974 edn, p. 65: this was
written and received its Imprimatur in 1928; my copy was published in 1986.

19 Paul Elliott, *Warrior Cults*, Cassell 1995, pp. 73–4.

20 See, for example, John J. Robinson, *Born in Blood*, Century 1989; Michael Baigent
and Richard Leigh, *The Temple and the Lodge*, Jonathan Cape 1989; Andrew
Sinclair, *The Sword and the Grail*, Century 1993, etc.

21 George, *The Encyclopedia of Heresies and Heretics*, p. 157.

22 Peter Partner, *The Murdered Magicians: The Templars and their Myth*, Aquarian edn
1987, pp. xx–xxi.

23 A.E. Waite, *A New Encyclopædia of Freemasonry*, 1994 reprint, vol. 1 p. 50.

24 Elliott, *Warrior Cults*, p. 77.

CHAPTER TWO
FROM THE RENAISSANCE TO
THE AGE OF REASON

1 See Ann Baer, *Medieval Woman*, Michael O'Mara Books 1996, for a powerful
fictional account of the constant grinding poverty and struggle to survive of
ordinary medieval villagers.

2 Robin Briggs, *Witches and Neighbours*, HarperCollins 1996, p. 101; here Briggs is
following the scholarship of historian John Bossy.

3 Ibid, p. 259.

4 Israel Regardie, *The Golden Dawn*, one-volume 6th edn, Llewellyn 1989, p. 23.

5 W.L. Wilmshurst, *The Meaning of Masonry*, John M. Watkins 1922, p. 100.

6 Frances Yates, *The Occult Philosophy in the Elizabethan Age*, Routledge & Kegan Paul
1979, Ark edn 1983, p. 82.

7 A.E. Waite, *The Brotherhood of the Rosy Cross*, Rider 1924, pp. 19, 33.

8 Mark L. Prophet and Elizabeth Clare Prophet, *Saint Germain on Alchemy: Formulas
for Self-Transformation*, 1985, pp. 446–8, 124.

9 Quoted in Jean Gimpel, trans. Teresa Waugh, *The Cathedral Builders*, Michael
Russell 1983, Pimlico edn 1993, p. 92. (Originally published in France by Éditions
du Seuil 1980).

10 Ibid, pp. 109–111.

11 'Architecture and City Planning' in M.I. Finley, ed., *The Legacy of Greece*, Oxford
University Press 1981, p. 389.

12 The concepts of sacred geometry and esoteric architecture are explored in some
depth in fiction by John Crowley in *Little, Big* (1981), and especially in *Ægypt*
(1987) and its sequels; and by Mary Gentle in *Rats and Gargoyles* (1990), *The*

Architecture of Desire (1991), *Left to His Own Devices* (1994), and two long novellas in her collection *Scholars and Soldiers* (1987).

13 The story of Christian Rosenkreuz's life is retold in fictional form in David Foster's *The Adventures of Christian Rosy Cross*, Penguin 1986.

14 See A.E. Waite, *The Brotherhood of the Rosy Cross*, Rider 1924, pp. 85–112, and the various dictionaries of symbolism cited in the Bibliography, for much more detail of the symbolism of the rose and the cross.

15 John Hamill and R.A. Gilbert, *World Freemasonry: An Illustrated History*, Aquarian Press 1991, pp. 98–101.

16 Michael Howard, *The Occult Conspiracy*, Rider 1989, p. 82.

17 From the Declaration of Independence. Thomas Jefferson's original draft read: 'We hold these truths to be sacred and undeniable; that all men are created equal and independent, that from that equal creation they derive rights inherent and inalienable, among which are the preservation of life, and liberty, and the pursuit of happiness.' (It should of course be remembered that 'men' meant men and not women, and white men not black men, and especially not black female slaves, including the one by whom Jefferson had a large illegitimate family.)

18 Many readers will recognize this scenario from the writings of Balgent, Leigh and Lincoln, Robert Anton Wilson, and others. It should perhaps be stressed that it is being offered here as an example of a conspiracy theory, and not in any way as a serious proposal of this book.

19 Massimo Introvigne, 'Ordeal by Fire: The Tragedy of the Solar Temple', Center for Studies on New Religions, Torino, Italy 1995, p. 17.

CHAPTER THREE
FREEMASONRY

1 Unless otherwise stated, quotations from John Hamill in this chapter are taken from an interview with the author, 7 March 1996.

2 Quoted in James Dewar, *The Unlocked Secret: Freemasonry examined*, William Kimber 1966, p. 164, and in Walton Hannah, *Darkness Visible*, Britons Publishing Company 1963, p. 136, my italics.

3 William Preston, *Illustrations of Masonry*, 1772, 11th edn 1804, Aquarian Press 1986, pp. 110, 111, 115–16, 6.

4 John Hamill and R.A. Gilbert, *World Freemasonry: An Illustrated History*, Aquarian Press 1991, pp. 24–5.

5 Robert Macoy, *A Dictionary of Freemasonry*, Bell 1989 reprint, p. 319.

6 Fred L. Pick and G. Norman Knight, revised Frederick Smyth, *Pocket History of Freemasonry*, 8th edn, Random Century 1991, p. 276.

7 Macoy, *op cit*, p. 361.

8 A.E. Waite, *A New Encyclopædia of Freemasonry*, 1994 reprint, vol. 2, p. 357; unless otherwise stated, all quotations from Waite in this chapter are from this work.

9 Pick and Knight, *op cit*, p. 240.

10 See, for example, Michael Baigent, Richard Leigh and Henry Lincoln, *The Holy Blood and the Holy Grail*, Jonathan Cape 1982; Michael Baigent and Richard Leigh, *The Temple and the Lodge*, Jonathan Cape 1989; John J. Robinson, *Born in Blood*, Century 1989; Andrew Sinclair, *The Sword and the Grail*, Century 1993; etc.

11   Waite, *op cit*, vol. 2, p. 219, p. 220, p. 222.
12   Robinson, *op cit*, p. 168.
13   Baigent, Leigh and Lincoln, *op cit*, p. 106.
14   Michael Howard, *The Occult Conspiracy: The secret history of mystics, Templars, Masons and occult societies*, Rider 1989, p. 31, p. 141.
15   Patricia and Lionel Fanthorpe, *The Holy Grail Revealed*, Newcastle Publishing Co 1982, p. 54.
16   For example, Peter Partner, *The Murdered Magicians: The Templars and their Myth*, Oxford University Press 1981; Edward Burman, *The Templars: Knights of God*, Crucible 1986; Paul Elliott, *Warrior Cults*, Blandford 1995, etc.
17   John Hamill, personal correspondence, 29 April 1996.
18   Baigent, Leigh and Lincoln, *The Holy Blood and the Holy Grail*, p. 133.
19   Waite, *op cit*, vol. 2, p. 356.
20   Bernard E. Jones, *Freemasons' Guide and Compendium*, 1950, Dobby 1994 edn, p. 343.
21   Hamill and Gilbert, *op cit*, p. 28.
22   John Hamill, personal correspondence, 29 April 1996.
23   H.L. Haywood and James E. Craig, *A History of Freemasonry*, George Allen & Unwin 1927, pp. 213–15.
24   Jones, *op cit*, p. 118.
25   Hannah, *op cit*, p. 45.
26   A.E. Waite, *The Brotherhood of the Rosy Cross*, Barnes & Noble reprint 1993, p. 442.
27   Foster Bailey, *The Spirit of Masonry*, Lucis Press 1957, pp. 132–33.
28   J.H.M. Dulley, quoted in James Dewar, *op cit*, p. 62.
29   Hannah, *op cit*, p. 85.
30   Joseph Fort Newton, *The Builders*, George Allen & Unwin 1914, p. 106.
31   Robinson, *op cit*, pp. 291–304.
32   Waite, *op cit*, vol. 2, p. 416.
33   Martin Short, *Inside the Brotherhood*, Grafton 1989, pp. 120, 121, 122.
34   Spoken at the 275th anniversary of the founding of the first Grand Lodge, Earls Court, 1992; video, *Freemasonry Today, Tomorrow*.
35   David Christie-Murray, *A History of Heresies*, Oxford University Press 1989 edn, p. 185.
36   In Britain, the *Rose Croix* is a specifically Christian Order; in parts of Europe, and in the United States and Canada, it has been adapted to be open to members of all faiths.
37   Keith B. Jackson, *Beyond the Craft*, Lewis Masonic Books 1994 edn, p. 40.
38   John Hamill, personal correspondence, 29 April 1996.
39   Jackson, *op cit*, p. 81, p. 84.
40   Knight, *op cit*, p. 236.
41   Ibid.
42   S.H. Hooke, *Middle Eastern Mythology*, Penguin 1963, p. 82.
43   Quoted in Dewar, *op cit*, pp. 200–201, and Hannah, *op cit*, pp. 181–2.
44   Hannah, *op cit*, p. 179
45   Short, *op cit*, p. 130.
46   Ibid, p. 131.
47   All quotations about Taxil are from Waite, *op cit*, vol. 2, pp. 251–64, 'Palladian Freemasonry'.
48   Short, *op cit*, p. 139.
49   Melanie Safka, 'Psychotherapy', Yellow Dog Music (ASCAP) 1972.

50 Short, *op cit*, p. 147.
51 Hamill and Gilbert, *op cit*. pp. 213–14.
52 Chalmers I. Paton, *Freemasonry, Its Symbolism, Religious Nature and Law of Perfection*, Reeves & Turner 1873, pp. 106–7.
53 Hannah, *op cit*, p. 37.
54 Summarized from J.D. Douglas, ed., *The New Bible Dictionary*, IVF 1962, pp. 477–80, 'God, Names of'. For a fuller explanation of the derivation of 'Jehovah', see the entry on Jehovah's Witnesses in my *Sects, 'Cults' and Alternative Religions*, Blandford 1996, p. 84.
55 W. Chalmers Smith (1824–1908), quoted from *The English Hymnal*, Oxford University Press 1914, No. 407.
56 Hannah, *op cit*, pp. 41–2.
57 Arthur S. Peake, ed., *A Commentary on the Bible*, Thomas Nelson & Sons 1919, 1937 edn, p. 723.
58 Robert Morey, *The Truth About Masons*, Harvest House 1993, p. 14.
59 Ibid, p. 46.
60 Ibid, p. 114.
61 Ibid, p. 36.
62 Waite, *op cit*, vol. 2, p. 278.
63 Morey. p. 25.
64 See my *Sects, 'Cults' and Alternative Religions*, Blandford 1996, pp. 46–50.
65 Newton, *op cit*, p. 180–81.
66 Short, *op cit*, p. 78.
67 Newton, *op cit*, pp. 182–3.
68 Subuh, founder of Subud, quoted in Robert Lyle, *Subud*, Humanus Ltd 1983, pp. 91–2.
69 Waite, *op cit*, vol. 2, pp. 416–17.
70 Newton, *op cit*, p. 211.

CHAPTER FOUR
THE RESURGENCE OF ESOTERIC SOCIETIES

1 Arthur C. Clarke, *Profiles of the Future*, Gollancz 1982, p. 36.
2 John Clute and Peter Nicholls, eds, *The Encyclopedia of Science Fiction*, Orbit 1993, p. 765.
3 The idea of the 'lost chord' is also related. In the Moody Blues's concept album *In Search of the Lost Chord* are the words, 'To reach the chord is our life's hope; and to name the chord is important to some, so they give it a word, and the word is OM.': Graeme Edge, 'The Word' (Palace Music), *In Search of the Lost Chord*, Decca 1968. OM, pronounced AUM, is a sacred sound used for meditation, mainly in Hindu-based religions. The 'lost chord' is related to Pythagoras's 'music of the spheres'.
4 *Book of Common Prayer*, originally written and compiled by Thomas Cranmer, 1549, revised 1662; *The Alternative Service Book 1980*, written and compiled by a committee, Hodder & Stoughton 1980.
5 Robin Briggs, *Witches and Neighbours*, HarperCollins 1996, p. 126.

6   Fred Gettings, *The Book of Tarot*, Hamlyn 1973, p. 139.
7   Brian Innes, *The Tarot*, Macdonald 1977, p. 7.
8   Éliphas Lévi, *Transcendental Magic: Its Doctrine and Ritual*, trans. A.E. Waite, Book One, *Doctrine*, chapter 10, p. 129.
9   Papus, *The Tarot of the Bohemians*, George Redway 1896, trans. A.P. Morton, chapter 9, p. 89.
10 Ibid, chapter 19, p. 298.
11 Ibid, chapter 9, p. 82.
12 Ibid, chapter 19, p. 300 (italics in original).
13 The pack designed by Paul Foster Case, founder of the occult school Builders of the Adytum, is very similar to Waite's – it is also based on the Mathers pack – but is much better executed; it is perhaps unfortunate that Waite published his first.
14 Francis Barrett, *The Magus, or Celestial Intelligencier*, 1801, Aquarian 1989 facsimile edn, p. iii.
15 Although *A Suggestive Enquiry into the Hermetic Mystery* has been reprinted more recently, copies are not easy to obtain; I have been unable to acquire one.
16 Beverly Hall Corporation leaflet: *The Rosicrucians*, pp. 3, 1.
17 *A Pilgrimage to Beverly Hall*, Beverly Hall Corporation 1955, p. 6.
18 Mrs Max Heindel, *The Birth of the Rosicrucian Fellowship*, pp. 5, 16–17
19 Marie-José Clerc, personal correspondence, 11 December 1995 and 23 April 1996.
20 SRIA leaflet, *Arcane Teachings offering the Mystic Key to Inner Truths*.
21 SRIA leaflet, *To Those Who Seek*, 11th edn, p. 5.
22 Booklet: *An Introduction to AMORC*, 31st edn, p. 16.
23 Gerald E. Poesnecker, personal correspondence, 12th January 1996.
24 Quoted from Francis King, *Sexuality, Magic and Perversion*, Spearman 1971, in Richard Cavendish, *A History of Magic*, Arkana edn 1990, p153.
25 A.E. Waite, *The Brotherhood of the Rosy Cross*, Rider 1924, pp. 613, 616.
26 Unless otherwise stated, quotations from John Hamill in this chapter are taken from an interview with the author, 7 March 1996.
27 A.E. Waite, The *Brotherhood of the Rosy Cross*, Rider 1924, p. 442.
28 Keith B. Jackson, *Beyond the Craft*, Lewis Masonic Books 1994 edn, pp. 73, 74.
29 Quoted in Israel Regardie, *The Golden Dawn*, one-volume 6th edn, Llewellyn 1989, p17.
30 In The Brotherhood of the Golden and Rosy Cross, when the lowest grade of Zelator was initiated 'he was presented as one whose spiritual being was imprisoned by an earthly body', a familiar Gnostic concept recalled in A.E. Waite, *Brotherhood*, p. 449.
31 *Lectorium Rosicrucianum* introductory leaflet, p. 2.
32 A.H. van den Brul, 'Gnosis – Forty years ago still hardly known', in *Pentagram* vol. 17 no. 3, pp. 9–10.
33 See my *Sects, 'Cults' & Alternative Religions*, Blandford 1996, p. 170, for further information on the Theosophical Society which, founded by H.P. Blavatsky in 1875, had something of a background influence on many later esoteric societies. It is not considered in any detail in this book for several reasons: it was an open society, not in any way secret; it was largely a study society, rather than an initiatory society; it drew much of its teaching from the East (Hinduism and Buddhism), rather than from the Western Mystery Tradition which is the substance of the societies in this book; and it was opposed to the practice of magic, which separates it from the HOGD and its successors.

34   Regardie, *The Golden Dawn*.
35   Gareth Knight, *A History of White Magic*, A.R. Mowbray 1978, p. 157.
36   Quoted in Russell Miller, *Bare-Faced Messiah*, Michael Joseph 1987, Sphere edn 1988, p. 153.
37   Quoted in Stewart Lamont, *Religion Inc: The Church of Scientology*, Harrap 1986, p. 21.
38   Most of the following esoteric movements are covered in more detail in my *Sects, 'Cults' and Alternative Religions*, Part 4.
39   *The Society of the Inner Light: Work and Aims*, p. 27; spelling and punctuation as in original.
40   *The Open Door*, BOTA introductory booklet, 1989.
41   Richard Cavendish, *A History of Magic*, Weidenfeld & Nicolson 1987, Arkana edn 1990, p. 151.
42   Source: Egon Larsen, *Strange Sects and Cults*, Arthur Barker 1971, p. 169.
43   Douglas Hill and Pat Williams, *The Supernatural*, Aldus Books 1965, p335; personal conversation between the author and Douglas Hill, 4 November 1995.
44   Personal communication from R&W Heap (Publishing) Company Ltd, 24 January 1995.
45   Geoffrey A. Dudley, booklet: *Realization*, R&W Heap, nd, p. ii.
46   Adelaide Pelley Pearson, daughter of William Dudley Pelley, personal correspondence, 11 December 1995.
47   Regardie, *The Golden Dawn*, p. 589.
48   Jean Beauchard, trans. Leon Shoolingin, *Le Tarot Symbolique Maçonnique*, France Cartes 1987, booklet p. 5.

CHAPTER FIVE
SECRET SOCIETY
– THE DARK SIDE

1   John Hamill, personal correspondence, 29 April 1996.
2   John Yeowell, *Odinism and Christianity under the Third Reich*, The Odinic Rite 1993, pp. 7–8.
3   Bernard King, *The Elements of The Runes*, Element 1993, p. 9.
4   Massimo Introvigne, 'Ordeal by Fire: The Tragedy of the Solar Temple', Center for Studies on New Religions, Torino, Italy 1995, pp.17, 5.
5   Matthew Kalman and John Murray in *New Statesman & Society* 23 June 1995, pp. 18–20, and *New Moon*, November 1995, pp. 24–7.
6   Quoted from the sleevenotes of *Society's Child: The Verve Recordings* CD, Polydor 1995.
7   Michael Baigent, Richard Leigh and Henry Lincoln, *The Messianic Legacy*, Corgi edn 1994, p. 273.
8   Joseph Fort Newton, *The Builders*, George Allen & Unwin 1914, p. 183.
9   Maldwyn A. Jones, *Destination America*, Weidenfeld & Nicolson 1976, p. 214.
10   Martin Short, *Inside the Brotherhood*, Grafton 1989, p. 651.
11   Short, *op cit*, p. 160.
12   Knight, *op cit*, pp. 124, 269–70.

13 Baigent, Leigh and Lincoln, *The Messianic Legacy*, pp. 377–9, 424ff.
14 David Yallop, *In God's Name*, Jonathan Cape 1984, p. 427.
15 See Paul Elliott, *Warrior Cults*, Blandford 1995, p. 160ff.
16 Det. Ins. Andrew Rennison, speaking at the Superintendents Association Conference in 1995.
17 12 and 19 February 1987.
18 John Hamill and R.A. Gilbert, *World Freemasonry; An Illustrated History*, Aquarian 1991, pp. 157 and 160.
19 *New Scientist*, 26 February 1987, p. 72.
20 *The Guardian*, 20 February 1987, p. 4.
21 W.E. Butler, *Magic and The Magician*, Aquarian 1959, 1991 edition p. 78; italics in original.
22 Lord George Brown, *In My Way*, Gollancz 1971, Pelican ed., p. 148.

CHAPTER SIX
THE ETERNAL QUEST

1   Max Heindel, *Rosicrucian Cosmo-Conception*, The Rosicrucian Fellowship 1909, 3rd edn 1974, p. 321.
2   A.E. Waite, *The Brotherhood of the Rosy Cross*, 1924 pp. 618–19, my italics.
3   A.E. Waite, *Encyclopædia of Freemasonry*, vol. 2, pp. 222–3.
4   A.E. Waite, *The Brotherhood of the Rosy Cross*, p. 22.
5   *The Society of the Inner Light: Work and Aims*, p. 12.
6   This book has not touched on a further mystery of southern France, Rennes-le-Château. It may or may not have anything to do with the Cathars, the Templars, the Rosicrucians, the Freemasons *et al*. Those interested specifically in Rennes-le-Château may find plenty of theories in the works of Baigent, Leigh and Lincoln; of Lionel Fanthorpe; of Elizabeth Van Buren; and of others, cited in the Bibliography.
7   Norris J. Lacey, ed., *The Arthurian Encyclopedia*, Boydell 1986, p. 257.
8   Chrétien de Troyes, *Perceval*, quoted in Lynette R. Muir, *Literature and Society in Medieval France*, Macmillan 1985, p. 69.
9   In their *The Holy Blood and the Holy Grail*, Jonathan Cape 1982, Baigent, Leigh and Lincoln go off in quite another direction; they throw away the cup entirely, and instead split the words *san graal* (Holy Grail) as *sang raal* (Blood Royal), and come up with the wonderfully enticing theory of the bloodline of Jesus and Mary Magdalene fathering the Merovingian kings of France – a theory to which few authorities, if any, give much credence.
10 J.D. Douglas, ed., *The New Bible Dictionary*, IVF 1962, p. 755.
11 Richard Cavendish, *King Arthur and the Grail*, Weidenfeld & Nicolson 1978, p. 137.
12 *The Society of the Inner Light: Work and Aims*, p. 22.
13 Foster Bailey, *The Spirit of Masonry*, Lucis Press 1957, p. 128.
14 Graham Phillips, *The Search for the Grail*, Century 1995, p. 107.
15 For more discussion on Tarot, see chapter four, pp. 142 and 175.
16 Rachel Pollack, *The New Tarot*, Aquarian Press 1989, p. 157.
17 W.L. Wilmshurst, *The Meaning of Masonry*, John M. Watkins 1922, p. 64.

18 Mrs M.W. Menger of the Lemurian Fellowship, personal correspondence, 8 December 1995.

19 Mrs Max Heindel, *The Birth of the Rosicrucian Fellowship*, p.16 (italics in original).

20 A.E. Waite, *Encyclopædia of Freemasonry*, vol. 2, p. 208.

21 W.L. Wilmshurst, *Meaning of Masonry*, pp. 68, 95.

22 H.E. Sampson, *Progressive Redemption*, pp. 171–4 (publisher and date unknown), quoted in Wilmshurst, *Meaning*, pp. 114–15.

CODA

1 Joseph Fort Newton, *The Builders*, George Allen & Unwin 1914, p. 211.

USEFUL ADDRESSES

I AM GRATEFUL to the following societies for providing illustrations for this book, and/or literature and personal correspondence from which I have both quoted and paraphrased relevant material, but which has been of most use in giving me a much greater understanding of the history, organization, methodology and motivations of the movements examined in this book. Especial thanks to John Hamill, curator and librarian at Freemason's Hall, and to Andri Soteri of INFORM, for their time and their invaluable assistance in providing obscure information.

AMORC Rosicrucian Order,
Greenwood Gate, Blackhill, Crowborough, East Sussex TN16 1XE, UK

Brotherhood of the White Temple,
PO Box 966, Castle Rock, CO 80104, USA

Builders of the Adytum,
5101–05 North Figueroa Street, Los Angeles, CA 90042, USA

Fellowship Press,
PO Box 192, Noblesville, Indiana 46060, USA

Fraternitas Rosae Crucis,
Beverly Hall Corporation, Box 220, Quakertown, PA 18951, USA

Freemasons' Hall,
Great Queen Street, London WC2B 5AZ, UK

INFORM,
Houghton Street, London WC2A 2AE, UK

Lectorium Rosicrucianum,
Bakernessergracht 11–15, 2011JS Haarlem, The Netherlands

Lemurian Fellowship,
PO Box 397, Ramona, CA 92065, USA

Philosophical Research Society,
3910 Los Feliz Boulevard, Los Angeles, CA 90027–2399, USA

Realization System,
R&W Heap, Bowden Hall, Marple, Stockport, Cheshire SK6 6NE, UK

Rosicrucian Fellowship,
2222 Mission Avenue, PO Box 713, Oceanside, CA 92049–0713, USA

Servants of the Light,
PO Box 215, St Helier, Jersey JE4 9SD, Channel Islands

Society of the Inner Light,
38 Steele's Road, London NW3 4RG, UK

Societas Rosicruciana in America,
RT1 Box 192-B, Preston Hollow, NY 12469, USA

BIBLIOGRAPHY

IT IS DIFFICULT to categorize the reference books in this field very precisely. Only those which are almost exclusively about either Rosicrucianism or Freemasonry have been listed under those headings, and even those sometimes overlap. Once the boundaries are extended, though, there is almost no way to sub-divide the subject matter; the largest section, then, entitled very loosely, 'Secret Societies, Alchemy, Magic, Esoteric and Occult', is basically a catch-all category.

No distinction has been made between serious scholarly works and speculative flights of fancy, though I have deliberately included very few of the latter. Also, no distinction is made between objective outside studies, antagonistic works, and deeply committed works by insiders. Those who wish to follow up the subject in more depth will need to examine books from all these various stances.

GENERAL REFERENCE, HISTORY AND RELIGION

Attwater, Donald (rev. Catherine Rachel John), *The Penguin Dictionary of Saints*, Penguin 1965, 1983 edn

Baldock, John, *The Elements of Christian Symbolism*, Element 1990

Barnstone, Willis, ed., *The Other Bible*, Harper and Row 1984

Barraclough, Geoffrey, *The Medieval Papacy*, Thames and Hudson 1968

Barrett, David V., *Sects, 'Cults' & Alternative Religions*, Blandford 1996

Becker, Udo, *The Element Encyclopedia of Symbols*, Element 1994 (originally published by Verlag Herder Freiburg im Breisgau, Germany, 1992)

Bossy, John, *Giordano Bruno and the Embassy Affair*, Yale University Press 1991

Briggs, Robin, *Witches and Neighbours*, HarperCollins 1996

Brosse, Jacques, *Religious Leaders*, W & R Chambers 1991 (original title *Les maîtres spirituels*, 1988)

Bruce, F.F., *The New Testament Documents*, Inter-Varsity Press 1943, 5th edn 1960

Chetwynd, Tom, *A Dictionary of Symbols*, Paladin 1982

Christie-Murray, David, *A History of Heresy*, New English Library 1976

Churton, Tobias, *The Gnostics*, Weidenfeld & Nicolson 1987

Comte, Fernand, *Mythology*, W & R Chambers 1991 (Original title *Les grandes figures des mythologies*, 1988)

Cotterell, Arthur, *A Dictionary of World Mythology*, Windward 1979, Oxford University Press 1986 edn

Cox, Michael, *A Handbook of Christian Mysticism*, Aquarian Press 1986 edn; first published as *Mysticism: The Direct Experience of God*, 1983

Cozens, M.L., *A Handbook of Heresies*, Sheed and Ward 1974 edn; first published 1928

Crim, Keith, ed., *The Perennial Dictionary of World Religions*, Harper and Row 1989 (originally *Abingdon Dictionary of Living Religions*, 1981)

Elliott, Paul, *Warrior Cults: A History of Magical, Mystical and Murderous Organizations*, Blandford 1995

George, Leonard, *The Encyclopedia of Heresies and Heretics*, Robson Books 1995

Gilbert, R.A., *The Elements of Mysticism*, Element 1991

Goring, Rosemary, ed., *Chambers Dictionary of Beliefs and Religions*, W & R Chambers 1992

Hinnells, John R., ed., *The Penguin Dictionary of Religions*, Penguin 1984

Hooke, S.H., *Middle Eastern Mythology*, Penguin 1963

Jones, Alison, *Saints*, W & R Chambers 1992

Julien, Nadia, *The Mammoth Dictionary of Symbols*, Robinson 1996 (originally published by Marabout, Alleur (Belgium) 1989)

Kelly, J.N.D., *The Oxford Dictionary of Popes*, Oxford University Press 1986

Larsen, Egon, *Strange Sects and Cults*, Arthur Barker 1971

Morris, Joan, *Pope John VIII – an English Woman: Alias Pope Joan*, Vrai Publishers 1985

Pagels, Elaine, *The Gnostic Gospels*, Weidenfeld & Nicolson 1980

Pardoe, Rosemary and Darroll, *The Female Pope: The Mystery of Pope Joan*, Crucible 1988

Shah, Idries, *The Sufis*, W.H. Allen 1964, Star ed. 1977

Waddell, Helen, *The Wandering Scholars*, Constable 7th edn, 1934

Walker, Benjamin, *Gnosticism: Its History and Influence*, Aquarian Press 1983

Whone, Herbert, *Church, Monastery, Cathedral: An Illustrated Guide to Christian Symbolism*, Element 1977, 1990 edn

SECRET SOCIETIES, ALCHEMY, MAGIC, ESOTERIC AND OCCULT

Baigent, Michael, Richard Leigh and Henry Lincoln, *The Holy Blood and the Holy Grail*, Jonathan Cape 1982, Corgi edn 1983

— *The Messianic Legacy*, Jonathan Cape 1986, Corgi edn 1987

Barrett, Francis, *The Magus, or Celestial Intelligencier; being a complete system of Occult Philosophy*, 1801, Aquarian Press 1989 reprint

Burman, Edward, *The Templars: Knights of God*, Aquarian Press 1986

Butler, W.E., *Magic and The Magician*, Aquarian Press 1991 (originally 1952, 1959)

Cavendish, Richard, *A History of Magic*, Weidenfeld & Nicolson 1987, Arkana edn 1990

— *The Magical Arts: Western Occultism and Occultists*, (Routledge 1967 as *The Black Arts*), Arkana edn 1984

Cavendish, Richard, ed., *Encyclopedia of the Unexplained*, Routledge & Kegan Paul 1974

Comte, Fernand, *Sacred Writings of World Religions*, W & R Chambers 1992 (Original title *Les Livres Sacrés* 1990)

Crow, W.B., *A History of Magic, Witchcraft and Occultism*, Aquarian Press 1968

Crowley, Aleister, *Magick in Theory and Practice*, 1929, Castle Books reprint 1991

Daraul, Arkon, *Secret Societies*, Frederick Muller 1961, Tandem edn 1965

De Givry, Émile Grillot, *Witchcraft, Magic & Alchemy*, 1929, trans. J. Courtney Locke, 1931, Dover 1971 reprint, *Illustrated Anthology of Sorcery, Magic and Alchemy*, Zachary Kwintner 1991 reprint

De Pascalis, Andrea, *Alchemy: The Golden Art*, trans. Shula Atil Curto, Gremese International 1995

De Rola, Stanislas Klossowski, *Alchemy: The Secret Art*, Avon 1973

Drury, Nevill, *Dictionary of Mysticism and the Occult*, Harper and Row 1985

Drury, Nevill and Stephen Skinner, *The Search for Abraxas*, Neville Spearman 1972

Fabricius, Johannes, *Alchemy: The Medieval Alchemists and their Royal Art*, Aquarian, 1989 (orig. edn Rosenkilde & Bagger 1976)

Gilchrist, Cherry, *The Elements of Alchemy*, Element Books 1991

Godwin, Joscelyn, *Music, Mysticism and Magic: A Sourcebook*, Arkana 1987

Gordon, Stuart, *The Paranormal: An Illustrated Encyclopedia*, Headline 1992

Guiley, Rosemary Ellen, *Harper's Encyclopedia of Mystical & Paranormal Experience*, HarperCollins 1991

Haeffner, Mark, *The Dictionary of Alchemy*, Aquarian Press 1991

Halevi, Z'ev ben Shimon, *Kabbalah: Tradition of Hidden Knowledge*, Thames and Hudson 1979

Howard, Michael, *The Occult Conspiracy*, Rider 1989

Introvigne, Massimo, 'Ordeal By Fire: The Tragedy of the Solar Temple', a report for CESNUR, Center for Studies on New Religions, Torino, Italy, 1995

King, Francis, *Magic: The Western Tradition*, Thames and Hudson 1975

Knight, Gareth, *A History of White Magic*, A.R. Mowbray 1978

Kramer, Heinrich and Jacob Sprenger, *Malleus Maleficarum*, 1486, Arrow edn 1971

Lethaby, William, *Architecture, Mysticism and Myth*, 1891, Architectural Press 1974 reprint

Lévi, Éliphas, *Transcendental Magic: Its Doctrine & Ritual*, trans. A.E. Waite, Redway 1896, Bracken Books reprint 1995 (Original title *Dogme et Rituel de la Haute Magie*, 1855 and 1856,

— *The History of Magic*, trans. A.E. Waite, Rider 1913, 1969 edn

Luck, Georg, *Arcana Mundi: Magic and the Occult in the Greek and Roman Worlds*, Johns Hopkins University Press 1985, Crucible 1987

MacKenzie, Norman, ed., *Secret Societies*, Aldus Books 1967

Matthews, Caitlín and John, *The Western Way: A Practical Guide to the Western Mystery Tradition, vol 2: The Hermetic Tradition*, Arkana 1986

Nataf, André, *The Occult*, W & R Chambers 1991 (Original title *Les maîtres de l'occultisme* 1988)

Partner, Peter, *The Murdered Magicians: The Templars and their Myth*, Oxford University Press 1981, Aquarian edn 1987

Powell, Neil, *Alchemy, the Ancient Science*, Aldus Books 1976

Prophet, Mark L. and Elizabeth Clare, *Saint Germain on Alchemy: Formulas for Self-Transformation*, Summit University Press 1985

Regardie, Israel, *Foundations of Practical Magic*, Aquarian Press 1979

— *The Golden Dawn*, one-volume 6th edn, Llewellyn 1989

Seligman, Kurt, *Magic, Supernaturalism and Religion*, Pantheon Books 1948, Allen Lane 1971, Paladin edn 1975; also as *The History of Magic and the Occult*, Harmony Books edn 1983

Shah, Idries, *The Secret Lore of Magic*, Frederick Muller 1957

Silberer, Herbert, *Hidden Symbolism of Alchemy and the Occult Arts*, Dover 1971 (Original title *Problems of Mysticism and its Symbolism*, Moffat, Yard & Co 1917)

Sinclair, Andrew, *The Sword and the Grail*, Century 1993, Arrow edn 1994

Singer, Charles, *From Magic to Science*, 1928, Dover edn 1958

Taylor, F Sherwood, *The Alchemists: Founders of Modern Chemistry*, William Heinemann 1951

Thompson, C.J.S., *Mysteries and Secrets of Magic*, nd, Studio Editions reprint 1995

— *The Lure and Romance of Alchemy*, G.G. Harrap 1932, Bell Publishing Co edn 1990

Turner, Robert *et al.*, *Elizabethan Magic: The Art and the Magus*, Element 1989

Underwood, Peter, *Dictionary of the Occult and the Supernatural*, Harrap 1978, Fontana 1979

Waite, Arthur Edward, *The Book of Ceremonial Magic*, William Ryder & Son 1911, reprint as *The Wordsworth Book of Spells*, Wordsworth 1995

Wilson, Colin, *The Occult*, Hodder & Stoughton 1971, Mayflower edn 1973

Yates, Frances A., *The Occult Philosophy in the Elizabethan Age*, Routledge & Kegan Paul 1979, Ark edn 1983

ARTHURIANA

Cavendish, Richard, *King Arthur and the Grail*, Weidenfeld & Nicolson 1978

Coghlan, Ronan, *The Encyclopaedia of Arthurian Legends*, Element 1991

Dixon-Kennedy, Mike, *Arthurian Myth & Legend*, Blandford 1995

Lacy, Noris J., *The Arthurian Encyclopedia*, Boydell 1986

Matthews, John, *The Elements of the Grail Tradition*, Element 1990

Matthews, John, ed., *An Arthurian Reader*, Aquarian Press 1988

— *The Household of the Grail*, Aquarian Press 1990

Wace and Layamon, *Arthurian Chronicles*, trans. Eugene Mason, Dent 1962

FRANCE

Duby, Georges, *The Knight, The Lady and The Priest*, Allen Lane 1984 (original title *Le Chevalier, la Femme et le Prêtre*)

Dunbabin, Jean, *France in the Making 843–1180*, Oxford 1991

Epton, Nina, *Love and the French*, Cassell 1959

James, Edward, *The Origins of France: From Clovis to the Capetians, 500–1000*, Macmillan 1982

Ladurie, Emmanuel Le Roy, *Montaillou*, Penguin 1980

Luchaire, Achille, *Social France at the time of Philip Augustus*, Frederick Ungar 1912

Maurois, André, *A History of France*, Jonathan Cape 1949, 3rd edn 1960

Muir, Lynette R., *Literature and Society in Medieval France*, Macmillan 1985

Seward, Desmond, *Eleanor of Aquitaine: The Mother Queen*, Dorset Press 1978

Taylor, W.C., *A History of France and Normandy*, Whittaker nd (*c.* 1830–48)

Tuchman, Barbara, *A Distant Mirror*, Macmillan 1979

TAROT

Case, Paul Foster, *The Book of Tokens: Tarot Meditations*, Builders of the Adytum 1934, 1989 edn

Dummett, Michael, *The Visconti-Sforza Tarot Cards*, George Braziller 1986

Gettings, Fred, *The Book of Tarot*, Hamlyn 1973

Innes, Brian, *Tarot: How to Use and Interpret the Cards*, Macdonald 1977

Kaplan, Stuart R., *The Classical Tarot*, Aquarian Press 1980 (original title *Tarot Classic*, US Games Systems 1972)

Olsen, Christina, *The Art of Tarot*, Abbeville Press 1995

Papus, *The Tarot of the Bohemians*, George Redway 1896, trans. A.P. Morton, Studio Editions 1994

Pollack, Rachel, *The New Tarot*, Aquarian Press 1989

Shephard, John, *The Tarot Trumps: Cosmos in Miniature*, Aquarian Press 1985

ROSICRUCIANISM

Heindel, Max, *Rosicrucian Cosmo-Conception*, The Roscicrucian Fellowship 1909, 3rd edn 1974

— *The Rosicrucian Philosophy in Questions and Answers*, 3rd edn L.N. Fowler 1922

Knight, Gareth, *The Rose Cross and the Goddess*, Aquarian Press 1985

Waite, Arthur Edward, *The Brotherhood of the Rosy Cross: A History of the Rosicrucians*, Rider 1924, Barnes & Noble 1993 reprint

FREEMASONRY

A Ritual and Illustrations of Freemasonry, William Reeves, no author, no date (Actually written by Avery Allyn, first published 1824)

Baigent, Michael and Richard Leigh, *The Temple and the Lodge*, Jonathan Cape 1989

Bailey, Foster, *The Spirit of Masonry*, Lucis Press 1957

Dewar, James, *The Unlocked Secret: Freemasonry Examined*, William Kimber 1966

Hamill, John and R.A. Gilbert, *World Freemasonry: An Illustrated History*, Aquarian Press 1991

Hannah, Walton, *Darkness Visible: A Revelation & Interpretation of Freemasonry*, Britons Publishing Company 1952, 1963 edn

Haywood, H.L., *Symbolical Masonry: An Interpretation of the Three Degrees*, George H. Doran 1923

Haywood, H.L. and James E. Craig, *A History of Freemasonry*, George Allen & Unwin 1927

Jackson, Keith B., *Beyond the Craft*, Lewis Masonic Books, 4th edn 1994

Jones, Bernard E., *Freemasons' Guide and Compendium*, George G. Harrap 1950, Eric Dobby 1994 edn

Knight, Stephen, *The Brotherhood*, Granada 1983, Grafton edn 1985

Knoop, Douglas and G.P. Jones, *The Genesis of Freemasonry*, Manchester University Press 1947

Lawrence, John, *Freemasonry – A Religion?*, Kingsway 1987, 2nd edn 1991

MacNulty, W. Kirk, *Freemasonry: A Journey through Ritual and Symbol*, Thames and Hudson 1991

— *The Way of the Craftsman: A Search for the Spiritual Essence of Craft Freemasonry*, Arkana 1988

Macoy, Robert, *A Dictionary of Freemasonry*, Bell 1989, originally published as *General History, Cyclopedia and Dictionary of Freemasonry*, Masonic Publishing Co., 1850

Morey, Robert, *The Truth About Masons*, Harvest House 1993

Newton, Joseph Fort, *The Builders: A Story and Study of Masonry*, George Allen & Unwin 1914

Paton, Chalmers I., *Freemasonry: Its Symbolism, Religious Nature, and Law of Perfection*, Reeves and Turner 1873

Pick, Fred L. and G. Norman Knight, *The Pocket History of Freemasonry*, Frederick Muller 1953, 8th edn edited by Frederick Smyth, Random Century 1991

Preston, William, *Illustrations of Masonry*, 1772, Aquarian Press 1986

Robinson, John J., *Born in Blood: The Lost Secrets of Freemasonry*, Century 1989

Short, Martin, *Inside the Brotherhood*, Grafton Books 1989, Grafton paperback edn 1990

Waite, Arthur Edward, *A New Encyclopaedia of Freemasonry*, University Books 1970, Wings Books edn 1994, originally published 1921

Wilmshurst, W.L., *The Meaning of Masonry*, John M. Watkins 1922, 1959 edn

INDEX